SHROPSHIRE UN

FLY-BOATS

The Jack Roberts Story

Fly-boat **Elector** *at Stourport, Staffordshire & Worcestershire Canal*

Canal Book Shop

SHROPSHIRE UNION
FLY-BOATS
The Jack Roberts Story

Editors:

Harry Arnold MBE   Sue Cawson

Tony Lewery   Peter Silvester

First edition July 2015
Second edition October 2015
Reprinted January 2016

Canal Book Shop
Audlem Mill The Wharf Audlem Cheshire CW3 0DX

ISBN 978-0-9574037-4-1

CONTENTS

THE SHROPSHIRE UNION FLY-BOAT PROJECT

The Shropshire Union Fly-boat Restoration Society Ltd - a voluntary charitable group - was set up to preserve one of the two then remaining Shropshire Union Canal fly-boats; rare examples of some of the finest boats to grace Britain's waterways.

Symbol was acquired but became too decayed to restore - although parts of her are preserved. *Saturn* - the last one - became available and was purchased by British Waterways. A partnership - The Saturn Project - was set up with the society to restore and operate the boat. Over four years and at a cost of £87,000, *Saturn* was professionally restored by Malkins Bank Canal Services, with assistance from society members. This was enabled by a fund-raising campaign with major contributions by British Waterways Wales & Border Counties Waterways, Heritage Lottery Fund, Waste Recycling Environmental (WREN), the Shropshire Union Canal Society, The Waterways Trust and the Manifold trust; plus other donations of money and materials from society members, other individuals and companies.

Relaunched in 2005, *Saturn* celebrated her 100th birthday in 2006, and is now the superb example of a fully operational fly-boat; travelling the waterways and fulfilling the partnership's aims to educate future generations about the history of narrow boats, horse-boating and our waterway network.

The combination of boat, crew and horse - and all the techniques and skills evolved over 250 years - demonstrates a unique unit of transport that served Britain from the 18th into the 20th Century. This boat and these traditional skills must be preserved for the future.

For more information, or to help in any way:
www.saturnflyboat.org.uk

4

FOREWORD

by Harry Arnold MBE

In early 1961, I bought a copy by mail of LTC Rolt's *Inland Waterways of England* from a company on the Bridgewater Canal at Stretford. It was defective, so on our way to Manchester, my friend from schooldays Ed Frangleton, and my wife Beryl called in to change it. There we met June Davies, who ran, on behalf of owner Pat Saunders (an early IWA campaigner) amongst other things, the horse-drawn hostelboat *Margaret*.

That day was a real life-changer. It led on to a lifetime on waterways, professionally for myself and Beryl, and for Ed a dedicated enthusiasm, and to him meeting his wife Margaret. But it also led to this book, because within a week we met for the first time Jack Roberts. Jack was to become a lifelong friend, mentor and trainer in all the skills and lore of horse boating. Not only that, but he would instil in us his love of all things canals, particularly the Shropshire Union network and especially what is now known as the Montgomery Canal.

Jack (John) Roberts was born on the *Quail* on 29 May 1894. He observed the passing boats from the family home, an SU company house at Wardle (Barbridge Junction), and during school holidays accompanied his father and uncles on various trips. So it was inevitable that he would go on to captain a fly-boat.

We are fortunate that Jack was blessed with a prodigious memory and retained vividly names, working practices, and events over the years, until prevailed upon to write it as a memoir in 1969.

So we have an authentic first-hand account of the operation of waterways in the North West and the Midlands during fly-boat days, until services were discontinued in 1921, and more of Jack's later life on waterway maintenance and the hostelboat.

We are indebted to the late Margaret Frangleton for not only transcribing Jack's notes into typescript, but working with him to check facts and awake further memories. Also to Ed for recording this process, so that we still have the sound of Jack's voice. Jack's daughter Freda transferred the manuscript into electronic form, which has helped considerably in the production of this book.

Jack's words have been completely retained, with the additional use of references in notes made by June Davies and myself, whilst also recording his stories, and in letters from him to me. You will read some accounts that may seem incredulous, but I can only say that in three or four specific instances I have obtained the official documentation and was able to do some checking. The official documents are wrong and Jack correct. So beware, you armchair waterway historians.

Our thanks go to Jack's family, who have been a pleasure to work with on this project, to other members of the Shropshire Union Fly-boat Restoration Society who have helped, and to all at Audlem Mill who have brought it to fruition.

I have been going on for years saying we are sitting on the best boatman's autobiography ever. Now it is in print, that opinion has not changed. Enjoy Jack's words – as some of us were lucky enough to hear in his lifetime.

ACKNOWLEDGEMENTS

The author's manuscript was not illustrated. The editors have included images appropriate to the text, and for specific images, thank the copyright owners: Ed Frangleton, Edwin Lewis, Eric de Maré, Fox-Davies Collection, Tom Godwin, Paul Higson, Kemsley Newspapers, Tony Lewery, National Waterways Museum, Peter Silvester, Waterways Archive, Freda Weyman, and David Williams.

The majority of photographs (except those older images believed to be out of copyright), are reproduced courtesy of Harry Arnold/Waterway Images.

The editors gratefully acknowledge the family's assistance in preparing this book, and for permission to use family photographs.

EDITORS' NOTES

The text is as written by Jack Roberts in his 1969 manuscript, and amended by him over the next few years, but with some editing, which mainly relates to punctuation and chronology.

Place names are largely as written, with some inconsistencies in spelling, and some disparity from modern spelling. For instance, Rode Heath is usually written in this book as Rhodeheath. Brumagem was the boatmens' name for Birmingham.

Some chapters relate to boating on what the author calls the "Welsh canal". This was built as the Ellesmere Canal, but has more recently become known as the Llangollen Canal.

The appendices have been added by the editors, where appropriate deriving information from the manuscript.

The author riding Mary, towing hostelboat Margaret *along the Bridgewater Canal in Stretford in early 1961*

AUTHOR'S NOTE

I would like to inform the reader that I cannot remember precise dates of past events, but I have tried to give a general picture of life on the canals, as I knew it. If I could remember everything, this book would be much longer.

Jack Roberts
1969

DEDICATION

For Frank

In Memory of Frank Roberts
Jack's Youngest Son

29 May 1946 - 6 August 2006

*"My two young daughters, Freda and Linda, myself and Molly by my home
at Grindley Brook, year 1955"*

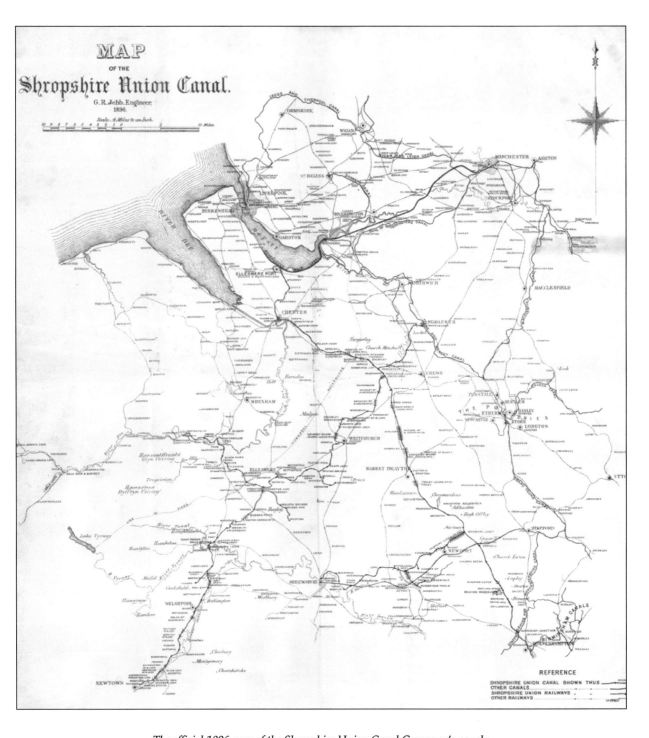

The official 1896 map of the Shropshire Union Canal Company's canals

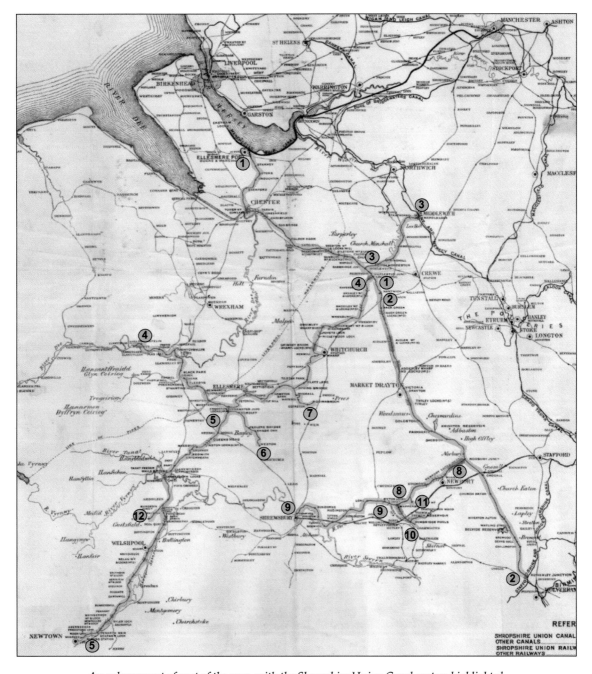

An enlargement of part of the map, with the Shropshire Union Canal system highlighted.
Constituent canals and arms include:

1   Chester Canal
2   Birmingham & Liverpool Junction Canal
    (1 & 2 form the Shropshire Union 'main
    line')
3   Middlewich Arm
4   Ellesmere (Welsh / Llangollen) Canal
5   Montgomery Canal

6   Weston Branch
7   Prees (Wem) Branch
8   Newport Branch
9   Shrewsbury Canal
10 Trench Canal
11 Humber Arm
12 Guilsfield Arm

Jack Roberts steering hostelboat Margaret *in 1961*

1

BORN TO A BOATING FAMILY

My family's connection with the cut [canal] goes back to my grandfather, Edward Roberts, who was born in Bala in 1819. He had a good home, living with his parents, until they both passed away when he was about 12 years old. As he was not old enough to manage his share of the inheritance, he was sent to a workhouse at Bala, together with the other children, two older sisters and one brother. They travelled in a two horse brake, such was the transport then. However, he did not arrive at the workhouse - he watched his chance, and dropped off the brake near Llangollen. He managed to get onto the canal towing path, and begged a ride to London on a canal boat. This boat was engaged in hauling slate slabs from Pentrefelin, near Berwyn, to London.

He worked several boats on what was then the Grand Junction Canal, and when he was a few years older, he got a job as mate on a Duke's Fly, running from London to Manchester. Later, he was engaged as a mate on a Pickford's Fly, running from London to Ellesmere Port. What their cargoes or time was, I do not know, but I understand that today's Pickford's Road Haulage was Pickford's Canal Carriers in the old days.

When he got older, and capable of taking charge of a boat, he made his way to Tower Wharf on the Shropshire Union Canal at Chester, and applied to the Canal Authority for a job as skipper on one of their commercial boats. They

Jack Roberts' grandfather Edward

wanted a skipper for a gunpowder boat, and asked him if he could take that. He agreed, and was engaged, and fixed himself up with a mate.

The boat's name was *Cato*, and it ran from Ellesmere Port to Pendeford, Wolverhampton. This boat was built with hatches like a flat. The boatmen and wharfmen wore flannel boots when they were loading and off-loading. A red light was fixed on each end of the boat. The warehouse at Ellesmere Port was situated by the china clay wharf, well away from the other buildings. I do not know where this powder came from, nor do I know its final destination, but I know where the boats moored en route. On the off-side of the canal there were red notices with 'Mooring Places for Powder Boats Only' in white letters. The powder was stored at Bunbury, and at Wheaton Aston, in a thick blue brick warehouse at the end of the valley. The last place was at Pendeford, a mile from Autherley Junction, where it was stored in a warehouse on the off side near the present aerodrome. After the carriage was stopped the three powder boats were converted to ordinary ones.

My Grandfather got married in Chester, and lived by Tower Wharf. He later moved to Basin End, Nantwich. At Nantwich Wharf there was a chapel for boatmen and their families, which still stands, by the present cheese warehouse. My Grandfather, Edward Roberts, lived in one of the cottages here, years previously, and my father, Alfred Roberts, went to Acton School when he was a boy. When he left school he was engaged at Worsey's bakery, Nantwich as an apprentice baker for a while, but he had to take over as mate on his father's boat in 1876.

After working on the powder boats, he was transferred to a Market Drayton Fly. The boat was named *Harriet* and was very small. His work involved three trips per week from Ellesmere Port to Market Drayton, with two horses which were changed at Nantwich. He had every Sunday at home. He delivered goods to Nantwich, Audlem and Market Drayton. The mileage was 228, and the pay sixpence per mile each way. It was a three-handed flyboat, and the Skipper paid the hands 8/- per week, together with their food. He also owned and fed the horses. His total earnings were £11 8s per week. I understand this was an excellent job in those days.

I never knew my Grandfather, as he was drowned at Bettisfield in 1890. Bill Ruscoe, another grandson, was steering, and Sam Rogers, the other boathand, was having a nap on the foot-plate. As they approached Cornhill Bridge, the horse was going by himself. Grandfather must have had a sudden stroke, and he fell off the hatches into the cut. His body was brought out near an old oak tree on the towing path side, and taken to the 'Nags Head' at Bettisfield. The inquest was held at Hanmer. He was afterwards taken home by canal to the bridge by Swanley No. 2 Lock, and buried at Acton Church. Both his house and the bridge were demolished before my time.

My father, Alfred Roberts, was born in 1862. He had three brothers and one sister, and I knew them all. They were all engaged on the canal at some part of their lives. One brother, Bob, left the Llangollen Fly to join the army. He was engaged in the South African campaign as an engine driver on an armoured train. When he was released, he went to Crewe Works, and later became an engine driver. Another brother,

George, was Skipper of a Pottery Fly, which I remember. He lived at Wheelock. I do not remember my grandma; she passed away in 1864. My grandfather later remarried. His second wife came from Guilsfield, near Welshpool.

Following the death of my grandfather at Bettisfield, my father was given the chance of the job as Skipper of the Llangollen Fly. This was his first boat as Skipper. After about three years, he was transferred to the Trench Fly. This was before I was old enough to remember much, but I do remember falling out of the hatches into the canal. This was at the Trench, where the old basic slag works were, at the bottom of the incline. My mother was there, and fished me out. I had my eyes open when I fell in, and the water was yellow.

Star *and Mallard at Christleton Lock, October 1965*

I was born on the canal boat *Quail* at Christleton, on the 29th of May 1894. My mother had been forced to leave the family at home at Barbridge in the care of Grandma as my father was without a mate, and she had undertaken to steer for him. The boat was working from Ellesmere Port to the Potteries, carrying general goods. During the journey, I was christened at Stoke on Trent, and on his return my father engaged a new mate.

My mother was then able to stay at home and send the older three, two sisters and a brother, to school. When I reached the age of five, I was also to attend school at Calveley, near Tarporley and Winsford. I can remember it quite well - my little short suit consisted of coat, vest and trousers. Fastened to my coat was a cord and whistle, which was placed in my top pocket. This was blown quite often, I was informed later! When I came home from school, I would go to the transhipping warehouse at Bunbury, and assist the boatmen with sheeting up, and shovelling stone etc. I used to take the horses

Ice breaker at Audlem, c.1910, outside the canal warehouse and canal employee houses (both now the Shroppie Fly pub).

to the blacksmith's and also give them their feed. I would be given sixpence or a shilling, which meant a lot to me in those days. Sometimes I would help the local farmers, and they would give me some coppers, and bread and cheese and a bottle of home-made pop.

On Saturdays, I would walk to Nantwich and spend my earnings on sweets. I always walked along the towing path, as it was a lonely road and we were afraid of tramps in those days. If I had to go to Nantwich to collect medicine, the local doctor would give me a ride there in his horse and trap, and I would walk back. However, I would come and go on a boat whenever possible. Monday was the least busy day for boats, until about seven or eight o'clock, when the fly boats would appear, although the Brumagem fly arrived at midday as usual.

I can well remember how many boats passed through Barbridge each day. There were the fly boats from Ellesmere Port - two Potteries, one Wolverhampton, one Trench, one Newtown, one Llangollen, one Maesbury, one Ellesmere, one Whitchurch, one Wrenbury and one Market Drayton. There was also one weekly Shrewsbury fly. In addition to these, there were reserve boats, called slow boats. They were all making for the same destinations as the flys, but with less urgent cargoes of every description. At normal times, there were fifty or sixty of these every day. The motto of the Shropshire Union Company was "Collect today, deliver tomorrow". Newtown and Birmingham were the longest fly trips, Ellesmere Port is 91 miles from Newtown, but they still maintained this standard. Shropshire Union boats were not allowed past Coventry, and goods for London were transhipped to Fellows Morton boats at their Fazeley Street Depot, Birmingham.

Before the Newtown fly, there used to be the "Welshpool Flyers". These ran daily to Welshpool, where goods were transhipped into a boat that went on to Newtown, making the trip twice a week. This was the *Cambria*, a boat built especially for the job.

There was quite a variety of goods stored at Ellesmere Port of many different kinds - raddle, stone, coal, iron ore, wheat, soap, copper and aluminium. If the reserve boats came upon a slack period, this found work for them. When the canal was frozen, the men would be engaged on the ice boat, with their horses, to keep the urgent traffic on the move. If the ice got so thick that the ice boat could not run, the men would be found work around the locks and weirs, and on the hedges and towing paths. The urgent traffic would be transferred to the railway, wherever possible.

The hardest frost I remember was in about 1902. I ran along the towing path, watching the men rocking the ice boat. There were twenty horses towing it. By Pool Hills, near Nantwich, the boat came out onto the top, on its side, and the men walked off. This particular frost lasted twenty weeks.

I can recall hearing of an experiment in towing boats, which the Shropshire Union tried at Cholmondeston. A narrow gauge track was laid on the towing path, which was about half a mile of straight at this point. Then a small locomotive was lowered from the railway bridge, by a crane from Crewe Works, and placed on the temporary track. A few boats were attached to the engine with a long rope. It proved a failure, however, as, when the engine started to move, the boats were pulled into the bank.

Dickie, *a narrow gauge railway locomotive, hauls six narrow boats along the Shropshire Union Canal's Middlewich Branch, near Worleston in 1888, under the watchful eye of F W Webb (left, by himself), the Chief Mechanical Engineer of the London & North Western Railway.*

2

THE BRUMAGEM FLY

As I grew older, I took more notice of the boats that passed by daily. Barbridge Junction was a transhipping depot to all parts of the Shropshire Union Canal, and other routes, mainly Newtown, Llangollen, all the Welsh Canal, Birmingham, Kidderminster, Manchester and the Potteries. Transhipment to and from the railway was at Calveley Station Canal Siding. This was a very busy station, two miles from Barbridge.

The special attraction on the canal passing Wardle and Barbridge was the Brumagem (Birmingham) Fly boat. It was timed to within a few minutes of midday Sunday going to Ellesmere Port, returning midday Monday to Birmingham; midday Wednesday to Ellesmere Port, and midday Thursday to Birmingham, where it arrived at about ten o'clock on Friday morning. After a night in Birmingham, it would leave between four and five on Saturday afternoon, to follow the same routine the next week.

The Captain lived in Birmingham. His name was Aaron Owen, and he was my Mother's uncle. He always had a word to call out to my mother as he passed Barbridge, sitting in the steering hatch with his watch in his hand. I only saw him a few times as he was in his sixties and later retired. The man who took his place was William Jarvis, who later had a weekly boat, *Beatrice*.

Owen's boat was the *Brocket*. Most of the Brumagem Fly Boats were named in series. Some were called after battles in the South

African War, and later the First World War, such as *Mons,* and others after newspapers such as *Express*, *Times* and *Mail*. The *Mail* and the *Brocket* both finished up at Welshpool.

The horses' names were Joe, who pulled from Birmingham to Autherley Junction, Sweep to Tyrley, Tiny to Bunbury, Vixen to Ellesmere Port; they covered the same stretch back again. Tiny was a light bay, sixteen hands high, half

Barbridge Junction, about 1960. Taken from the Nantwich side; straight on for Chester, and turn right under the bridge for Middlewich. The former transhipment shed and warehouse were behind the photographer

legged with four white socks and a white face. It had a lovely black harness, with brass buckles and red, white and blue bobbins. It had no face brasses, to avoid carrying unnecessary weight. The boats had black tarpaulins, neatly put and tied down where the planks joined. There was a five foot gangway covered with small thin boards to make it level to walk along if required. To step up off the cabin to the gangway, which we called planks, there was a cabin block, painted with diamonds down each side, and a painted picture of Lord Kitchener, about sixteen inches high, which looked very neat. The water can was painted with roses, and tied by the chimney with a white rope spliced to a ring on the end of the cabin. The handbowl or dipper was hung up inside the cabin, near the steerer.

The drinking can, or tot, was also hung on a little brass hook inside. The copper and brass bugle was also within reach of the steerer. The tiller was painted red, white and blue, and made in a half bow shape. The helm was painted to match, and decorated with one Turk's Head, and a white cow's tail. The name of the boat , *Brocket*, was in black paint on white on either side of the counter. The stern stud, onto which was attached the stern rope when tying up, was painted signal red. The prevention strips were made of white ash, as also were the hatches, coal-box top, and foot-board - that is the entrance to the cabin and steering position.

The fore-bows were painted white with a black dot, and the stem bar red with a white rope fender. The cratch was five foot high, at the other end of the gangway from the cabin. Over the cratch were four white glittering ropes, with rosettes on each rope, rolled under the rope after making secure. These cratches were never pulled down. The black covers were marked:

"S.U.R. & C. Co." in white letters. At the stern cabin end, the full name: "SHROPSHIRE UNION R. & C. Co. General Carriers" was painted in black letters, with white over a white panel, and "Registered at Chester 342" in black letters. The trademark, painted light brown, was a wheatsheaf.

The interior and cabin doors were oak grained, and the cabin floor was white deal. The light was a brass lamp set in a candle stick. It had a shade which tilted to direct the light towards the bull's eye glass which was set in the cabin roof. At night the steerer would have to jump down into the boat after opening the lock gate, and this light showed him where to jump. If it was very dark, he could easily jump in the lock. All boats were fitted with this.

There was a black lead stove in the cabin which was cleaned and polished every morning. The two draw plates, jockey bar, ash pan and steel top were burnished. There were also cupboards and drawers for clothes. These were all fitted with brass knobs and handles. The table cupboard, which closed and opened, was decorated. There was a closed up bunk for the bed, but this was only used one night a week, Friday at Birmingham. There were two day-beds to rest on. You just removed your shoes and socks, coat and vest, and dropped on it.

The crew's food was brought to the boat by the Skipper before leaving, and consisted of about ten pounds of roast beef, mutton or pork. In addition, there would be two fruit cakes and two

Cheese fly-boat Saturn *at the Gathering of Historic Boats in Audlem in 2009. Built in 1906, and restored just under a century later, Saturn is the only remaining Shropshire Union fly-boat in near original condition.*

pies or tarts each, and bread, butter, tea, sugar, bacon and all the necessaries for four men. This was purchased on Saturday afternoon before leaving for Ellesmere Port, and also at the start of each return journey.

Nothing stopped the Brumagem Fly, not even the weather. The gauging stops in Birmingham were closed from Saturday night until Monday morning, but the fly was allowed through, unhindered. Once, the boat *Tariff* was sunk at Market Drayton. The ice was thick, and the ice-boat had not arrived on time so the fly decided to go on without it. He was allowed six horses if necessary, to get him to Birmingham on time. However, the boat was not plated for ice, and it cut right through the oak planks. The

goods had to be unloaded at Market Drayton Wharf, and sent on by rail. There was not much damage to the boat, and it was soon repaired. The incident was reported in the papers, with the comment "All the crew were saved"!

The distance from Ellesmere Port to Birmingham was 84 miles, with 53 narrow locks, 14 barge locks, and two into the Ship Canal at Ellesmere Port. Two trips per week brought the total mileage to 336 miles, 264 locks, 128 hours travelling, and 16 hours loading and off-loading cargoes. 144 hours, with four men and four horses meant less than forty hours per man per week. The Skipper's wages were £6 per week. This fly boat was the only one paid by the week, except the Stourport boats. The three crew

Mail, *a Brumagem fly-boat, at Chester, around 1900*

17

earned 10/- each per week, but food was included and paid for by the Skipper. In those days this was the equivalent of £1 per week. A lengthsman's or lock-keeper's would be 17/6 per week, with 2/6 per week house rent.

Two canal book authors together, in May 1969. Jack Roberts (left) with John Liley, who wrote the seminal 1971 book Journeys of the Swan, *alongside Swan Line Cruisers' hire boat* Mute Swan.

Boatmen's strike, Ellesmere Port, 1911

3

FIRST TRIP TO NEWTOWN, 1904

By the time I reached the age of ten, my father was Captain or Skipper on the Newtown fly. The name of the boat was *Broxton*, a nice shaped small boat, built to travel at a fair speed. The captain of a boat used to be called Skipper, although he was graded as "Steerer" on the Company's Time & Way Bill. He had Saturday evening and Sunday morning at home, starting off after dinner on Sunday for Ellesmere Port. I was anxious to go for a trip, and my father and his three mates agreed that I could go during my annual school holidays. We started from home with my father's horse, Tommy, and when we arrived at Bunbury stables, we put him in a private stable by the railway bridge. This was Mr Worral's. He had a smithy, and also a shop for groceries, boatman's clothes, women's shawls, whips, thrums and provender. The relief horse for the last twenty two miles to Ellesmere Port was Albert, a lovely grey, about fourteen hands high, and owned by the Shropshire Union Company.

Albert was quite fresh when he was hooked on, and started to trot and play. One of the mates was ahead, getting the locks ready, so that there was no waiting. There was a driver, a deckman and a steerer and I was the passenger. After passing down six big locks, we came to an eight mile level, and all the men came on board, one to steer and three to relax. Albert knew the way and trotted to the next lock at Christleton, by Rowton Moor. All the traffic which was held up there from ten o'clock in the morning until six o'clock in the evening on a Sunday had cleared, and we passed down the next five big locks unhindered and arrived at Northgate Locks, a mile into Chester city. The lock-keeper, F. Roberts, had the lock ready. I stopped on the boat while we passed down these three deep

locks. I found that they were cut out of red rock. The gates were enormous, and there were two paddles at each middle gate. I learned that these were the deepest, wide canal locks in the country.

I heard the mates and my father discussing whether to take Albert to the stable at the Dee Basin, Tower Wharf, and wait for the tug at five o'clock the following morning. However, they decided to take him on to Ellesmere Port, as they then stood a chance of collecting their cargo earlier. The Docks commenced working at six o'clock.

We arrived at Ellesmere Port at eleven o'clock just as it was growing dark. Albert had brought us from Bunbury in seven hours, and was still quite fresh and full of play. Everyone adored Albert. You could talk to him like a human being, and he was well known on this, his regular route. We had had a meal before entering Ellesmere Port, and were all ready to rest, after making Albert comfortable for the short night. About twenty horses had already been bedded by the stable attendant. All the stables had clean sawdust bedding, and were lit by gas lamps.

When we went to bed, I slept across the top of the bed, which was about 5 foot five inches wide, with two of the crew in the bed. I was quite comfortable. One man slept on the side bed, and one on the cabin floor. The steerer and the driver for the first length next day were appointed when we moored for the night. Typical working lengths were from Welsh Frankton to Carreghofa, and Carreghofa to Welshpool.

On the Monday morning, I heard the hooter or buzzer blowing from the Hydraulic Pump House at six o'clock. I also heard the ganger call the boat's name, *Broxton*. The boat was placed in berth at the large top warehouse together with other fly boats, and loading commenced.

I was out and about, anxious to see all of this. I heard that the gang loading our boat had been out at midnight to load the Brumagem Fly, who was now well on his way to Birmingham. As it was a nice morning, I went round the docks, and arrived at the Pier Head. I saw two tugs whose names were *Lord Clive* and *Ralph Brocklebank*. They were the tugs engaged in bringing the flats from Liverpool and Birkenhead, through Eastham lock to the canal. These flats were loaded with different kinds of goods, timber and flints.

Period postcard of the lift bridge by the entrance to the Whitchurch Arm

When I arrived back at the boat, it was loaded and ready. Before breakfast, we pulled it by hand to the stable, where one of the mates had already harnessed Albert ready for his journey back to Bunbury. As we were leaving, I heard the buzzer blowing for half past eight. We passed through the locks in Chester, and later by Beeston Castle with Peckforton Castle in the distance. We arrived at Bunbury at six o'clock in the evening, and left Albert at the stable there. Hooking on Tommy again, we passed our home at Barbridge at a quarter past seven, and called out, but did not stop.

Turning off at Hurleston Junction for Wales, we passed up the four Hurleston locks, and two miles further on, came to the two Swanley locks.

I heard the clock on Acton church strike nine. After another short pound and three locks at Baddiley, we came to Wrenbury. I heard the church clock there strike ten.

After a four mile pound, we reached Marbury Lock, and my father said it was bedtime for me. I had already had my supper, so I went to sleep in the usual place. At times during the night I heard the crew changing, and passing through the locks, one at Quoisley, two at Willeymoor, and six at Grindley Brook. The Llangollen Fly had accompanied us from Ellesmere Port, and was close behind. She was a three handed fly boat, with only two horses owned by the Skipper, John Hones. However, I was asleep when he left us, and when I awoke at Bettisfield I asked where he had gone.

I understood that we had parted company at Whitchurch, where he turned left at the drawbridge, up the branch to the town. This was his first call to offload goods. Next meeting at Bettisfield, I heard the church clock six, as we passed under Cornhill Bridge. In the distance I could see the Monument on Breidon Hill.

The crew changed over, and we had breakfast. The horse had a feed while going along. He ate out of a special feed tin, hung on his head with a strap, which you had to keep tightening up until he had finished. He then had a drink out of the canal, and the muzzle was put on to stop him grazing.

The last workers could now go to rest, leaving the two others to clean out the cabin, polish the brasses, and mop the boat off. If they had not reached Cornhill Bridge by six, the rule was that the last workers would have to do this. The horse carried on without a driver.

It was a lovely morning as we passed Hampton Bank, Lyneal, Colemere, and Ellesmere Tunnel. Here there were meres, close to the canal, and I thought it was a lovely sight, going through the

Aston Locks, before restoration

woods, hearing and seeing nature. At the tunnel, the horse was unhooked and led over the top while the Steerer pulled the boat through the short length. The horse was then hooked on again. I asked why the horse did not haul the boat through the tunnel, and was told that owing to it being seventeen miles from lock to lock, i.e. Grindley to Frankton, this short break eased the horse's shoulders. This was quite right and fair.

Passing Ellesmere and the repair yard, Tetchill and Val Hill, we came up to Frankton Junction, and turned left down four locks. We had entered the Montgomery Canal. At the bottom of the locks was Lockgate Bridge Junction, where the main canal turned right, and the Weston Branch, which went to the left towards Baschurch.

All four men were busy when we passed down Frankton Locks, two working the boat, one lockwheeling, and one cooking the second breakfast. After that two men would go to rest. This was ten o'clock on Tuesday morning, 25½ hours after

leaving Ellesmere Port. I had the job of driving Tommy, who was a black horse. We passed along Perry Moor, where the river Perry, not much more than a wide brook, runs alongside the canal. When we came up to Keeper's Bridge one of the men, Tom Scragg, came off the boat to attend to the horse. The reason for this was that the horse could smell Richard's Bone works, and it made him nervous; there was also a little swing bridge across the towpath crossing the little branch that went off the main canal into the work's basin.

All went well, however, and a little way further on we came to a railway bridge and Rednal Wharf. There were no trains passing over at the time, though this was the main Paddington line. Here there was a roving bridge, and the towpath crossed over to the other side of the cut. Next we came to Queen's Head Wharf, where we made our first delivery - a few bags of sugar, one bag of bacon, two boxes of oranges and onions, four boxes of fruit and four boxes of kippers. We did not call one of the sleeping crew men out except at a busy warehouse, or on a long flight of locks. After the goods were delivered, the shopkeeper would sign for them. Here, it was Mr Gittens.

Trench Locks, showing guillotine gate

We started off again, and came to Aston Locks, numbers 1, 2 & 3, where we changed horses, putting Tommy for a rest and hooking on Charley. Charley was a cream coloured cob, very pretty but very fat and a terror to catch in a field. There were two or three horses stabled at this point, which was also a Toll Office, where private owners were charged. Edward Lea was the lengthsman, stableman and a Toll Clerk.

Continuing our journey, we arrived at Maesbury Wharf. The horse was tied to a fence, and given a feed while we off-loaded, having called up one of the sleeping crew. There was about two tons of goods including six hogsheads of Guinness stout, sugar, bacon etc. This was loaded straight on to a two horse dray which took it to Oswestry. There were three more boats waiting to be off-loaded here, but the fly boat had priority. There were two porters at this wharf, and a drayman, and they stabled two lovely horses. Our delivery of goods was signed for on the Time Bill, which was a pink one. The delivery note from Queen's Head, our first delivery point, was also handed in, and the Time Bill signed again. As this was a Shropshire Union Wharf, the men were engaged by the Company.

When we left Maesbury Wharf, one man went to rest again. We passed the end of a short branch by Maesbury Mill, owned by the Peate family, and came to Redwith Wharf. Next we passed Crickheath Wharf, which was convenient for Porth y Waen. It was stone traffic

only here, and there were two boats loading. About a hundred yards from the end of this wharf there was a sunken boat whose name was *Usk*. It was practically a skeleton, but you could still see the name, the knees and also the helm.

There was a story attached to this boat. My father explained that it was built for the Trench

Llanymynech Wharf

branch, with a six foot four inch beam so that it would go up the Trench locks, which had guillotine gates. The bottom gates had to be wound up with a winch, and the boat had to pass under them to enter the lock. The Steerer had to drop into the cabin, as the gates were very low. There was no place to turn the boat round up the Trench branch, so boats had to be navigated helm first (something which I experienced in later years). The man steering this particular boat, George Salmon, forgot to drop down into the cabin as he entered the lock, and so hit the gate and severed his head from his body. After the tragedy, no Shropshire Union Canal boatman would work on *Usk* because of superstition, so it was sold to a private owner, Tom Moody, cousin to John Moody of Ellesmere, and was engaged in carrying coal and slack from Black Park Colliery to Newtown, Montgomeryshire. After a few years, and the worse for wear, it was placed to sink at Crickheath, and the remains of it are still there.

To return to our journey – we came next to Waen Wen, where there was a small malt warehouse, owned by Jones Maltsters of Shrewsbury, across a wide water. From there we went to Pant. Just above the canal was Pant Station, a country railway. As we passed peacefully along, we came to the rocks and white stone houses. On the rock, a lovely bloom of wild flowers was hanging down, and I thought this was a lovely sight on my first canal voyage.

We sailed under a railway bridge, a road bridge, and passed a brickyard on the offside, which was very busy with Company boats and loading bricks. As we passed under another railway bridge, which connected Chubbs Lime Works and Quarry, I saw to my amazement a most unusual sight. A boat was coming towards us with two donkeys abreast hauling it. The name of the boat was *Vulcan* and it had a load of lime for Staffordshire. This had been loaded from Chubb's Works, and the boat was owned by Chubbs. The boatman's name was John Cloxon.

We passed through Llanymynech and came to Wall's Bridge Warehouse. We had about 10 cwt [hundredweight] of sugar and a few other goods to deliver there, and when this was signed for, we set off again. We called the two sleepers up as we arrived at Carreghofa Locks. At No. 1 Lock, there was a Toll Office, and a feed of water coming from the River Tanat. The Toll Clerk was Mr Beddows and he attended to the paddle which was situated up the small stream, which was the feeder. At No. 2 Lock, there was a stable and a lengthsman's cottage. The lengthsman's name was Moody, another cousin to John Moody of Ellesmere Yard. After passing down the two locks, it was meal time again and the workers changed over.

At Newbridge, we made another delivery. Then we crossed the aqueduct over the River Vyrnwy, and rounded a big bend. Here we passed under two ornamental bridges, named Pentre Heylin. These were pretty, but very low bridges, with just room for Charley to get under.

Our next call was at Four Crosses Canal House Warehouse, where Mrs Lloyd was waiting to collect her goods. I understood she was paid tonnage, and had the canal house as tenant. She was assisted by her husband, who was employed at a local farm. Quite a quantity of wheat was stored here. There was a parrot in a cage, hanging from the house door. I said "Hello Polly" to it and it answered "Gee up Charley" as it knew our horse from previous trips. It knew my father's name, too, and wished us good day. We set off again, and met another fly boat on his return journey. The Skipper's name was Ellis, and he told us that all the locks were set ready for us.

The next place that we passed was the Maerdy. Just under the bridge was a privet hedge, growing almost into the canal, and over this hedge I could sees a very low cottage. There was a gap in the bottom of the hedge for the occupant to take water from the canal, and a peacock cut carefully out of the privet, on the top. The man who lived in this two roomed house was Alfred Maddocks, who married Anne Pugh. His daughter, Liz, came out to call to us – her uncle was my uncle too. There was also a Public House here, and a wharf and lime kilns, and the boat *Hilda* owned by Charlie the Mardu. I do not know the man's real name. He used the boat to fetch a load of coal from Black Park or Littleton for his own works. This was a fairly busy wharf, but it was private and not for ordinary goods.

A little further on, we came to Arddleen. I was attending to the horse, and when we came to an orchard on the offside, I halted him, and the boat came to a stop. There were a few goods to deliver here. There was a chain and pulley fixed to a big oak tree, to make a home-made crane to lift the bags of sugar from the boat into the orchard. The local grocery shop was at the end of the orchard on the main road, owned by a Mr Davies. He came to the boat, and collected the goods on a small truck, as there was no warehouse.

Two hundred yards further on, we came to a small warehouse on the towing path side, by Dragon Bridge. Halting Charley again, I was sent to the shop over the bridge to inform them of our arrival. They were expecting us - as they all were on this route. Here was Mr Alfred Davies, brother to Mr Davies at the orchard. There were quite a few goods to deliver here, including ten bags of sound Indian corn. As we hung them on the small stationary crane and wound them up, one of the

"a small warehouse on the towing path side, by Dragon Bridge"

bags caught on an iron nut on the boat side, ripping the sack and letting the corn run out. Mr Davies made the sharp remark "Be careful, it's 17/- a sack." Now what would he have said today! When he signed the note, he gave me sixpence.

Moving on again, we came to Lock 1 at Burgeddin. On the right was the branch to Tyddyn Wharf, Guilsfield. The lengthsman's house and a two stall stable were situated in the fork. We then passed down No. 2 Lock. Next we came to the Wern Mill., on the towing path side. Here there was a paddle, which was open and drove the mill. From Newtown, the canal runs down to meet the water coming from Junction. At this point, the surplus is let off to drive the mill, and then goes into the River Severn. As we came along the Wern Valley, we

passed Breidden Hill, and I could see the monument that I had seen from Bettisfield first thing that morning. We were now just going past it.

We now came to Pool Quay Railway Station on the towing path side, and entered No. 4 Lock, rising up to No. 3 Lock. Here there was a brickyard, and another boat had been loaded. This was Mr Finney's private brickyard. We rose up again to No. 2. Lock, where the lock-keeper closed the gates for us. He was called George Lloyd, and he knew which fly boat it was and the time. He would have the lock ready at all times, whether it was during working hours or not. A little further on was Pool Quay church, with a lovely little churchyard close to the towing path. After passing up to No. 1 Lock, we had a word with the lock-keeper and his family, and were given some lettuce and onions. Here there was a small warehouse, but we had no delivery to make on this trip. I heard the church clock chime eight.

On our way again, we came to the draw-bridge, and I went ahead to hang on the chain and raise it. It was quite easy, owing to the weather being dry. Charley was on his way, and seemed to be putting speed on, as he knew where he was making for, and the canal was wide and deep

Bank Lock No. 4, Pool Quay - with 1970s Market Harborough built holiday boat Clifton

George Morris, who was steering, told me that a boatman had committed suicide over that stile a few years before. His name was Dick Lewis, and he was Skipper of the Welshpool Fly. No.-one knew the reason he committed suicide. Just before arriving at the wharf, we passed under the Llanfair Railway bridge, as a small engine and passenger coaches passed over. Next we crossed the short aqueduct over a small river, a tributary of the Severn. On the off side was the Stone Wharf for the Welshpool Standard Quarry, and two Shropshire Union Canal boats were waiting to load stone the following day. We passed under the new Town Bridge, completed in 1901, and arrived at the wharf. I

here. We trotted for a short time, and then we came to another draw-bridge. I went ahead again, and raised it. After lowering it, I came over, and saw two lovely blue peacocks in a field on the offside of the canal. This was Buttington – a big farm, and another small warehouse, but we had no delivery here this time. My brother-in-law's father used to work from the lime-kiln at Buttington to Black Park Colliery and back – four days work for 15/-. However, I do not remember the lime-kiln working. On the offside was Abbey Bank, and forestry, a lovely bloom of wild flowers, and two white stone cottages.

A mile further on, we entered Welshpool. Opposite the factory by Gallowstree Bank Bridge, there was a wooden stile on the towing path.

Looking north from Severn Street Bridge, Welshpool, about 1900, with wharves on both sides of the canal, a working boat at the builder's yard and a rowing boat

unpegged the horse, and led him over the bridge to the stable, which was for the convenience of the fly boat for one night only. Harry Owen brought a feed for him, and I had already taken the harness off, so he could now have three hours rest. The Town clock struck nine. It was Tuesday night.

I heard Harry and George discussing a pint, and they decided to ask my father and Tom, who were resting, whether they wanted a drink before closing time. So the four of them went, together with Jim Lloyd, the porter. I went with them for a mineral (children were allowed in a pub in those days), but I had a drink of beer off Tom, while my father was not watching. That was the first time I had tasted beer. Father was keen and particular, and would use a boat pole on your shoulder, or the double end of a whip,

This six ton had been brought by one of the slow "mileage" boats. This was for economic reasons, as the fly boat was paid by the mile and could deliver on his regular route and thus save the Company about 12/-. While the men were busy transhipping, I was told to go to bed.

When all was done, and they had a meal, one man pulled the boat into the lock, while the other went to harness Charley. After three hours rest, I had got out of bed, and came outside. I found quite a different type of lock-gate here – there were two gates instead of one, and they were all of iron, the beams shaped like the muzzle of an artillery gun. The Canal Inspector, Mr W Baker, lived by the lock, and there was a footplank across the weir that led to his house. The canal maintenance yard was on the opposite towing path side. The two mates

went to rest, as my father and Tom were the workers to Newtown. I did not go to bed again; I did not want to miss anything as it was the last length, and a nice night. We came to a bridge on the bend of the canal, which was difficult for the steerer, but we went through alright. On the offside of the canal was Powis Castle, the residence of the Earl of Powis.

A canal camping expedition at Belan Locks, just after the second world war, which went up to Newtown. It was organised by an IWA member, Bill Thistlewaite

if you displeased him. You never dared tell him a lie, or let him know you had smoked a cigarette.

At closing time, we all came back to off-load the goods - about six tons of sugar, bacon, cheese and fruit; lard and butter in buckets, and lump sugar in boxes. There were about six tons to load afterwards, for various places to Newtown.

Half a mile further on, we delivered ten cwt (hundredweight) of goods at Belan Wharf, a private wharf, shop and lime-kilns. After the note was signed, we entered the lock, and as we rose up, I heard the clock in Powis Castle chime one o'clock a.m.. The lock-keeper's name here was Bob Jabb. We now passed along a two mile pound, and it was such a light night that I could see the small white cottages just above the canal on the offside, and also Belan School, a very small school, situated by the canal bridge.

Next we came to Brithdir Lock, where there were a few more goods to deliver. There was a small warehouse on the lockside, and the lock-keeper's house opposite. The lock-keeper, Thomas Roberts, was waiting for us. He was responsible for the handling of the goods, and signed for them. Close by this lock, there was a pub called the "Horse Shoe", a Coal Wharf and Lime Kilns. There was a Company boat moored here, loaded with coal from Cannock, Staffordshire. Some say that Brithdir Lock was the original place where roses and castle were painted on boats, as Powis Castle is in the background.

Now we passed over a very small iron aqueduct, all painted white, bridging another tributary to the Severn. The next lock was at Berriew. The porter, Edward Windsor, lived at the lock, and we had to call him up. We passed through a small tunnel, and came to the wharf. Tom told me that there was the devil's foot under the tunnel, and he would show me on the way back. We called George, the sleeper, up and began to off-load. There were six tons of goods here, as Berriew was a large village. After our Time Bill was signed, we set off again, just as day was breaking.

We passed a coal wharf owned by Mr Thomas Rowlands, and entered another fairly long aqueduct which went over the River Rhiw. I heard Berriew church clock strike three a.m. We next came to Evelvach Stone Wharf and dry dock on the towing path side, and a mile further on we arrived at Garthmyl Bridge. There was a sharp right hand turn to enter this bridge, which was very low, with only just space for Charley on the towing path, and about seven foot six inches width for the boat. Rounding a sharp left hand bend, we reached the wharf which was on the offside. We had to use the boat pole to get there. We called Mr Leo Owen up to unlock the Warehouse, and attend to the goods. Mr Owen and his family kept the

pub "The Nag's Head" and also the Post Office and a Stud Farm. While we were off-loading, the Mail Van approached from Montgomery Station, four miles away. It was a horse drawn red van, run by Mr Rowlands of Berriew. When he had collected the mail, Mr Owen came to attend to the Warehouse. He was not employed by the Company, but was paid tonnage. While I was inside the Warehouse, I saw an old notice fixed on the beam with the words "This man, Thomas Jones, is not to be employed on any of the Company's boats. By Order. Signed Thomas Hales, Tower Wharf, Chester." I asked my Father about it, and he told me that Jones had been to Shrewsbury Prison for pilfering. He was now a boatman for a private concern.

With all the goods signed for, we were on our way again, passing up Finney Straight. We came to Halfway House, a very small shop situated between the canal and the main road to Newtown. I was sent to the back door to knock and ask for the key to the tiny warehouse. The Missus lowered the key from the window in a little round cup and asked if I could manage.

Glanhafren Bridge No. 143, August 1969

I said yes, and went across twenty yards and unlocked the small hut. These people always trusted the boatmen. My father and Charlie put the goods in, one bag of sugar, one back of bacon, one box of onions, two boxes of figs, a box of oranges and a case of tobacco. We locked up and I took the key back. The cup was lowered and I put the key in it and also the note to be signed, and up it went and was returned duly signed. I said good morning and we set off. By the boat was a small swing bridge, and on the offside was an orchard and two lovely

Brynderwyn warehouse and (restored) lock, 2009

walnut trees in full leaf and full of young nuts, but not then ready to eat.

The next bridge we came to was Breezes Bridge, a very low road bridge, and then another swing bridge. On the off side was a great high wall, separating the main road from the canal, and covered in wild bloom. This wall went from the swing bridge, nearly to the next bridge, which was Glanhafren. This bridge had a flat top with ornamental stone rails and pillars, and the walls were covered with red ivy. It was the very lowest bridge on the canal, being only six foot high, so that we had to take the chimney down. Newtown boats were low boats anyway and had low cabins, and their gangways, cratches etc. were gauged especially for this bridge when the boat was light. Boats that had not been built specially for this canal had to be very careful of the low bridges when they came this way. When we passed under this bridge, the main road was on the offside and the mountains close by on the other. Now there was another swing bridge, and then the flat topped roving bridge which took the towing path to the opposite side

for about a hundred yards, and then another roving bridge which changed the towpath again.

At five o'clock on Wednesday morning, we reached Brynderwyn Lock, a warehouse, and four very small cottages below the lock. The River Severn ran close by. The country postman, Mr Price, lived here with his wife, and two lovely young daughters. He also attended to the warehouse, but there was not a delivery

"....four very small cottages below the lock" - below Brynderwyn lock in 2009

to be made today. As we came into the lock, he came out on his bicycle to go and collect the mail from Newtown, six miles away.

We now followed the River Severn, and passed under a long iron bridge which took the main road over the canal and the river. After a quarter of a mile, we came to Byles Lock, and a lock keeper's cottage. In the background was a mountain, with a road leading up it. We went up the lock and along the foot of the mountain and came to Newhouse Lock. Mr Joe Thomas was lock keeper and lengthsman here, but there was nobody about at this time of the morning. We left the river for nearly a mile, and came to Aberbechan, a warehouse, lime-kilns and a coal wharf owned by the Severn Valley Company. We called John Edwards who was engaged by the Severn Valley Company. He collected our goods, about two tons, and signed the note. His daughter, Nessie, still lives in that house today. We used to fetch coal from Littleton, Cannock and the Black Country to Aberbechan. The last load of coal I took there was in about 1923, on the boat *Francis* which is still at Berriew now.

We passed over a small iron aqueduct, and under a road bridge, and came up to Freestone Lock. This was where the River Severn feeds the canal to Pool Quay. It was a very quiet lock. There were two houses, but they were rented to farm labourers. The next lock was Dolfer Lock, where there was an old white stone cottage and an orchard. Price-Bebb was lock keeper here. Next were Llanllwchaiarn or Rock Locks Nos. 2 and 1, which was the last. Here there was a cottage rented to a railway man. Above the lock we came to a very small bridge, and a pretty little old church. The churchyard came close to the canal on the offside, with overhanging beech trees. We now entered Newtown.

First we came to the Pump House with a little footbridge over the canal for the access to the house. Mr Goff was the attendant at the pumping station and was employed by the

The Pump House at Newtown, with "a little footbridge over the canal for the access to the house".

Company. This was a steam pump, and fed the canal for two miles to Freestone Lock, where it was then fed by the level of water in the Severn through a water pipe. At Factory Bridge, we had to unhook the horse and take him round by road to the end of the canal, leaving the steerer to pole the boat the rest of the way. We passed two boats offloading slack at the coal wharf, another bridge, and a pub called "The Wagon", and then went across the wide basin to the wharf. All around the basin was a coal wharf, a timber wharf and disused lime kilns. It was a large basin, a quarter of a mile round, and a terrible place to cross when it was windy. I noticed some very old sunken boats that had been there before my father's time.

While the boat was offloading, I made my way to the town, and came to the entrance of Ha'penny Bridge, where I paid ½d to go over. At the other end was Skinner Street, and a tannery. It was only a small Welsh town, but pretty and surrounded by hills. After a walk round I paid ½d to re-cross the bridge, and came back to the boat.

Mr Taylor was the Porter and Clerk, and Mr

Ireland at Welshpool was the Agent for Montgomeryshire. There was a horse and dray here, but it was privately owned and paid by the ton – Tommy the Dray they called him. Facing the wharf was the Cambrian Wool Factory, where mostly girls were employed. It was now dinner-time, and a few came across to the boat for a chat with us. They looked forward to seeing the fly boat, as there was one each day, and they knew all the boat's names, the horses and the men. I got to know them well in later years, and I still go to Newtown to visit one of them – a friendship of sixty years.

We were now ready for our return journey to Ellesmere Port. Mr Taylor informed my father that we had to take a full load of wool from the Cambrian Factory to Calveley Railway Station. It was bound for Huddersfield. There were a dozen great bales, a very bulky cargo. We loaded six tons, and were on our way again. My father told me that we had to be back at Newtown the next Sunday, and would have a night in. Tom and father were sleepers back to Welshpool.

When we arrived back at Berriew, I was told to ring the bell on the wharf. This called the attention of the attendant at the lock beyond. We had to collect two cases for Liverpool from Montgomery. Away again, we arrived at Welshpool, and called at the wharf, as usual. Frank Windsor, the porter who was on duty at that time, said there was a load of empty sacks for Ellesmere Port Flour Mills. When he signed our Time and Way Bill, he could see that we were well loaded. It was now six o'clock on Wednesday evening.

At various warehouses on our way, I saw the word "STOP" hanging out on a narrow board over the canal. There was a cord fixed inside the warehouse to pull it out with. This drew the attention of the up and down traffic. If you were light (empty), and passed one of these boards, you were fined 2/6. When we reached Aston

Locks we changed horses again, putting Charley in the stable and taking Tommy out. He had had a good rest. It was almost midnight, and I had a few winks of sleep.

We met our fellow fly boats as we came up to Rednal. Tom had to attend to the horse again as he went over the turnover bridge, and under the railway bridge. An express train came over, and my father informed me that it was the Zulu Express from London to Birkenhead, named after the Zulu War. I went to bed again, and when I got up, we were coming to Grindley Brook Locks. It was still lovely weather. We passed down nineteen locks to Hurleston, and reached the main canal again.

We called at home at Barbridge to collect our basket of roast beef, cakes, pies etc, and went on to Calveley Railway Station to tranship our cargo of wool for Huddersfield. This left us light again. When we arrived at Bunbury Locks, we changed horses. We hooked on Mac, not Albert. He was a lovely little grey cob, like Albert. It was half past six on Thursday evening.

Mac took us to Ellesmere Port, arriving at two o'clock on Friday morning. We put him in the stable, and we all had a few hours rest. At six o'clock the hooter was blasted out, and we commenced loading for Newtown again. The previous trip had been a quick one as there was no weekend. We loaded from Ellesmere Port on Monday and Friday. There were eight berths for loading. At this time there were seven fly boats loading at once, the Newtown, Llangollen, the Trench, the Shrewsbury, the Brumagem, and two for the Potteries. All the Skippers were at the old offices by the top warehouse settling for their wages and doing their shopping at the shops which were conveniently near at hand in those days. The crews were loading the boats.

As I was up and about, I went into the big warehouse and saw printed on the huge beams the various destinations of the goods stored below. The flats from Liverpool put the goods into the correct place to await collection. Below, under No.'s 1 and 2, the hoists were raising the cargoes from the flats to boats. All around the other part of the docks there were ships, barges and narrow boats collecting and discharging their traffic, from all parts of the Midlands, Wales, the Potteries, Trench and Shrewsbury, and also from abroad and for abroad. I made my way back to the boat which was almost loaded. The two Pottery Flys were leaving, and the Llangollen and Newtown Flys were getting ready for away. They mostly went butty to Whitchurch. The remaining fly boats were usually the last, as they had a little more weight.

Off again, we came the nine miles to Northgate Locks, and had a clear way to Bunbury. We changed horses again, and went on to Barbridge, where I had to leave and return home. I watched my father's boat disappear from sight, bound for Newtown again.

Barbridge Junction, looking south towards Nantwich. The arm to to the Trent & Mersey Canal (the North Staffs in this book) at Middlewich, via the Wardle Canal, leads off to the left under the bridge. The transhipment shed, demolished in the 1960s, covers the canal. The photo was taken during a strike, hence all the boats lined up

4

TRIPS WITH GRANDFATHER OWEN - BIRMINGHAM AND MANCHESTER

I still had three weeks holiday left, and hung around the boats at the wharf, doing little jobs for different boatmen. One day, my mother's father came along with his boat. His name was John Owen, but he was mostly called Nixon on the canal. He was brother to Aaron Owen, who ran the Brumagem Fly. My grandpa had also been Skipper of the Brumagem Fly, and of the Wolverhampton Fly and the Kidderminster Fly.

I went to meet his boat, as I usually did, and he told me he had just had orders to proceed to Malkin's Bank, near Sandbach, to collect twenty tons of soda from Brunner Mond for Birmingham. I arranged with my mother to go for another trip, and collect my clothes for the fortnight.

We started off next morning at six o'clock. My Uncle Bill, Grandpa's son, was mate. He was the youngest in the family, being about twenty years of age. Grandma had passed away before my time, and Grandpa and Uncle Bill both made their home with my mother when they moored at Barbridge. We set off down the Middlewich branch and passed down Cholmondeston Lock, and Minshull Lock and over the River Weaver. Then we came to Stanthorne Lock, and the end of the branch, a distance of ten miles from Barbridge.

Here we entered the North Stafford Canal, now known as the Trent and Mersey. We passed up King's Lock in Middlewich, and went by Brunner Mond's Salt Works and Cledford Bridge. At Rump's Lock, called Joe Lowe's Lock by the boatmen, there was a pub "The Kinnerton Arms", and a shop. Grandpa and Uncle Bill

went for a pint, and I was treated to an Eccles cake and sweets. Traffic was quiet at this time. We went for about a mile to three locks at Booth Lane, where we met quite a lot of traffic, including the Salt Union Fly, Anderton Company boats, Potters and Fellows Morton boats. The Salt Union Company which later became the Mersey Weaver & Ship Canal Company, ran four flys a day from Anderton to Longport and Etruria. My Uncle George had one of these boats. We passed Rookery Bone Works, and I was shown where the Canal Company had commenced cutting a canal to Crewe, but only went a hundred yards. We now came to Wheelock, passed the wharf and Lees Mill, and entered Cheshire Locks.

To my surprise the locks were in pairs, and we entered the nearside, which is inside to a boatman. The steerer pulled the tiller out, stepped off the boat on to the steps, and went up to draw the two paddles [between the two locks] with the windlass – these were rather big ones but light. I made an attempt to close the lock gate, but I was told the paddles would do the job. The steerer looked down into the lock, and waited until the helm was clear, whereupon he drew the centre paddles connected to the other lock, and the bottom gate closed in a second. The driver then raised two top gate paddles. When the lock was half full the steerer dropped the centre paddles. These connected with the other lock, which had been full, but was now half empty. This system saved wasting water, and was in use at all these Cheshire double locks. I do not know of any other locks that were arranged in this way, apart from those with side pounds. In two minutes, the boat had risen up, and we were off again, passing up three more locks to arrive at Malkin's Bank.

We turned the boat round, and berthed to commence loading soda. While the boat was loading, I was allowed to go into the Works. Beyond the next lock were four Brunner Mond boats discharging stone from Froghall on the

The paired Cheshire Locks, here at Malkins Bank. The paddle mechanism that connected the two chambers can be seen by the left hand lock, but it was probably out of use by this time

Caldon Canal into small trucks. The noise was terrific, even from that distance. I returned to the boat which was almost loaded, taking twenty tons on completion. We were soon on our way back again.

At this stage, traffic was quite busy, but we managed to get a turn in. There was a boat in every lock, meeting each other, going in opposite directions, one rising and one lowering, with the bottom gates closing automatically as one lock filled the other through the centre paddles. We went down four locks, the bottom four of the twenty one Cheshire Locks.

We went back down the three locks at Booth Lane, Kinnerton Lock and King's Lock. Then we turned off onto the Shroppie, and entered Wardle Lock. We moored for the night at about seven o'clock, and took the horse, Darky, to the stable. This was August 1904, and it was still

very warm and dry. We had travelled twenty seven miles from Barbridge and collected our cargo. However this was not a fly boat so time was not so important. I went for a stroll and stood by King's Lock. Traffic was still very busy. One boat I noticed was a Gandy Fly coming from Preston Brook en route to Derby. The Skipper's name was Albert Jones, an ex-Shropshire Union man, who lived at Stone. My Grandpa knew him well.

On Wednesday morning we were on our way again, and after ten miles and four locks we arrived again at Barbridge. This was the depot for this boat which was known as a Barbridge Ton Boat. We moored for a short while, and the Skipper went into the office to see Mr Wyn and settle for his previous trip and his pay to this point. His previous trip had been with cattle food from Calveley to Platt Lane, Dobson's Bridge, Waterloo Wharf and Edstaston near Wem, which is three miles down the Prees

Branch of the Welsh Canal, and then back light to Barbridge. I was told that this was paid at a rate of 1/6 per ton for 15 tons, but he was paid for twenty tons owing to the bulky nature of the cargo. He got 5d a mile from Barbridge to Malkin's Bank, and back to Barbridge as this was the rate on the North Stafford Canal. On the Shroppie, it was 3½d per mile with a Company-owned horse.

Having a little provender to take us to our next stable, we went on our way for seven and a half miles, passing Nantwich and reaching the two locks at Hack Green. Here we collected a few feeds of provender. There was stabling for about twenty horses here, and ten relief horses were stabled for emergencies. Two horse-keepers, who were also lock-keepers, worked in twelve hour shifts for seven days and nights a week. At all stables on the main canal your time-sheet and Way Bill were signed, and your time of passing through noted.

Three miles further on, we reached Audlem No. 15 Lock, Moss Hall. We passed the wharf at Audlem, as the village church clock struck four. Billy went for a pint at "The Bridge Inn", by the lock – a quick one while the lock was filling. Pubs and shops were open all day and up till

Audlem warehouse (left) and two staff houses (right), shortly before conversion into the Shroppie Fly pub in 1973

ten o'clock at night in those days. Darky was eating grass by the lock. We passed the Carpenter's Shop at No. 10 Lock and went on up to No. 1 Lock at Coxbank. As he had a mash of food, Darky was going by himself – what the boatmen called "baccering".

At the bridge before the Adderley flight, Billy and I stepped off the boat onto the towing path, leaving Grandpa to steer. Billy ran ahead to get the locks ready, as they were against us. However, we soon met a Trench Fly, which meant that the next four locks would be in our favour or ready, as we say on the canals. The lock-keeper's bungalow at the middle lock was built in blue brick, and was the same pattern as five other bungalows at various other places on the Norbury section. At No. 1 Lock was a hut for the night man who was on a twelve hour shift.

We went on, and came to a roving bridge, which took the horse over to the other side. Everyone was now on board, so we came through Betton Wood, passed under a railway bridge, and arrived at Victoria Wharf. This was owned by William Rogers, of the Corn Mill, Market Drayton. He also owned two boats.

The next place was Market Drayton Wharf. This was the Company's Wharf. There were six boats waiting to be off-loaded, and light boats in the basin; there were also two boats off-loading coal on Skitt's Wharf. I was told this coal came from the Humber Arm, Donnington, on the Shrewsbury Canal.

At the end of this four mile pound, we approached Tyrley Lock, No. 5, which was cut out of the rock. I saw the birds, swifts or sand martins, going in and out of their nests, which were small holes in the rock. Rising up the locks, we came to Tyrley No. 1. Here there was a long stable, with twenty horses standing, and another stable on the side of a by-lane near the lock, which was for

"The Shops" (Carpenter, blacksmith, stonemason) at Lock, 10, Audlem, with hostel boat Margaret, *which Jack Roberts steered for some time*

closing time was ten o'clock. Then we had a meal and went to bed.

We started off again at four o'clock on Thursday morning. It was very foggy, and we had to walk with Sailor in case we met any traffic. The pound from Tyrley to Wheaton Aston, which is nineteen miles long, was low, owing to its being a very dry summer, and our speed was not very fast. This seemed to worry my Grandpa Owen, and he told me that he had taken a week to pass up the fifteen locks at Audlem a few years before, owing to drought.

As we came up Grub Street cutting, and arrived at Norbury, the mist disappeared. We passed the Wharf, the old pub "The Junction Inn", the Engineering Yard and the stables. There were ten standing horses here. The Brumagem Fly changed horses at Norbury in those days. Jack Tyrler was horse-keeper, and Mr C Palin was the Maintenance Inspector.

We now entered Norbury Valley. At the entrance was an emergency stop-gate, and another at the far end. This was in case there was a breach along this mile-long valley. Next was Gnosall where we passed "The Bridge Inn", and the "Boat Inn". Then we went through the tunnel, which is cut from red rock, and a cutting, which was very narrow, but lovely. Near Bridge 32, on top of the cutting, was a brickyard, with a wharf at the bottom. There was a steam-powered tramway to lower the bricks in small trucks. This brick company was Belshaw's, and I was told it was quite busy. We saw a private boat loading brick. Private boats took more coal and stone, as the Shropshire Union Company was keener on carrying goods and farm stuffs.

Company horses only to spend the night in. On the opposite side was a privately owned stable for the boats which owned their own horses. These were mostly hired boats. The stabling fee was 3d per night. We had a word with Arthur Talbot, the horse-keeper, and he decided we should leave Darky for a rest, and take another horse to Birmingham and back. We changed the harness over to Sailor, another black horse, with four white socks, and a white face, and collected more provender to last to Autherley Junction.

The Skipper decided to go a few miles further, so that he would be in front of the tug next morning. This was a tug which left Ellesmere Port at three o'clock in the afternoon with a fleet of boats for Wolverhampton and Birmingham. It went to Chester, and they were drawn by horse from there to Tyrley, and then by tug to Autherley Junction, leaving Tyrley at five o'clock on the second morning.

We passed through Woodseaves Cutting, and arrived at Goldstone Wharf on Wednesday evening at nine o'clock. We stabled Sailor for the night, which cost 3d. The Skipper and mate had a pint, and I had a mineral [water], as

The Shrewsbury Fly at High Bridge, Shropshire Union Canal

Sailor had been eating his food as we came along this quiet stretch, and now he stopped and asked, in his way, for a drink. Billy attended to this, and then put the muzzle on so that he could not stop to graze. This meant that he could go by himself - "baccering". Billy got back on board, and we all three had our second breakfast. All was quiet as we came through these lovely woods, and arrived at the turnover bridge at High Onn. Billy went along to the mast, and swung the rope over the front end of the boat as Sailor changed sides and went off on his usual pull. We passed High Onn Wharf and Bridge, and saw the five o'clock tug from Autherley coming to meet us. Billy left the boat to look after the horse, and slow him down if required. The tug was the *Rocket*, and was pulling fourteen commercial boats. The tug driver was Joe Challoner. We exchanged a few words in passing, as we came up to Little Onn

Bridge, and a small wharf for the convenience of the farmer.

After going through a lovely stretch of woods, we arrived at Wheaton Aston, and passed the old powder house with its faded old notice "Mooring Place for Powder Boats Only". Passing "The Hartley Arms" on the offside, we came to Wheaton Aston Lock, the first for nineteen miles. Sailor had another feed, and we had to walk with him. A boatman never left the horse unattended while it was carrying its feed-tin as, if the horse fell into the canal, it would be drowned instantly with the feed-tin hung on its head. My father told me that this stretch of canal from Wheaton Aston to Autherley Junction was owned by the Stafford and Worcester Company when it was first built, but later turned over to the Shropshire Union. This was before his time. There was a row of

Avenue Bridge, Chillington ("Fancy Bridge" in the text)

to Chillington Hall. We passed Chillington Wharf, where another Company boat was off-loading goods. I saw a notice on the front of the warehouse "Goods Carefully Handled"; this is still plain to read today, though somewhat faded. As we went through the small rock cutting under Bridge No. 5, the air began to take on an unpleasant smell. I asked the Skipper what it was, and he said we were now entering the Black Country, and would soon be passing the Wolverhampton Corporation Sewage Disposal Works. We went through the "Figure Three", a wide water shaped like the figure, and passed another powder house at Pendeford. At No. 3 bridge, we changed towing paths again, and when we came to No. 2 bridge, Billy stepped onto the bank again, having had a good rest. He went ahead with the Time and Way Bill, to get the shallow lock ready. We entered the lock and collected a few feeds for Sailor at the stable.

houses at Wheaton Aston that still belonged to the Staffs and Worcs.

After his feed, Sailor was baccering well, and we came to Brewood Aqueduct, "The Aqueduct Inn", and a private coal wharf with a boat off-loading coal. This business was managed by the publican. In the distance, I could see Belvide Reservoir, which fed the canal. The Skipper pointed out a cottage on the roadside near the reservoir, which I thought was for the attendant, and told me he had been born there in 1844. Both his father and grandfather were boatmen. Further on we passed the feeder from the reservoir, and arrived at Brewood Wharf and village as the clock struck three. This was a busy wharf for coal, and there was also a warehouse for cattle food and goods. There was a Company boat off-loading goods here.

We went through more lovely woods, and passed under the "Fancy Bridge", an ornamental bridge which carried the drive

Thomas Clayton (Oldbury) Ltd. boats at Autherley Junction, looking north up the Shropshire Union Canal. The toll office is on the extreme left, facing the middle of the stop-lock, which only has a 6" rise from the Shropshire Union Canal to the Staffordshire & Worcestershire Canal

There were ten standing horses here, and three big stables.

This was Autherley Junction. We collected our permit from Ern Parr at the Staffs and Worcester Canal Toll Offices, and Mr Lovekin at the Shropshire Union Canal Office, and entered the Stafford and Worcester Canal. After about half a mile we came to Aldersley Junction on our left, and entered the Birmingham Canal Navigation,

Working boats at Broad Street, Wolverhampton, September 1961

at Gorsebrook. Billy and the Skipper went through the door into the street, and had a quick pint. When they came back there was a Railway Fly Boat waiting for the lock. It was an L.N.W.R. vinegar boat, named *Havana*, going from Wolverhampton to Stourport with three men and a lovely horse. However, all the locks to No. 1 would be in our favour, and the ones we had already come up would be ready for the fly. We passed the Gasworks Basin, the Corporation Works, and other works, till we came to No. 1 Lock. I was told that No. 2 Lock was the fighting ground, as it was well away from the high road, and under the signal box.

We moored the boat by the "Rotten Road Bridge", and I took Sailor across Broad Street to the big depot. There were trams running along the busy street. The horse-keeper took off Sailor's harness and gave him a good wash with the hose, and then examined his shoulders before giving him a clean sawdust bed. This was half past seven on Thursday night. I boarded the boat again, and had a good meal of fish and chips, as the Skipper had been up to town. We had already taken it in turns to have a wash as we came through the locks. The Skipper and mate went to the "New Inn" for a couple of pints. I went into town for a little walk, but I was told not to go far as I had not been before. I was too late for the Empire Theatre. I saw boys of my own age with bare feet, selling matches and newspapers in the street. I returned to the boat and got into bed. Traffic was still busy and there were about twenty boats of different firms moored along both sides of the canal.

going into No. 21 Lock of the Wolverhampton flight. Leaving half of our Staffs and Worcester permit, we collected the permit for the B.C.N. to Birmingham at the Aldersley Toll Office. Luckily we were not bothered with traffic, but the locks were against us.

I walked with Sailor, and Billy got the locks ready. He also raised the top paddles to fill the lock, and I shut one gate for the steerer. We were sailing alongside Dunstall Park Race Course, and then under a high railway bridge

At four o'clock next morning we were away, while traffic was very quiet, as we wanted to be in Birmingham for after dinner. I had to take it in turns to be with the horse, as this part was all side-bridges and branches. It was also very industrial on both sides of the canal. The water was hot and steaming for quite a way coming up to Rough Hills Stop. Here we had to be gauged by the Toll Clerk with a staff, and produce our Birmingham Canal Permit. After being gauged, and setting off again we saw the Brumagem Fly from Ellesmere Port catching up with us. We allowed him to pass as he could travel much faster than we could. We passed through Bilston where the noise and steam from Alfred Hickman's great steel works was terrific, and the water was yellow and hot for a mile. Next was Deepfields Stop, and here our weight and permit were checked again. These checking stops were to find out whether the cargo had been increased or decreased between points. The B.C.N. was a Toll Canal, and very alert for discrepancies. Traffic was very thick here. I saw five Company boats loaded with stone from Trevor, Llangollen, waiting to be off-loaded at a great works with hot furnaces. We now entered Coseley Tunnel which is 360 yards long. It had a towing path on each side, and lamps fixed into the top, though these gave very poor light. There were boats travelling both ways in the tunnel, and you had to be careful with the steering. We next came to Tipton Gauging Stop.

We entered Dudley Port Valley, and passed Dudley Port Station where quite a number of Corporation boats were being off-loaded. Women were on the wharf, searching for coal which had dropped out of the barrows as the men were shovelling, and putting it into baskets on their heads. We passed the junction for Stourbridge on our right, and I could see the New Tunnel (Netherton) in the distance. On the opposite side was Barnett's Blue Brickyard, which was very busy burning, and also quite a number of boats loading bricks. There used to be a big notice by the works "Beware of Mantraps". Towards the end of this valley was Dunkirk Gauging Stop, which was built in the middle of the canal, with a toll office in the centre for the two way traffic.

After being gauged, we went on again and passed Soho Station, and a hole in the wall

Near Albion Bridge, Dudley Port, March 1969, with a British Waterways motor boat towing a Joey boat

When we arrived at the three Tipton Locks there were four boats in front of us, so we had to wait our turn. This gave Sailor time to eat a feed of corn and have a drink, and also gave us time to collect clean water for ourselves. After we had passed down the locks, we entered the bottom summit, which had a towing path on each side of the canal, all the way to Birmingham. This was very convenient when meeting traffic.

where hot bars came from the rolling mills across the towing path. You had to make sure all was clear before you passed in case the horse was frightened. We passed the junction of the Wednesbury Old Canal, and after a mile or so came to Spon Lane (Bromford) Gauging Stop. Here we had to change sides owing to the Junction with the junction. At the Junction to Spon Lane, we changed to our right side again. The Spon Lane Locks Branch branched again for

Oldbury, crossed the main line on the aqueduct and also connected with Stourbridge for Stourport. I noticed the three locks in the distance. We came to a deep cutting, with the Railway Main Line above us on our right, and the top canal on our left. We passed under a very high bridge, which carried the Engine Branch. Traffic was very thick at this point. We reached the Weighing Stop, which weighed all the boats by arrangement, and gave them a

Thomas Clayton's Umea *between locks 7 and 8 of the Wolverhampton flight of 21 locks*

B.C.N. number on a thick plate, which was usually fixed on the side of the hatches where it could be seen. These were mostly newly built boats, or new arrivals from various parts of the Waterways.

We passed the junction to the Smethwick Locks, and the G.K.N. Works, and arrived at Winson Green Gauging Stop. This was the last stop to Birmingham. In the distance, looking up a branch to Scribbon's Flour Mill, I could just see Winson Green Prison. We entered another cutting, with the railway on our towing path side and the backs of houses on the offside, behind a high wall covered with

advertisements. At the end of the cutting was a branch to the Corrugated Iron Works on the offside, and on our side, the branch to Phillip's Bedstead Works. After another half mile we passed Monument Lane, the Railway and Canal Transhipping Depot, and on the offside, a branch to Canning and Wildblood's Jam Factory, and other industries. Still further on, we passed Todd and Watson's great Flour Mill, and on the offside a branch to Tilby's Timber Yard. There were a few S.U.C. [Shropshire Union Canal] boats waiting to be off-loaded of wheat from Ellesmere Port. There were also boats from Gloucester, with more wheat for Todd's.

We now passed the junction for Worcester on our right, and came up to Tindal Bridge. Here there was a flight of thirteen locks. There were about three boats waiting to enter, so we moored to take our turn. We did not yet know which part of Birmingham was our destination, so the Skipper walked around to our depot at Crescent Wharf, which was just this side of the locks, to find out where to take our cargo of soda. When he came back, he told us we were to deliver at Johnstone Wharf in the Hospital Pound, about a mile away, but down the thirteen locks. It was now one o'clock on Friday, and we took our turn to enter, as was wise in this case.

We entered the locks and met traffic in every lock. There were only two gates on the locks, and very short pounds in which to pass. It was a busy industrial area, and the canal passed under the buildings in places. We arrived at our destination and managed to off-load half of our cargo. As there was no stabling, Billy and I walked through the town to Crescent Wharf to stable the horse for the night. After we had taken his harness off and allowed him to drink at the trough, we handed him to the horse-keeper who was employed by the Company, and made our way back to the boat. We arrived to find a good feed waiting for us. My Grandpa had cooked some mutton chops. I managed to have a quick stroll round the city as I had never seen such a large place before, and returned for supper and bed. Next morning the men were busy off-loading the rest of our cargo, and we set off on our way back, after collecting the horse from Crescent Wharf. We went up the thirteen locks again, and arrived at the Company's Depot, Crescent Wharf, for the weekend.

It was midday, Saturday. There were fifteen boats here from Ellesmere Port, waiting to be discharged. These were loaded with sugar, bacon, flour etc., timber, and soap from the Lever Brothers at Port Sunlight. There were a

Gas Street Basin, and Worcester Lock and Bar (with the telegraph pole) - the SUC depot at Crescent Wharf was just off the basin

few men engaged in loading the Brumagem Fly during the afternoon, and he was on his way back to Ellesmere Port by four o'clock. After this all was quiet until six o'clock on Monday morning. On Saturday afternoon I had a walk round the city while Billy washed the boat off and cleaned out the cabin for Sunday. The Skipper went shopping to get provisions for the following week. I returned to the boat and had my tea and then had a good look round the

stables. There were about thirty horses here, all at rest for the weekend. These horses were heavy draft horses, and half-legged "vanners", but the best part were boat horses, all under the care of the horse-keeper, with a watchmen on duty all night. The boatmen could go and groom his own horse or clean the harness, but the feeding was supervised by the horse-keeper until the commencement of the next trip. Next, I found my way to the Alexandra Theatre from seven to eleven to see a play called "Australian Nell", which I enjoyed very much. I had a seat in the gallery for 4d, and I had a few coppers left for sweets as the Skipper had given me a 1/-. When I returned to the boat again, the Skipper was a little upset wondering where I was. He and Billy had been for a few pints.

Sunday morning came, and we rose about nine o'clock. After breakfast, I went round the stables again to have a chat with the boatmen while grooming. Those who had no cooking range on their boats brought their Sunday joint to be roasted. There was a big galley with a large oven, quite a big fire, and also gas. All was spotlessly clean, and cared for by the women who were engaged on the boats. There were quite a few with families, and a number of children attended Sunday School at the Mission. In the afternoon there came a group of people and a preacher with a small church organ. They stood on the Wharf in the centre of all the boats moored there, and held a service. All the boatmen and their families were seated on their own boats listening. I remember the first hymn they sang was "What a friend we have in Jesus", and after several others, the last was the lovely old hymn "Abide with me". I later learned that there were three places on the canal where these services were held every Sunday – Chester, Wolverhampton and Birmingham – and these hymns were always sung as they were the boatmen's favourites. They were also sung at boatmen's funerals.

Monday morning at six o'clock, all the staff were at work on the boats preparing to off-load, some at Crescent Wharf, and some around the district. If our load had been for Crescent Wharf, we should have had to wait our turn, and might have been there for two or three days. There were five wharves here, owned by the Shropshire Union Company, and about six or seven boats could be engaged at one time. Of course, some were loading for Ellesmere Port with various kinds of traffic for export, mostly urgent. On average there were two of these per day. There was also a "gathering" boat which brought in goods from different works as far afield as Oldbury and Smethwick. The name of this boat was the *Skye*, the Skipper T. Scragg, the mate, George Wood, and the horse Arthur. This horse knew his route like a human being, and would do anything for his Skipper when asked, even lying down. There was one private wharf at the Crescent, rented by Pictons Limited. They had two boats which travelled only at night, taking special traffic around the Black Country, one each night. The boatmen would rest in the day, while the boat was being loaded.

It was now nine o'clock on Monday morning, and the Skipper went to the office for orders for our next route. On his return, he told us we were to proceed to Chance and Hunt of Oldbury to collect a cargo of naptha for Manchester, Castle Fields. We arrived at Oldbury at midday, and loaded with fourteen enormous barrels, which I learned were filled with high explosive. We were not allowed a fire, and had to show a red flag, which was fitted on the gangway, and a red lamp at night. We left Oldbury, and managed to reach Broad Street,

Wolverhampton, which was a quick day's work. Here we were told to moor in the wharf, away from the other traffic in the Hay Basin. We put the horse up for the night, and had to have our kettle boiled in the horse-keeper's mess room. We did not care for this, as we had to depend on other people for our hot water all the way to Manchester. It was a good job it was summertime.

We started off from Broad Street at six o'clock on Tuesday morning, and we entered the twenty one locks. We had our B.C.N. Permit, as we had on our uphill journey. We arrived at Autherley Junction at about eight o'clock in the morning. There was a fair amount of traffic about, but we were not delayed as about twelve of the boats were waiting for the tug to Tyrley. These were "Hampton" boats, all heavy loaded and bound for Ellesmere Port. After collecting our provender, we made off again, and when we had put the horse over No. 3 turnover bridge, we allowed him to go by himself with a muzzle on to prevent his grazing. We had had our kettle boiled at Autherley, and we took our second breakfast. After this, I was put to steer for the first time while the Skipper and mate had a nap. I was told to call them up if we should meet uphill traffic, as it was the rule that those going downhill should attend to the horses on those occasions. After coming up to Brewood, I saw a couple of boats in the distance, and called one of the sleepers up. We passed them alright; they were two hired boats from Tipton – W Foster and Sons – loaded with copper ingots for Selly Oak. We then came up to Wheaton Aston Lock, gave the horse a feed and had our kettle boiled for dinner, as it was midday.

The Inspector, Mr Talbot, often travelled all the way from Autherley Junction to Manchester with a naptha boat. If there was no Inspector with you, old Tommy at Hack Green would put his hand over the chimney to see if you had a fire in the cabin range. One day some kids got some paraffin and rags in the stove, and lit it when he put his hand over. They got into trouble over that. He was only doing his duty – he was a very conscientious man.

We set off from Wheaton Aston at a fair rate, as our load was only fifteen tons, and we let Sailor go by himself. I was told to go inside and get a nap. At this point there was a change in the weather; it had been very hot, and now there came a thunderstorm and heavy rain, the first for a month. The Skipper was steering, and we two were inside the cabin. When we came to High Onn, we had to meet the five am tug from Tyrley, with a train of boats that had left Ellesmere Port late on Saturday, and were going to Wolverhampton, Birmingham and other places. They would collect their horses again at Autherley Junction. We passed Norbury, and when we came up to Knighton, we had the kettle boiled again by the lengthsman in his hut, and also gave the horse a feed. We set off again and arrived at Tyrley Locks at eight o'clock, and stabled the horse.

Wheaton Aston Lock. The telegraph poles carried GPO telephone wires alongside the Shropshire Union Canal, linking Birmingham to the north west

Next morning, we harnessed our regular horse, Darky, who had had a few days rest, collected our provender, and had the kettle boiled. We entered the lock, and went on our way, passing Market Drayton, five locks at Adderley, and fifteen locks at Audlem, and reached Hack Green. Here we collected a week's provender to last us to Manchester, and back again to Barbridge Junction. We arrived at Barbridge at three o'clock, and while the Skipper was settling for pay, I went home to take all our laundry, and to collect our clean things. My mother came down to the boat with a few cakes, pies etc., and to see if we were alright. We started off again, and arrived at Wardle Lock, Middlewich. This time we turned left down three locks, passed Henry Seddon's Salt Works, and came to Big Lock. We were accompanied by a fly boat from Derby, a Gandy

Anderton Lift, 1970s, prior to closure and subsequent restoration. It connected the Trent & Mersey Canal (above) with the River Weaver (below)

Fly. He carried on with his journey to Runcorn, but we moored for the night opposite the Tip Top Milk Factory. It was about nine o'clock. We stabled the horse at the Big Lock Inn. There was also a large stores here, for food, clothes, brass, ropes and complete outfits for boatmen.

We were on our way by seven on Thursday morning, passing through the woods. There was traffic in both directions – Anderton Company boats, Salt Union boats, Potters, Meakin's and Brunner Mond's. We passed Marston Salt Works, I.C.I. and the Boat Dock, and came to Dock Bridge, and the Anderton Boat Lift. There were boats to go down to the River Weaver and Weston Point. Next we reached Barnton Tunnel. We had to wait for the tug to come out with a few boats from Runcorn and Preston Brook, the previous days' traffic. When the tug had turned round, we hung on together with a number of other boats, mostly loaded with earthenware from the Potteries, but also including a Shroppie Cheese Fly for Manchester, Castle Fields. Barnton and Saltersford were fairly low tunnels, but quite wide, and there was a very sharp bend on entering Saltersford. They were each about a quarter of a mile long, with a quarter of a mile between them. The same tug hauled us through both tunnels. It ran about every hour and a half each way. We loosed from the tug at the end, pulled our tow rope in and attached to the horse again. We now followed the River Weaver, away below us. I could see the ships and barges passing along, and going through the river locks at Acton Bridge and Saltersford, and also the great swing bridges and railway arches over the river. These last carried the main railway line to Liverpool and Scotland. This four mile length

was all bends to the right and left, and, as I found in later years, very dark at night owing to the wooded surroundings. We came up to Preston Brook Toll Office, and the Shallow Lock. We had to produce our permit, and pay 1/8 for the tugs hauling us through the three tunnels.

In tow again by the other tug, we entered Preston Brook Tunnel. This was about three quarters of mile long. We hung a feed on the horse for him to eat while going over the top.

Bridgewater Canal packet boat Duchess Countess *on the bank at Frankton, after conversion to residential. The boat was broken up in 1956*

All the other horses here had the same. The horses which belonged to the Cheese Fly came over unattended, and both men rode under the tunnel. This was his regular route, and he knew the way, as the boatmen had to leg on the return journey, which was after six on a Sunday evening when the tug did not run. The two men legged the boat through, while the horse made his own way over, eating his feed. He would not stop until the exact right spot at the end of the tunnel. There was a pub on the top of this tunnel named "The Tunnel Top". Some of the horses would try and stop here as their boatmen were used to calling for a pint! We came to the end of the tunnel, and the end of the North Stafford Canal.

We pegged our horses on, and entered the Bridgewater Canal at Preston Brook, collecting our permit at the Toll Office. We passed the large warehouses and transhipping depot, and the junction to Runcorn, and were now in the wide and deep canal, with no more locks all the way to Manchester. We travelled with our friend and butty, the Cheese Fly, passing Moore, Walton, London Bridge, Stockton Heath and Grappenhall. There was quite an amount of traffic going to and from Manchester Docks, including a Bridgewater Tug hauling a dozen flats, Simpson Davies of Runcorn, Rathbone's of Manchester, Union Acid boats, all one-horse flats, mostly laden with coal or sand. Several times I saw one horse pulling two boats, hung together. Sometimes we had to moor to the side, when we were meeting or being overtaken. There were stumps every 80 feet to moor to if necessary, and every mile there was a shuttering to raise, should a horse fall into the canal, as this canal had a wall along the edge to protect the embankment on the towing path side.

We now passed through Lymm, a pretty little town, and as we were coming up to Agden we saw the *Duchess Countess*, which loaded with fruit and vegetables for Manchester at this point each day. This boat was horse-drawn, with a riding saddle for the driver, and therefore the horse could trot along, as it was only a light cargo. We also saw a few market boats from Preston Brook, which called at all the farms en route to Altrincham and Manchester. We passed over the River Bollin, and Dunham Park, and moored for the night at Broadheath with our butty, the Cheese Fly. We stabled the horses, and everyone went for a pint. It was just before dark. These stables were very well cleaned out. They belonged to the Bridgewater Canal, and kept a relief horse for the *Duchess Countess* only. After having supper, we all retired for the night. The Cheese Fly went on

his way again at three o'clock in the morning, to arrive at Castlefields, Manchester by six o'clock to meet the horse wagons which came from London Road Station [now Piccadilly] and distributed the cheese for home and abroad.

We started off at seven o'clock, and arrived at ten on Friday morning. Our friends, the Cheese Fly, were already off-loaded. Our cargo was taken away in wagons which were ready and waiting, but I do not know its destination. We were pleased to see it off, as we could now light a fire in the cabin. During the latter part of the day, we were engaged in loading with macbar, cattle food mixed with treacle which was very sticky to handle, and got all over your clothes. This was for Ellesmere, and Weston in Shropshire. The Cheese Fly was loaded with goods for Market Drayton and Shrewsbury. The men engaged at this wharf were railway men, except for two who were employed by the Shropshire Union. They were Tom Gittins, who had been transferred from Pontcysyllte, near Llangollen, and Albert Oldham, and was an ex-sailor and a Manchester man. Having completed our work by five o'clock, we decided to go to the theatre in Manchester Piccadilly.

We left Manchester at seven o'clock on Saturday morning with our butty, the Cheese Fly whose name was *Tit*. We managed to catch the three o'clock tug at Preston Brook, and the five o'clock tug at Saltersford and Barnton. We arrived at Broken Cross near Northwich by eight o'clock, and stabled the two horses. We had a jolly Saturday evening in the local with songs and music in the company of other boatmen on different routes. On Sunday morning we were on our way again at seven, and having passed through Middlewich and re-entered the Shropshire Union Canal at the junction, we did the ten miles to Barbridge by three o'clock. The horse was stabled here until Monday morning. During my month's holiday, I had travelled 486 miles and passed through 304 locks. My annual holidays had now come to an end, and I had to attend school again. My Grandpa went on to deliver his cargo direct to Ellesmere, Frankton, Pedlar's Bridge, Shade Oak and Weston Wharf near Baschurch.

During the weekend, I groomed Darky and oiled the harness. I also painted the bobbins of cheese from Nantwich the following Thursday. He had to be in the right place for the Cheese Fairs which were held at Whitchurch, Market Drayton and Nantwich in turn. The boat was fitted with special sheets, one of linen and one of heavy white stuff to keep the sun out. There was a cut in the cratch for

Whitchurch Cheese Fair

which were attached to the harness on a strong rope, which we called sides, but were correctly named traces. This stopped the ropes chafing the horse's sides. The horses also wore little caps, fastened on top of the bridle, to keep the flies off their ears. The boatwomen used to knit these. They also made rosettes for the horses in red, white and blue, and collars for the donkeys.

Part of the Cheese Fly's cargo was transhipped at Barbridge into a boat bound for Shrewsbury. This was arranged with the other depots, Ellesmere Port or Calveley Station Sidings, as the Cheese Fly was only allowed to deliver to Market Drayton on his way to collect his cargo

the air to get through. All the shelves were numbered, and the cheeses were stowed only two high to avoid damage, and not in boxes as they were when they came from abroad. After delivering his cheese to Manchester, he could lay these fittings in the bottom of the hold and make it more convenient for his return cargo. This boat could take twenty tons of cheese, but an ordinary boat could only take six or seven as they were not fitted out properly. This was a two-handed fly, and the Skipper's name was Isaac Lowe, and the mate, his nephew, John Lowe. The horse was owned by the Skipper in those days, and the rate was 6½d per mile each way, on an average 160 miles per week.

On the following Friday evening my Grandpa returned from his trip to Weston via Glyn Ceiriog with a cargo of Macadam Stone. He found me a job offloading onto the wharf. This stone was for Nantwich County Council. I was given a small shovel, and learned how to use it! When the job was complete, the Skipper went into the office to settle his Time and Way Bill, and get his pay. He gave me 2/- which was quite a lot in those days. I heard him discussing the trip with his mate. He was paid by the ton from Barbridge to Weston at a rate of 1/6 per ton. He only had fifteen tons weight, but was paid for twenty tons, which he could carry when full. This was the agreement for bulky traffic only. The whole amount came to 50/-, which included his twenty ton return cargo of stone with a red Time Bill, paid at 1/- per ton. If you had a red Time Bill, your journey must be completed in a certain time; if your cargo was not so urgent you would be issued with a white Time Bill, and this reduced your tonnage by 3d per ton, or your mileage by ½d per mile. This boat was a tonnage boat, when working on the Shropshire Union Canal. When it left this canal, it would be paid mileage.

On Monday morning, it was school again. The days were getting shorter as it was coming winter, but I still saw the fly boats passing. I now went back to school with my older brother, George, who was twelve. During the holidays he had been helping the farmers with the harvest, and playing in the local football team on Saturdays. This did not interest me much. My brother was very keen on sport, but he would go on the boat at times too.

I still had four years at school, but I went for short trips at weekends whenever I could. I went with my Grandpa, and also with my brother-in-law who had just become Skipper of the *Brett*, a boat taking timber from Ellesmere Port to Birmingham. It was the custom to start with a timber boat in those days. He had his own horse, Crusader, from the Newtown Fly. During this time I learned to steer a boat, drive a horse, and raise a paddle correctly.

"Passing down Bunbury Locks on Chester route, Daughter Freda in rear on top of Boat." 2 May 1961

5

DOWN TO SHREWSBURY 1906, AND IN THE ICE 1907

In 1906 I remember going on a trip on the Shrewsbury Canal as far as Uffington. My father had a Trench fly named *Opal*. The mate was a chap of about twenty called Jack Stubbs, engaged by my father. When we got to Berwick Wharf there was a bucket, clean as new, placed by the wall. It was full of water that ran very slowly from a spring, and was kept there for the local people as well as the boatmen. We tipped it into our water vessel.

We then passed through Berwick Tunnel, and Dad took the horse over the top. It was quite a

Both portals of Berwick Tunnel,
970 yds long, 6' 10" headroom (Bradshaw, 1904)

long walk as the tunnel was over half a mile long. When we left the tunnel, we passed under a railway bridge that carried the main G.W.R. Paddington line. To the right of the canal was a big hall with Upton Magna mountain in the background. Near the next bridge there was a brickyard busy firing bricks, and an old boat called *Eva* loading bricks for Pimley, which was not far away.

We arrived at Uffington with a load of mixed corn for Mrs Geoffrey's Mill, which was on the side of the river Severn. We reported our arrival at the Mill, and a two-horse wagon came to the boat to collect the load. The load was collected in two journeys. It was only a short distance. There was no warehouse, only a small crane by the canal. Nor was there much space for the wagon between the side of the canal bridge and the small cottage and Post Office. When we passed this shop, I heard a little girl's voice say: "I go to sea and Hanover, who's put rice in my tea". It was teatime. We turned the boat at Sundorn Wharf, as we had a few goods for the shop there.

On our return journey, we entered the tunnel again, and I was put to steer so that Jack could leg the boat through, and Dad take the mare, called Wren, over the top. When we neared the other end and were passing under the last light hole, someone on the top dropped clods down onto the boat. This angered Jack Stubbs, who was easily aroused, and he used some foul language. I copied him, using the same language. Next thing I heard a voice coming down: "Wait till you get out, I'll learn you better than that". We came out, and I learned. I was given a few strokes across my shoulders with the double of the whip. I wonder what Dad would think of the language today!

When this was all over, I asked why there was no towing path in this tunnel. Dad told me that there had been a very narrow one, when the tunnel was made just big enough for a man and a donkey to haul the tubs through. When the commercial boats started coming, it was taken out, and chains were fixed to one side to pull short tub boats through. Each tub could take four tons of coal from Donnington Colliery. I remember the chains, and also the tub boats. There are a few of them sunk at Rodington and Sundorn Wharf.

Lock 2, Norbury Flight, 1965

The Skipper of the Shrewsbury Fly, Evan Powell, trained his horse to walk into the canal, and had a galvanised collar made for the purpose which he fixed on the horse's shoulders. It would then haul the boat through the tunnel, as the depth was only two foot six inches, and it had a hard bottom. I knew Mr Powell, and he told me this himself. Three brothers worked this Shrewsbury Fly, Evan, Jim and Dick. I saw the horse too. It was fourteen hands high and its name was Coot. Evan had the Llangollen Fly in later years and passed away while at work at Grindley Brook Locks in 1920. Dick passed away near the Aqueduct at Nantwich after going for a pint of beer on the main road in 1922. Jim died at Ellesmere Port.

As I have been talking about the Shrewsbury Canal, I will record my memories of the second trip I made, when I was about thirteen, in 1907.

Our boat's name was the *Crescent,* after Crescent Wharf. It was an ex-Brumagem Fly and a good swimmer. We were taking a load from Manchester Castle Fields to Shrewsbury Castle Fields, the G.W.R. joint wharf, and into the basin. The load was cattle food from abroad to be distributed at different places from Newport onwards.

We first came down the seventeen locks from Norbury. These included one at Mosspool, and Old Hannah's and Tom Moore's Lock above Newport Lock. In charge of Newport Wharf was Joe Tonkinson, who was assisted when necessary by Tom Moore and Charlie Oakley, the lock-keepers who took alternate weeks. They were on the locks all night in those days. The next was Polly's Lock, where there was a hut for the lock-keeper to go in at night. There were quite a few houses at Bloomfield Place where two boatmen who worked the Trench Fly lived, and also a bungalow for Joe Tonkinson.

At Newport Lock there was a pub called "The Wharf Tavern". It was a jolly good pub for the

Newport Lock, Basin and Warehouse, winter 1965

boatmen at nights. Mrs Felton was the proprietor. This was a very busy wharf, and there were a few shops on the canal bridge. One was a confectioners, and always had a lovely variety of cakes which was very convenient for the boatmen and their families.

Wappenshall warehouse at the junction - July 1965

over Kynnersley Aqueduct. Under Preston Bridge we could see a work-house, and also a Hall, and a wide patch of water with a few rowing boats moored in the boat-house. The canal was covered with water lilies. There was plenty of depth from here to Wappenshall, and all wide water and pike galore.

When we entered Wappenshall Junction, Bill Salmon was waiting for us. He was the porter here, and lived at the cottage. He had a few tons for Shrewsbury, transhipped off a Trench Fly. We collected this. The warehouse was a great high building, erected over the canal. It belonged to the Duke of Sutherland. To our left were the nine Trench Locks with their guillotine gates, which I was to experience in later years.

From Newport, we passed down two more locks, and arrived at Edgmond Wharf. This was a private wharf and warehouse owned by the Lilleshall Coal Company. In charge was Frank Owen, a very conscientious chap. He was a bomb-thrower in the First World War, and was killed. There were several private boats here, hauling coal from the Humber Arm to different places to Shrewsbury. We left four ton here.

We then passed down Edgmond Lock. This was the widest single lock on the Shroppie. It was wide at the top, and the lock walls were built on the slope so that it was much narrower at the bottom. I do not know the reason for this, but I suspect it was either built on sand, or to accommodate some little flats that used to run between Humber Arm, and Edgmond Lock, with coal. It was six miles to Wappenshall, all open flat countryside. The fields were covered with mole-hills, and the mole catcher was busy with his traps at Crabtree Bridge and Buttery Valley. Changing towing paths at the bridge, we passed

We turned right through the drawbridge, and came to Eyton Lock. This had a guillotine gate, and we had a special big windlass to wind it up. My father and brother George attended to this.

Wappenshall Junction

Below the lock was a drawbridge which was awkward for the boatmen as it was so close to the lock. You had to pull it up before you came out of the lock. Isaac Clark, the lengthsman lived near it. I managed to swing the bridge by jumping on the chain. Any boat can pass down these locks, but not down the nine Trench Locks. The second lock was at the end of a stretch that ran through a lovely spinney. This also had a guillotine gate, with a long box weighted with scrap iron to make it easier to wind up. The paddle to empty the lock was fixed on these gates.

It was wintertime, and a little frosty, and thin ice was appearing in the water, which caused the Skipper much concern. Two nights of frost meant stop. At Longlane, there was a small iron bridge on the towing path side. It was very low – just high enough to allow tub boats to enter the basin and coal wharf which were run by the Lilleshall Coal Company. There was a very small warehouse here, which held a couple of ton, but we had no traffic for it. The canal now became very narrow, and there were two low bridges. The first was a new one which led to "The Buck's Head", where you could stable the horse and have a good pint. The road went round and crossed the canal at the next bridge. We then passed under a railway line, the branch line from Nantwich to Wellington. Next was a draw-bridge which required two of us to lift it. The second draw-bridge was by the little church at Longden, where the headstones were so close to the offside of the canal, one could read the inscriptions. Just before the bridge were two cottages, where the Skipper who worked the Shrewsbury Fly lived. This was William Musson, but they called him Peggy Musson as he had a peg leg. We exchanged words with his missus, who was expecting him home that night.

The next bridge was a fairly high iron one, where we had to unpeg the horse and swing the rope underneath as there was no towpath. We now entered an unusual aqueduct, where the horse walked along the bottom of the tank. There was a long wall of strong iron, with iron supports fixed across the towpath to hold the water in. The horse could comfortably take a drink out of the canal in the tank, by simply turning his head. This was about seven foot six inches wide, and was built over a brook and marshy ground.

We now arrived at Longden Wharf, and we had a couple of ton to leave here for Longden Mill, a short distance away. Mr W Arnold used to collect it. This was a busy wharf for wheat and coal, and there was also a brickyard owned by Mr Finney of Poolway, near Welshpool. All his requirements were carried by canal. The wharf was owned by the Lilleshall Coal Company, which employed Mr Arnold. We stayed here for the night. There was a good stable for Tim, the horse, and also a country pub, called "The Pheasant".

Longdon-on-Tern Aqueduct, August 1966

Next morning the canal was frozen over, about a quarter of an inch thick, which made it a little difficult for Tim. However, we only had a light load. We went along with the Wrekin in view, raising and lowering the drawbridges, and leaving another ton of meal at Rodington and Withington, two small wharves and a shop. Withington was very pretty, with a lovely church by the canal. When you pulled the drawbridge up, the end just touched the church wall. There were three drawbridges fairly close together here. We saw the lengthsman, John Venables, busy cutting the hedge.

Jack Roberts' father, with horse Bobby, outside the family home at Basin End, Nantwich, where daughter Freda was born

We kept on going steadily, as there was not much depth along this part of the canal. The next bridge was a small foot-bridge over the canal, near Upton Magna station. It was called "Gallows Bridge", as an old man had hung himself there years before. Next was Upton Magna Railway Bridge which took the main line to Paddington over. Near this point was a large Hall. We passed under two more low bridges, and changed sides with the horse. Our next stop was at Berwick Wharf. Mr Wild, who owned the wharf, collected our cargo into a small warehouse. There were also a coal wharf here, and several small country cottages. Mr Wild and his wife and family were very pleasant

people, and always pleased to see us come. He gave us a drink of home brewed beer.

At the next bridge, the towpath changed sides again. We collected the bucket of clean spring water, and passed on to the tunnel. I took the horse back to the last bridge, and found my way over the top of the tunnel to the other end. Dad and brother George legged through, and were out by the time I arrived. The tunnel was about half a mile long, but the distance over the top was about a mile and a half.

Our next stop was Shrewsbury, five miles further on. We passed Uffington and Sundorn, and came up to Comet Bridge which had just been rebuilt by the Shropshire Union Company. We passed Jones Malters Mill, Factory Bridge, the Gasworks and Brown's Flour Mill, and arrived at Castlefields, the G.W.R. wharf and basin, where we winded off the bridge. Here we delivered the rest of our cargo. The main Railway Station and Junction, His Majesty's Prison, and the canal wharf and depot were all situated in this area. The horse was stabled at the old "Canal Tavern", overlooking the canal.

While we were here, we heard of a railway accident that had recently occurred on Crewe Bank, near Shrewsbury Railway Station and the canal. It had happened on October 15 1907; the 1.20 am mail from Crewe to the West of England had over-run the signals just outside Shrewsbury Station, and failed to negotiate the sharply curved approach to the platform. The engine and coaches overturned, and eighteen lives were lost. As we had a little free time, old Tom from the wharf, offered to escort us to the scene of the accident. There a few broken parts from the coaches, but otherwise everything had been cleared away. Father also took us both around the Quarry and Dingle, which looked very pretty, although it was winter.

We loaded the boat again with bundles of paper and a few bales of rags for Edgmond Paper Mill, and completed our load with meal from Brown's Mill, through the bridge. In part of the basin were tub boats unloading coal. Loading at the Gas Works was a Thomas Clayton boat from Oldbury. It was the boat *Usk*, worked by a husband and wife, Harry and Polly, who were a very clean couple. They had no family.

In the morning we found we were frozen up, and could not go. We were told that the ice-boat was on its way to relieve us, bringing the Shrewsbury Fly with it. The Skipper knew we could not move that day without it. The ice-boat arrived at about four o'clock together with the Fly and two Trench boats. These were *Mentor* and *Spot*, Skippers John Wood and Dick Wooley, and had loads of barley for Jones the Malters. They all stopped here for the night.

The following morning we all set off. We went a short distance behind the ice-boat, which was hauled by six farm horses. Harry, the Gas boat came last, but we had to keep helping him as he was loaded with eighteen tons, and could not put speed on owing to the shallowness of the canal. The ice was now two inches thick. We arrived at the tunnel, and helped one another through, managing to make Withington for "bait" i.e. dinner for men and horses. The horses were stabled at the big farm on the canal bank opposite the church. All the ice-boat crew had their sandwiches and a pint in the local pub. While they had their dinner, we unloaded part of our cargo from Shrewsbury.

We went on and unloaded at Rodington and Long Lane, and the ice-boat waited for us each time. The crew of the ice-boat consisted of eight rockers, a steerer and a rope-man, all working on the boat, and three horse-drivers. The latter were all farm hands, but the boat crew were lengthsmen. The ice-boat was named *Wappenshall* after the village where she was stationed. It was built of iron and was the smallest on the canal, as it had been constructed to navigate the narrow locks of the Trench, though it would, of course, go through to Norbury Junction as well. After a gruesome day, we made Wappenshall at about nine o'clock in the moonlight. The farm hands took their horses home for the night to the farm nearby. We stabled our two horses at the Company's stable at the wharf. We had

Ice-boat (breaker) Wappenshall

managed fourteen miles that day, from Shrewsbury to Wappenshall.

Next day, we covered the ten miles from Wappenshall to Norbury. With a few exceptions, the canal was much deeper and wider on this stretch. The ice-boat set off at a gallop for a couple of hundred yards, and then came to a near stop, forcing a flush of water to lift and loosen the ice from the sides. It was rocked at the same time to break the ice. This was the correct way to go, and it could not be done with a motor-driven boat. Going was much easier and faster this day, and we soon arrived at Edgmond wide lock, where we had to stop and deliver part of our cargo of rags and paper. When we had unloaded we had to collect another load of paper for Liverpool. The ice-boat and the other traffic went on their way to Norbury Junction to relieve all the traffic from Trench, Humber Arm, and Newport, who all carried cargo.

The Skipper went up to the village which was a mile away, to explain our position and ask them to send our load down as soon as possible if it was ready. They started right away and it was delivered to the boat in a few hours being hauled by two horse-wagons. Thanking them, we set off again loaded with sixteen tons of solid paper in blue bundles. We had difficulty going along with only one horse, and a load, as the canal was almost frozen over again, but we managed to make Newport, two miles away. I had to go ahead and work the paddles at the first lock to move the water and loosen the ice. If there had been snow on the ice, we could not

have managed this, as the ice will not crack under snow.

When we arrived at Newport, Dad said there was going to be a change in the weather. My brother asked him how he could tell, and he said it was by the smoke coming from the chimneys. He was right. It was thawing next morning, so we were able to travel. We met the ice-boat in the seventeen locks. There were quite a few obstructions owing to ice getting behind the lock gates, which jammed the boat at times. We had to use the paddles often. However we managed to reach Market Drayton for the night.

This was an urgent load for shipment. We called at home at Barbridge next day and made Ellesmere Port by midnight, where we were unloaded straight into the ship, which was already loaded with many different classes of cargo for export. It was Thursday night.

Next morning we were ordered to Chester Cow Lane Depot light. There we were loaded for Welshpool and Newtown, half for J Hughes of Llanfair, Welshpool, and half for Newtown. I had to leave the boat at Barbridge to attend school.

George No. 1 at the Welshpool Standard Granite Company's wharf in Welshpool

6

LEAVING SCHOOL

I cannot remember my odd trips in much detail, but I do remember one week when my Grandad came from Ellesmere Port with a load of sugar, sultanas, currants, lard and other food stuffs for Nantwich only. As it was a Saturday, I went for the day and returned at night.

On Sunday we were back again at Barbridge after our day at Nantwich. This gave me a chance to feed and groom the horse again. My grandfather made his home with our family at Barbridge, as he was a widower and in his sixties. After another week at school, my brother, George, left and was engaged on the Newtown Fly with my father. He went as kid, which was the grade to a boatman in those days, and saved my father the cost of a hand, and also saved my mother's pocket with regard to food and clothes. My father gave him half wages, 4/- per week, and his food.

I was the next one to leave school, and I was anxious for that day to come as I did not like studying very much. Towards the end of my school days I often had a holiday of my own accord, though I never got into mischief, and always returned home with those who had attended! However, there was trouble when the School Board bloke checked the register, and my mother had to pay on the last occasion, so from then, I ceased to be absent. Once I had walked after the boat, and told my Grandfather I was on holiday, but the second time I was told I was holidaying too often, and my excuse would not wash!

About this time we had sad news concerning my cousin Alfred Roberts. He was drowned at Pharum's Lock, which was one of the Cheshire Locks. He had been engaged on a Salt Union Fly and lived at Wheelock. My Uncle George

and Aunt were very upset. They were engaged on a Pottery Fly, having previously left the Shropshire Union Fly. In a few months my Uncle returned to the old firm, and was engaged on a slow boat named *Beatrice* on the Pottery route from Ellesmere Port. Not long after there was sad news again. Their second son, Harry, was drowned at Tilston Lock on the Chester branch near Tarporley. My Uncle came with the boat the same day, and broke the news to us. The body was sent to Sandbach Station from Calveley Station. This was a terrible tragedy as they were both in their early youth and strong and healthy. The family will never forget these bereavements.

In the second instance, Harry had raised the paddle, gone across the foot-board, slipped and fallen into the fore-bay, the entrance to the lock. He then went through the paddle hole into the lock and under the two boats. This was a big lock, and if it had been free from boats he might have had a chance. While I am on this subject, I would like to give some advice to present holidaymakers on the canals. Never get on the wrong side to raise a paddle. If your windlass comes off when you are standing on the right side, you will only fall to the ground, but if you are on the wrong side you will fall into the canal. If the spindle is wet, just dip your windlass or key into the ground, or any gritty substance, and it will grip the spindle better.

Nick Jones of Barbridge once told me he had been through the paddle-hole at Queen's Head top lock. He was ahead, drawing the paddle when he slipped and fell in. He went right through the paddle hole, and was there standing up in the bottom of the lock when his dad came with the boat. He was lucky! I had an experience at that lock when I was running in the dark to get it ready. I fell over two donkeys which got up and started braying. I've never run so fast!

It was one evening in 1904 at Barbridge

Warehouse that I learned that the Shropshire Union Canal Company had arranged for a new wall to be erected around Hurleston reservoir. It was quite a long job, and thirty men were engaged from the locality for about two years. The stone for the walling came from Trevor, Llangollen, and also from Llanymynech and Crickheath on the Montgomeryshire Canal. It all came by canal of course, and was carried by the Company's boats. A wharf was built at Hurleston Junction, and still exists. A railway was built to take the stone to the site in small wagons, which was about a mile round. A few of us boys went to see it whenever we could, and begged a ride on the wagons which were pulled by a Tom Pony engine and rope near the workings. The job was completed in 1906. All the boatmen who were employed by the Shropshire Union Canal Company on this job lived at Barbridge, Burland and Swanley.

The first breach I ever remember hearing about was in 1908. The canal breached near Newport, Salop, on the embankment at Meirtown opposite the church and near the river. This meant a fortnight's work and the urgent traffic to Newport, Trench and Shrewsbury had to be despatched by rail. The urgent goods traffic that was stranded near the breach had to be hauled away by the railway horse and dray. What was

not urgent or perishable was kept in the boats until the breach was mended. The men from the boats were engaged on the repair work.

Also around this time, I heard from the boatmen engaged on the Manchester routes, that there had been a serious breach on the North Stafford Canal at Marbury near Marston. The towpath went, and took one of the returning cheese flys [see Appendix 6] over the edge with it. The boat, whose name was *Ruth*, Skipper Joe Jones, was now on dry land. The two other cheese boats had to return to Manchester, and go up the Peak Forest Canal via Marple and Kidsgrove Junction, down Cheshire Locks to Middlewich, and the Shropshire Union canal to Barbridge again. This breach was a three weeks job, but the boat was recovered safely.

It was in 1908 also, that there was another serious breach at Chirk Bank, by the Quinta Bridge. This took the embankment, and about six miles of water, down the hundred foot drop to the River Ceiriog, a quarter of a mile across the fields, and over the main road to Holyhead. This point was near Chirk Aqueduct and Viaduct, on the Shropshire and Denbighshire border, where there is a lovely view of the hills, forestry, church and Chirk Castle. I was to see all these places in later years. There were no casualties on this occasion, but it took a few weeks to repair the breach. The food and goods traffic that had already arrived was taken by horse drays, but the remainder was allowed to stay in the boats. The men from the boats were again engaged in mending the breach, as was usual in such cases.

In the following year, 1909, the culvert collapsed close to No. 2 Lock at New Martin, near Whittington. This was not quite so serious, as it was noticed by

Canal breach at Marbury, 1907

Canal breach (Bryn Howell)

the lengthsman at the time. There was a short delay while a wooden trough was sent by boat from Ellesmere Yard and placed over the culvert. This was then piled, and the canal bed puddle with clay at each end. When it was completed, the dam which had been placed across the canal was taken out, and the water and traffic returned to normal. Later a new culvert was erected, and the trough was taken away. I have not known this method to be used since, but I did see it on this occasion, as I was on the boat for a week.

It was at Pendeford, one Sunday during the second World War, that an enemy aircraft mistook a white shed near the canal for a house that was used as a landmark, and dropped a bomb on the towpath. Two oil boats were going past at the time. Sid Gibbons was one of the Skippers. The water started going out of the cut,

and both boats got stuck. Fortunately it was not a high embankment, and the towpath was soon patched up again. The plane was shot down at Nuneaton.

May 29th, 1908 was my fourteenth birthday, and also the day I left school. The previous day we had been sixteen miles to Chester on a Sunday School outing in a two-horse brake. This was our form of travel in those days. There were about four vehicles in all, and it was just a country outing from the Mission Room at Barbridge. This had only just been opened, and was converted from an old warehouse known as Black Shed, and run by the Church Army. Captain Phippin was the preacher allocated, and various other preachers would take service on Sunday. These were mainly arranged for the boat people, but local residents also attended.

Two or three years later, this preacher emigrated, and was replaced by an old Navvy preacher, who was allowed a Company house to live in. He could preach an excellent sermon, and was well liked by all. If an incident occurred, and two boatmen started fighting, he would go and talk to them and all would be well. He had experienced a rough and tumble life himself, and preached accordingly. He stayed until he retired, but I never heard where he went then.

I now entered my working life, and started on the boats. The evening before I went, my school-master came to see me on his bicycle and tried to persuade me to stay another year. I told him I had been waiting to leave school for too long, and would not entertain the idea. He smiled, and wished me well and left me, but I often wish I had taken his advice. I remember I had just started to learn the metric system, and now today the government is introducing the scheme in reality.

7

A BOATMAN AT LAST, TO LEEK, EDSTASTON AND KIDDERMINSTER

My father had previously decided to give up the Newtown Fly, and was at that time engaged on a reserve North Boat, running to North Wales mostly. He was working with my brother George, who was now sixteen. George became engaged on another Newtown Fly, *Fancy*, as mate to my Uncle Jack Owen, my mother's brother. This was a lovely little craft, specially lightly built for speed on a shallow canal.

My first trip in George's place as mate to my father was on the boat *Times*, an ex-Brumagem Fly placed for this section. We were bound for Leek on the Caldon Canal, with a cargo of sugar and flour. We left Barbridge on a Sunday morning, went down the Middlewich Branch, and entered the North Stafford Canal to go up the twenty one Cheshire Locks.

We passed up the first locks, and came to Hassall Green, where there were two single locks. As was expected, traffic built up here, both up and down, and there was about half an hour's delay. A mile further on, after a quick bite of food, we came to two double locks at Rhode Heath, then after another mile we passed up Lawton Church Locks, Red Bull Locks, and Plant's Lock at the last. Here we moored for the night, as it was nine o'clock. This was near Kidsgrove, a gloomy smoky place.

We rose at six next morning, gave the horse a feed and had our breakfast. Then we entered Harecastle Old Tunnel. At this time the tunnel was for uphill traffic only. I took the horse over the top, and my father legged the boat from the cabin roof with half a sack of provender to lie on. No fire was allowed in the cabin, but we had a home-made lamp, called a "duck". This was a golden syrup tin, with an inch of round pipe and a short piece of cotton rope fitted through the lid. This was filled with paraffin, and gave a fair light, but smoky. We had a clear run through, and it took nearly an hour to leg it as this tunnel is about a mile [and three quarters] long – 2,897 yards.

Hooking on again, we passed Tunstall, Longport and Burslem. There were quite a few pottery works, and a big dock repair yard belonging to the Anderton Company. As we passed Shelton Steel Works, there was a deafening noise, and the water in the canal was

Rode Heath Mill, with internal wharf for unloading; demolished relatively recently

yellow, dirty and hot. We were pleased to get away from there. When we had passed Etruria, we left the main canal at Stoke Top Lock.

We called at our office at Etruria Wharf for instructions and our permit for the Caldon Canal. All being well, we entered the rise of two locks. This was where one of my school-mates had been drowned a few weeks before. He was Aber Poole from Barbridge, and had been engaged working with his father the same as me. We next passed Joiner's Square, where there were a number of boats off-loading flints and china-clay from Ellesmere Port and Runcorn. We also passed the Robert Heath Colliery and Ivy House and came to Hazlehurst Junction where we turned right for Leek. It was lovely countryside again. We went through the tunnel, and arrived at our destination. It had

A recent photo of both Harecastle tunnel northern portals at Kidsgrove. Until 1914, when mining subsidence caused James Brindley's "old tunnel" (right) to be closed, both were used - Brindley's for uphill/northbound traffic, with boats legged through. Thomas Telford's later tunnel, also subject to severe subsidence over the years, is still in use, although the final disconnected sections of towpath were not removed until the 1980s.

been a long busy day. We stabled the horse, which was our own, at the wharf there.

The following morning, we off-loaded with a hand-crane and our own man-power, two bags at a time. After a break for breakfast, we continued and completed our cargo, and had the road notes signed for. One they kept, and one was signed and handed back to the skipper. We turned the boat around for the return journey, having been informed by telephone to proceed to Ivy House to collect 18 tons of coal for Edstaston near Wem, Salop. We arrived at the colliery the same evening, reported our

arrival, and were told we were to be loaded next day. Wednesday morning came and we were loaded by ten o'clock, and made Etruria that evening. We stabled our horse at "The Bird in Hand", which is situated by the Etruria Lift, the last locks on the Caldon Canal.

On the Thursday morning, the Skipper reported to the Company's office. This was a Shropshire Union Wharf, and quite a few boats were waiting to off-load their cargoes of goods, flints etc. The Pottery Fly was being attended to, as he had priority. We received our uphill Time and Way bill, and signed for our road note. We were given a new Way Bill and our cargo was entered. This was a white bill as the cargo was not urgent. It meant a penny a mile less, so we had sevenpence a mile to Barbridge, and fivepence instead of sixpence on the Shropshire Union. Our boat was graded as a North Wales boat, and whatever part of the canal system we travelled on, we would always take our cargoes on that route. On this occasion however, we were engaged on this other route, as the Welsh Canal was not so busy as it was summer time and the cattle did not require meal etc.

We left Etruria on Friday morning at nine o'clock, and went back past the Shelton Steel Works. We arrived at Harecastle Down Tunnel, which we could take the horse through. About half-way through, I could hear the horse's feet on the planks, proddling through water, which he did not like. The Skipper had to speak roughly to him, and used the stick at this point. The horse had not been through this tunnel before, and was not aware of the conditions. It was a temporary towpath, as the old path had sunk. Also, the roof of this part of the tunnel was very low for about a hundred yards. There were other boats ahead and behind us. We reached the end, and daylight, and we all raced for the locks.

At Plant's Lock, we allowed them to pass, as they were mostly light-loaded with crates of pottery for Runcorn, Ellesmere Port and Manchester Docks. We had to wait behind a dozen boats for our turn at the lock. This was the junction for the Macclesfield Canal, and boats from that area were waiting too. We entered the lock and continued our journey. Each boat drew a paddle to fill the lock for the

Wardle Canal and Lock, Middlewich, looking from the junction with the Trent & Mersey Canal, July 1962

boat behind him. This was the boatmen's rule in Cheshire Locks, where a friendly attitude prevailed. However, they did not open the gates, the following boat had to do that.

We arrived at Middlewich on Friday night at eight o'clock, and entered Wardle Lock. We were "on our own ground" as the boatmen said. I took Dick, the horse, to King's Lock Stable with his supper and also a drink of clean water. The water on the North Stafford here was dirty and salty, and you had to pick your places for the horse to drink. This did not apply on the Shroppie where the water was always clean. After a good meal, the Skipper went for a pint or two and a chat with the other boatmen at "King's Lock Inn". I went for fish and chips at the shop opposite the main road, which was owned by a boatman. We both made our way back to the boat and bed.

We left on Saturday morning and arrived at Barbridge at eleven o'clock. We stabled the horses at "The Jolly Tar", and looked forward to a weekend in. The Skipper required money for the following week, both for the home and for the boat. He was allowed to draw the amount necessary in advance at Barbridge Office. You were allowed this anywhere on the canal system. If you were not at your settling office, it would be entered on your Way Bill. In this case, Ellesmere Port was our depot. Sometimes you could be away from the depot for a month or more. You could also collect money at Railway Stations, where you were also allowed a quarter rail fare if you wanted to visit home at a weekend or any other time.

On Saturday afternoon, I had to wash and clean out the cabin and do the brasswork. This was the usual routine. The Skipper was very fussy in this respect – too much so, I thought! The interior was all white woodwork, and not painted. You would scrub the coalbox white, and then put coal in it! The footboard and hatches were white ash, and looked very nice, like a mackerel's back when dry. You would put either a piece of thin board or white paper there to step on when steering. There must not be a spot on the paint, and when steering, you were not allowed to touch the paintwork with your boots. The tarpaulins were mopped and the white ropes were scrubbed too.

The Skipper expected me to wash my feet every night before going to bed. I did this in the canal in summertime. Sometimes, when travelling, I would have a swim, holding on to the stern rope. This was great fun. After removing my clothes, I would go along to the fore-end, dive in, and grasp the rope at the helm. To get out again, I would climb up the helm, and dress on top of the cabin. I must not make a mess inside, oh no! One of our hobbies on a Sunday at Barbridge was jumping the village brook. This was quite a physical feat. If you failed to co-operate, you were thrown in. Another pastime was jumping over the barrels, either beer or oil, which were stored on the wharf. We would start with one, and add another and another. I would manage four, which would be roughly twelve feet. Another youth, Potter, could manage five or six, equal to eighteen feet. We certainly could spring! Our other occupation was arguing who had the best horse or boat, as we were practically all boatmen's sons. This would end up with a fight, shirts off and bare fisted in the boatman's style. Sunday would then end in the mission room!

Back to work on Monday, those who were already for their next voyage set off at about six o'clock. We were for the Welsh Canal. I was the driver, and hooked Dick on again. At Bridge 98, I collected the windlass, trotted ahead and

made the lock ready, and then came back to attend to the horse, leading him over the bridge at Hurleston Junction to the entrance to the locks. We passed through these locks rather slowly owing to our heavy cargo, and arrived at Grindley Brook at the end of nineteen locks, and a lovely stretch of scenery. It was about four o'clock. We moored for the night at Platt Lane, Whixall, at eight o'clock. It was June, and lovely weather, and after doing my usual jobs on the boat, I was able to spend a while fishing. The Skipper had a little chat with the local shop-keeper and other boatmen who were moored there for the night. There were also a

Jack Roberts repairing the wooden hostel boat Margaret *at Grindley Brook in the 1960s*

few private boatmen who lived locally at this little country place. The industry was mostly peat and agriculture. The local pub was "The Wagonners", a very old Inn in black and white with beams and an old-fashioned fire-grate.

We set off again next morning, came to the junction on the left, and entered the Wem Branch. We took the horse over the roving-bridge, and raised the lift up bridges. The next three miles were very slow and heavy for the horse – "a snail's gallop", the boatmen called it. Just ahead, I saw some smoke over the hedge, and remarked upon it to my father. He said it was old John Wild boiling his kettle for breakfast. They called him "Forty Patches". He lived along the canal all summer, moving from place to place. We stopped the boat to give the horse a feed and rest, and have our breakfast as it was half-past eight. We had a little chat with old John. He had collections of song books and Old Moore's Almanac, which he was selling at a penny for a song book and threepence for an almanac. This was his living. I bought one of each. His breakfast was egg and bacon, served on a clean white plate, and cooked in a small frying pan. He had already had a wash, and his bed was rolled up and placed by the trunk of an oak tree. His towel, socks etc., were placed on the hedgerow. His old coat was all patches that he had sewed on himself. He was a very nice old man, rather big and aged about sixty. He spread the old songs about that you heard on the canal. I saw him several times in the following years, but only on the Welsh Canal, which was his favourite spot. No-one was allowed to interrupt him in any way, or move him on, by order of the Shropshire Union Canal Company. They knew his history, and all the boatmen knew him too. I never heard where he ended up.

We went on our way again, and passed the Clay Hole, where there was an engineering boat loading clay. It was Sam Rogers, who had been my father's mate on the Llangollen Fly. The clay was used on the Ellesmere Section of the Welsh Canal. There was a tramway where the wagons were pulled by a long wire rope from a stationary engine. Still going steady, we came to Waterloo Wharf, and shop owned by Mr Hall. There was a Company boat here off-loading corn and a few goods from Ellesmere Port. We passed a few words with Ned Owen, the boatman and his wife, Lizzy. We now came up to our last mile, the Wren's Nest. This was most difficult of all as we were almost full up and the canal was very shallow. We carried on in stages, stop and go, giving the horse a blow. It took us two hours to reach our destination, Edstaston; by twelve o'clock, dinner time.

Edstaston Wharf buildings, 1968

We had our dinner, and left the horse on the towing path to graze. We first took his harness off, and he had a good roll in relief. There was a coal wharf and warehouse on one side here, and a stone warehouse on the other. The wharf, warehouse and cottage were rented by Platt and Dobell. The chap in charge was Fred Mannering. He was not a Company man, but was paid by Stubbs of Stone, though he was also paid tonnage by the Company. Fred was occupied in receiving another Company boat with a full load of cattle cake and corn. The boatman was Tom Evans. Offloading on the other side of the canal at Dobell's warehouse, was a boat belonging to Griffith Brothers, Corn Merchants from Chester. Bill Carter and his wife had this boat *Crane*, which had to pay toll. Griffiths Brothers also engaged Company boats at Chester, and had four flats running from Liverpool as well. There was a private boat off-loading macadam on the same wharf as ourselves. This was *The Gleaner*, run by Bill Baines from Chirk, and owned by the Ceriog Granite Company from Glyn Ceriog, Chirk. They had ten of these boats which also had to pay toll.

After lunch, we each took a shovel and commenced to off-load. There were only the two of us, but we had to off-load our cargo at a private wharf, and in fact anywhere except in the docks or at a corn or flour mill. The two commercial boats delivered their cargo and went on their way again, both light. Our friend the stone boat also off-loaded his cargo of 20 tons. We delivered our coal and then washed the boat out, after which we took our dusty clothes off and jumped into the canal for a bath, as it had been a very hot day. The water here was very clean – you could see the bed of the canal, and also the fish. When our load had been signed for, the Skipper decided to remain for the night. It was Tuesday. After our usual meal, we relaxed, leaving Dick on the towing path for the night. He would not leave the boat as he knew where his food was kept!

This was a pretty country place, with a road bridge and a pull-up bridge side by side. The latter was used by the canal customers when they collected their corn etc. from the wharf. There was also a lovely old church near the canal, and a few farms. The end of this branch was three quarters of a mile further on. Here there was a wharf and a large lime kiln, and a small country pub called "The Harp Inn". My father and Mr Baines went there for a couple of pints. I heard afterwards it was a jolly good pint. A while ago, this place had been busy and there was still a coal wharf with a boatload of

coal per week on average, but business at the lime kiln had ceased a short while previously. The pub missed the boatmen. The small town of Wem could be seen in the distance, together with the spires of several churches and Grinshill Hall. I spent an hour fishing with my friend, Mr Baines' son.

We left next morning at seven o'clock, and turned around. Fred Mannering was up and about, as he had been called to the telephone by Tower Wharf, Chester, and asked to tell the Skipper of the boat *Times*. We were to proceed to Ellesmere to collect a quantity of cheese for Ellesmere Port, as the Cheese Fly was in dock. This was quite a good order for us, as we would be paid mileage. We arrived at Ellesmere at ten o'clock and reported to Mr J Pixton, the Agent. He told us to berth at the Cheese Warehouse, and start loading the cheese. This was a Company Depot, and John Wood was the porter. We collected the cheeses from the warehouse, and a few out of farm conveyances. We were quite full up with about seven tons, as we were only allowed to place them two high. The Cheese Fly *Peel* was fitted with sections for cheese carriage and could take twenty ton. Before we left, Mr Pixton told us this cargo was for Liverpool, and entered it on the Way Bill. We could not call at Whitchurch for their cheeses as we were full up, but these would be sent on the Whitchurch Fly. We were told to be at Ellesmere Port by midday Friday.

That evening, we moored at nine o'clock at Grindley Brook, and were off again at six next morning down the nineteen locks to Hurleston. Here we entered the main canal, collected our necessaries from our home at Barbridge, and went on our way again. At Bunbury big locks, we connected with the Shrewsbury Fly, the boat *Rhoda* and the Skipper Tom Sutton. His cargo was a few bales of oakum from Shrewsbury Prison for Chester Dock Repair Yard. We buttied together down the four locks to Wharton Lock. Then there was eight miles level, past

Beeston Castle, Peckforton Castle and Smith and Sons Bone Works at Tattenhall Road, the only tall chimney on our route since we left the Potteries a week earlier. The two horses were a little upset at this point. They did not like the smell of the bone-works, and we had to lead them until we were clear of it. There were two or three boats discharging slack here, and one loading fat in barrels for Liverpool. We passed under the bridge, and went by a busy brickyard with a boat loading bricks. After this we met the Fly Boats from Ellesmere Port, two Pottery Flys, the Newtown Fly, the Llangollen Fly, the Trench Fly, the Brewood Fly and the Wolverhampton Fly.

After a break, we reached Halfway Bridge and the gipsy camp. On a wide patch of grass between the canal and road, there was a caravan or two, and camp fires. Some of the gipsies wanted to exchange horses with us, but we said "nothing doing". They also wanted to beg a bit of rope. Next we saw Waverton church across the fields, and passing Egg Bridge Corn Mill and Rowton Moor, we entered Christleton Locks. It was a lovely June day. We passed down five more locks, and went a mile through the city of Chester, meeting several slow boats bound for different routes. Then we came up to Northgate Locks, cut out of red rock, with King Charles' Tower above the towing path, and the small Execution Bridge over the canal. Below the locks, and above the canal were the city walls on one side, and the Shropshire Union General Offices on the other. We had to separate from the Fly here as two boats met us, and only one can meet two [*see explanation in panel, right*].

After a sharp right hand bend under the wide bridge carrying Sealand Road, we came to a great patch of wide water on the offside which was a mooring place for tugs, flats and boats. On the towing path side were two big locks, the entrance to the River Dee. We tied up for the night by the Tarpaulin Shed, opposite the big repair and building dockyard, and stabled the horse at a boat-builder's private stable.

The boat-builder rented his cottage from the Company and was known as "Tom the Quarter". I never knew his surname. At nine o'clock, Tom Sutton appeared with the night-watchman, George Porter. We gave him a hand to off-load his small cargo of oakum. Then he went on down the nine mile pound to Ellesmere Port to collect his next cargo early in the morning. The Shrewsbury Fly was three-handed, and had a trip and a half a week to Shrewsbury, changing horses at Coole Pilot [Pilate] where the Skipper's son-in-law had the black-smith's shop. All the horses from Hack Green were shoed here.

We set off again at about seven next morning, and arrived at Ellesmere Port at nine-thirty. We entered the locks and went down to the Bottom Dock. While we were passing down the lock, Tom Gary, one of the dock foremen, ordered us to berth alongside the flat *Snipe* and tranship our cargo of cheese. This was done in about an hour at No. 1.

A modern, but almost timeless image - fly-boat Saturn *at Grindley Brook*

We brushed up the straw that was left in the boat, and bagged it for horse-bedding for our next voyage. We had to wait our turn for a cargo as the Welsh Canal was not very busy at this time, and we had to be prepared to go anywhere. Some of the boats waiting were ordered to load flints and clay for the Potteries, others soap from Levers at Port Sunlight for Spon Lane, West Bromwich, and others, iron ore for the Humber Arm. All these products were stored at Ellesmere Port and transported at slack times.

I had a little time to look round the Top Dock, and in the Top Warehouse over bays No. 1 and No. 2. On the beams I saw the names of the places the goods were for, and their destination. The warehouse was separated into sections, with an office in the centre where the clerk would hand you your Time and Way Bill with the cargo entered accordingly.

Our turn came after dinner on Friday. Tom Shoan called out *Times,* and told us to go to North Wall for a load of wheat for Harveys at Kidderminster. After feeding the horse, we made our way across the docks to the huge blue brick warehouse on the side of the Ship Canal. This was the grain warehouse. By four o'clock we were loaded with eighteen tons of Russian Wheat, and went back across the docks again, and up the locks. Here we tied up for the rest of the day in order to collect our food and provender, and settle up for our previous trips to Leek, Edstaston and Ellesmere Port. The full amount was £5 8 2, but as we had had an advance at Barbridge, we had £3 8 2 to draw. We had our own horse, but if we had had a Company horse, we would have had half this amount. Our next voyage to Kidderminster would be at 6d per mile.

The total number of days worked was twelve, from Sunday to Sunday in one week, and Monday to Friday in the next. The total pay was £5 8 2.

Summary of Journey's Mileage and Rates

	Miles	Rate	
Ellesmere Port - Leek	68	8½d	Fly
Leek - Barbridge	44	7d	Slow
Barbridge - Edstaston	24	5d	Slow
Edstaston-Ellesmere	11	4½	Light
Elesmere - Ellesmere Port	51	6d	Over 6 ton

On Saturday morning we commenced our journey at four thirty, in order to get away before the tug which left at five o'clock with traffic for Wolverhampton and Birmingham, which it towed to Chester. They were then pulled by horse to Tyrley, and then by tug again to Autherley. We got well ahead, and were buttying a Trench boat. This was the *Mentor,* run by John Wood, with a load of copper for the Shropshire Iron Works at Trench. He was urgent, as he had to be there on Monday morning, and this meant two long days for him. We stayed with him to Barbridge where we arrived at four in the afternoon, having had a clear run. We wished John and his son good-day, and went home for Saturday evening. We prepared our food and laundry and were ready to start off again on Sunday morning.

We gave the horse time to have his breakfast, and were on our way by nine o'clock, passing

Hurleston and Nantwich and entering Hack Green Locks. There were two locks here, then a two mile pound, then fifteen locks at Audlem, five at Adderley, followed by a four mile pound, and then five more locks at Tyrley. At about eight o'clock, we tied up at Goldstone for the night.

On Monday morning we passed through some lovely countryside. Traffic was fairly quiet, it being Monday. We had seventeen miles to go before the next lock at Wheaton Aston, and then six miles to the shallow lock at Autherley Junction the end of the Shroppie. Here we handed our Time and Way Bill to John Masson,

Wheaton Aston lock, with Telford designed lock cottage (left)

the Toll Clerk and Stableman. He gave us the ticket to pass onto the Stafford and Worcester - Toll Clerk, Mr E Farr. He then gave us our Permit and we went on. We passed Aldersley Junction and the B.C.N. and went on beside Dunstall Park racecourse for a short distance.

We passed through Tettenhall, and then down Compton Lock. The next two locks were at Wightwick. I noticed that the paddle gear was quite different. We had to wind the opposite way at the bottom gates, and there were four paddles on the top gate which was not very convenient. It was a lovely stretch of countryside, but the air was not so sweet, as it

was a wet afternoon, and we were near the Black Country. When we arrived at Bob's Lock at Dimmingsdale near Wombourn, we tied up for the night. It was a quiet little spot, and we found a clean dry stable for Dick at the lock-keeper's cottage. Bob and his wife were a very sociable couple, and invited us in for an hour for a cup of tea and a chat. We paid the stabling fee of 3d and retired to the boat for the night. I woke in the night, hearing the paddles at work, and feeling the movement of our boat. My father told me that Harry Goram had been through with his boat *Gertrude*, a Stourlifter. This was a railway boat from Stourport with a load of vinegar for Wolverhampton. My father had been on this route many times before and knew all the boatmen. It was my first trip on this canal and I was not familiar with every place and lock.

We rose early on Tuesday morning, and decided to have our breakfast, and give the horse his, before we set off, owing to the locks ahead and the traffic. We left at about seven, went down two locks, and then came to the Bratch. This was three locks, separated by very short pounds with extra side-sluices and overflows. They were very deep and tricky for a stranger. The horse had time to rest and eat while we passed down them. Next we passed down Bumble Hole Lock near a Public House, and then entered a mile pound. At the end of this were the double locks at Botterham, and two more at Swindon where we passed the Steel Works of Thomas Baldwin.

There was another railway boat here, loading steel plates for Wolverhampton Railway Wharf, where it was transhipped. The name of this boat was *Swindon*, after the village, and George Wood was the Skipper. I knew this was a new

Kidderminster Church and Wharf, Staffordshire & Worcestershire Canal

boat, as I had seen it pass Barbridge on its way up. She was built at Chester at the same time as the *Berriew*. *Berriew* was built for Inspector W Baker at the Engineering Department at Welshpool, and the boatman who had her was Edwin Middle.

For the next ten miles we passed through lovely scenery, woods and sandstone outcrops, and many locks. First was Hinksford, and next Greensforge with the Navigation Inn close by, if you wanted a pint. Then we came to Rocky Lock, where I noticed the circular weir peculiar to this canal. After Gothersley Lock, we passed Stourton Junction where the Stourbridge Canal went off into Birmingham. Then we passed down Stewpony Lock, through Hyde Bridge, Kinver and Whittington Locks, and arrived at Cookley Tunnel. This was only 25 yards long, but it was cut out of the rock and was fairly low. There was a row of houses built on the top of it. After another three locks, we reached Wolverley Court, and another of Thomas Baldwin's Steel

Works. At four o'clock we reached Kidderminster, and tied up at the Railway Wharf. Harvey's Mill was below the next lock. The Skipper went to inform them of our arrival and arranged for off-loading the following morning. We had to make sure of our turn in the event of another boat arriving from Gloucester, or any other route. The arrangements gave the horse and ourselves a good night's rest.

Above and behind the wharf was the church, and the bell-ringers were practising. They played several hymns and it was a wonderful sound. Boatmen always say that Kidderminster bells, together with those at Marbury, near Whitchurch on the Welsh Canal, are the sweetest in the country, as the water below collects the sound. Marbury is situated on a mere.

At the wharf, the Railway boat *Edris*, with its Skipper Tom Clerk, was collecting a quantity of

67

Saturn at Kidderminster. Note the Scammell Mechanical Horse on the right.

goods and carpets for Wolverhampton Railway Tranship Depot. He completed his cargo and went on his way to arrive there in the early hours of the next morning. There were three men engaged on these Railway Fly Boats, and they were all paid weekly by the Railway Section. The Railway also owned some lovely horses.

Next morning, we pulled the boat through the one lock, and under the street, and arrived at Harvey's Mill. It was eight o'clock on Wednesday, and we were off-loaded by nine thirty. We rolled our side-cloths along the side of the boat, and fastened them with thin knee strings, all neat and tidy. We were then prepared for our return journey, and reported to our Canal Office for orders. The Skipper was told to proceed to Wilden Iron Works for 20 ton of sash weights for Liverpool. This was another three miles towards Stourport.

We left Kidderminster and went down two locks to the River Stour Junction, where we left the main canal. We passed down Pratt's Wharf Lock onto the Stour. The Steel Works were a mile down the river. It was so narrow here that it was known as The Brook. What a place to come to, I thought! We turned left and right around bends that seemed impossible to me. We had a light boat going down, but what about coming back loaded! However, we managed to reach Wilden Steel Works at about two o'clock, with some difficulty. After stabling the horse, the Skipper berthed the boat, and went to report our arrival. Meanwhile the boat *Wilden* arrived. This boat was named after the small village, and this was his regular route. The Skipper's name was Joe Bradley, and my cousin Alfred Morris was engaged as one of the hands. The foreman told our Skipper that the Fly was to load first. This was arranged, and within the hour he was off again up "The Brook".

We berthed our boat again, and commenced to load, and were finished by six o'clock. We had discussed the navigation of the Stour with the boatman, and he had told us that when returning, the water ran away and put you on the bottom on occasion. There was a man with a donkey who helped to pull the other end of the boat round the bends. The Fly Boat was well aware of the conditions, and acted accordingly. We returned to our boat, having collected our notes with the nature and weight of our cargo marked down, and settled down for the night.

Next morning, we had an early breakfast, and proceeded up "The Brook", with the chap and his donkey. He was a great help, but we still got stuck a few times, when the water left us. We arrived back at the lock, and entered the main canal again at eleven o'clock. The donkey and his master returned home. We reached our Kidderminster Office at one o'clock, and after dinner we collected our Permit and a red Time and Way Bill, with the uphill load signed for and the return load entered. There were 89 miles and 72 locks from Ellesmere Port to Wilden, and now we had the same journey back. We tied up at Kinver on Thursday night, Shebdon on the Shroppie again on Friday, and arrived at Barbridge at five o'clock on Saturday evening. We were back in Ellesmere Port again by midday Monday, and our load was transhipped into a foreign cargo ship. The pay for this trip, with a red Time and Way Bill, was £4 9. 0 at 6d per mile each way. There were no stoppages, as there was no P.A.Y.E. or Insurance Stamps in those days.

A posed photo of Saturn *and crew on the Staffordshire & Worcestershire Canal, probably at Wolverley Lock.*
The barrels contain vinegar bound for the HP sauce factory in Aston, Birmingham

8

THE SHROPSHIRE UNION FLEET AND RATES OF PAY

I will now leave my boating experiences for a while, and explain a little about the boats we saw around the Shroppie. The Cheshire Farmers Association owned three small steam flats. They were 26 tonners, 69 feet in length and about 10 feet in beam. The beam was based on the width of the railway bridge at Bunbury which was 13 feet 3 inches wide. These boats were named *Cambria*, *Petrel* and *Mafeking*, and were engaged in carrying corn, wheat etc. from Ellesmere Port to Nantwich. These were built at the time of the Boer War, together with two narrow boats *Faith* and *Diver*. They were all toll payers. The flats could only navigate as far as Nantwich, but the narrow boats went to Grindley Brook. They all supplied Egg Bridge, Calveley and Nantwich.

The Shropshire Union has three big boats build to supply Cow Lane Wharf, Chester, Butler's Mill, Christleton, Whalley of Tilston, Bates of Tiverton, Beeston, Barbridge Depot and Nantwich. They could not go any further than Nantwich either. These three were built like an ordinary boat, but their beam and length was similar to that of the flats mentioned above. They were horse-drawn by big half-legged horses, 16 and 17 hands high and used for that work only. Their hours were twelve hours per day until twelve o'clock on Saturday,

which made a sixty six hour week for which they were paid weekly at 36/- per week. This was a fairly good job in those days as the Company supplied the horse, rope and bedding. These three boats were also built at the end of the Boer War and were named *Kimberley*, *Ladysmith* and *Cestria*. The S.U.C. also had a number of narrowboats such as *Kitchener*, *Khartoum* and *African Gordon*. *Kitchener* was fitted with two moveable saloons, and was used for inspections when necessary. When not required, these saloons were taken out and the boat was worked liked the others.

The Welsh Canal was registered as a 15 ton canal, but we could and did take 20 or 22 tons

Hurleston Reservoir, and the spillweir which takes water from just above the top lock of four, immediately before the Ellesmere (Llangollen) Canal flows into the former Chester Canal at Hurleston Junction

according to the state of the water supply from Llangollen. If it was a dry time and the reservoirs at Hurleston or Belvide Brewood were low, we would be ordered to reduce to 15 tons. This also applied to all craft carrying 20 tons on the main line of the Shroppie to the Black Country and the Potteries. However you would still be paid for 20 tons as if you were full, and for 18 tons on the Welsh Canal. These were the conditions at all times, including bulky traffic, but excluding mileage boats.

There were several grades of boat. Boats to the Welsh Canal and North Wales were known as North Boats; boats to Trench and Shrewsbury, Salop Boats; boats to Birmingham and Wolverhampton, South Staffordshire Boats; boats around the Black Country, Gathering boats; from Wolverhampton to Kidderminster, Stour Lighters; all railway boats were fly boats. All maintenance boats were called engineering boats, including ice-boats and hand dredgers. Lastly there were two packets, the *Neptune* and the *Inspector* which were the Manager and Director's business boats.

If you had a mileage boat, and found your own horse, you were paid 6d per mile when you loaded over six tons and had a Fly Time Bill. This was pink, but was called a Red Ticket, and it placed a time limit on your journey. If you did not keep within the time allowed, your mileage rate would be reduced to 5d per mile. When you were given a white ticket or Way Bill, the journey was not so urgent. If you were light on your return journey, the rate was 4½d per mile. In the industrial areas like Birmingham, Wolverhampton, the Potteries and Manchester there was always a back cargo, but not so often on the Welsh Canal. There were seventy Pottery boats carrying flints and china clay, goods and grain. Their back cargoes were pottery, basic slag, coal, iron and steel, all for export.

If you worked a Company horse, your mileage was 3½d per mile, and 2½d per mile light; as opposed to 6d and 5d above. The Shropshire Union Company paid all mileage boats in this way, whatever canal they went on.

All Fly Boats who owned their own horses were paid 6½d per mile each way, whether loaded or light. The only exception was the boats running from Ellesmere Port to the Potteries, who got 8½d per mile with cargo, and 6d light, if they owned their own horses. The Pottery Fly was paid 6d per mile each way, and all horses were owned by the Company. If a boatman had a bigger boat and could carry say 25 tons, he would be paid 1/9 per ton over 20 ton. This did not include Pottery Fly boats. The rates and charges for the Pottery run were higher than those for other routes, although it was not so long, being only 54 miles from Ellesmere Port to Stoke-on-Trent. I think this route was more highly paid owing to Cheshire Locks, and Harecastle Tunnel, where we had to leg or pay leggers. Also, the Company had to pay toll on the North Stafford Canal from Middlewich in those days.

Jack Roberts' father's fly-boat Ruth *at Nantwich*

While I am on the subject, I will touch on the rates of the tonnage boats. First, the Wolverhampton, Birmingham and Black Country areas: - from Ellesmere Port to Birmingham and Wolverhampton, all had 1/9 per ton, and 3d per ton fly money. Thirty six hours were allowed from Ellesmere Port to Autherley Junction, and if they went over that time, they lost the 3d per ton fly money. Autherley Junction was the end of the Shropshire Union Canal , and your way bill was signed there by the clerk, Mr Lovekin, or the horsekeeper, John Musson at night. Way bills were signed at all the Company's offices and stables on route. On the return journey from Autherley Junction to Ellesmere Port, you were only paid 1/- per ton.

After leaving Autherley Junction for the Black Country, you would make the best of your way to reach your destination, otherwise other boats would pass you and you might have to wait a day or two to off-load your cargo. Once the cargo was delivered, you would make straight for the Office at Wolverhampton, get everything signed for, and receive your orders for your next load back. When you had collected your load, you would make your way back to Wolverhampton to get your pay, and then go down the 21 locks to Autherley. Here you were timed and listed for your following turn or your next trip. If, by any chance, you had collected or taken your cargo through Netherton Tunnel, you would be allowed 6/8 District money. Hampton Boats mostly got this, but all traffic was paid the same on that route.

I will now give you the names of the Engineers, Agents and Managers as I remember them up to 1969.

S.U.C./B.C.N.
Civil Engineer - Mr J R Jebb, Paradise Street, Birmingham

L.M.S.
District Engineer Crewe - Messrs Turnbull, Bullough and Everett
Assistant Engineers - W Massey, W Phillips and
Mr Harbottle, Tower Wharf, Chester

B.W.B.
Divisional Engineer - Mr E Marsh, Lime Street Chambers, Liverpool

S.U.C.
General Managers - Messrs Sales, Whitlam, Mattnison, Thompson and Talbot, Tower Wharf, Chester

Agents   Ellesmere Port Docks -
      Mr Whitridge
    Cow Lane Wharf, Chester -
      Mr Chalton
    Barbridge -
      Messrs W Wyn and S Moore
      Assistants - Messrs B Clay
      and J Johnson
    Market Drayton -
      Mr Bennet
    Norbury, and later Autherley -
      Mr W Lovekin
    Wolverhampton, Tipton and Walsall -
      Mr Trafford and Mr Bourne
    Birmingham, Crescent Wharf -
      Mr Wedge
    Potteries, Tunstall, Burslem, Etruria, Stoke -
      Mr Evans
    Manchester Castle Fields, Tower Wharf and London Road Station
      Mr Tom Gittens
    Whitchurch -
      Mr Wyn from Barbridge
    Ellesmere -
      Mr J Pixton
    Oswestry -
      Mr Bloomer
    Welshpool -
      Mr W Ireland and Mr Trafford

Trench and Wellington -
Mr Whitehead

Inspectors for horse traffic, stables, boatmen and engaging men for various grades of employment:

Tower Wharf, Chester - Mr Talbot
Whitchurch - Mr T Bailey

Superintendent and Veterinary Surgeon.for the purchasing and selling of horses -

Mr Llewellyn, Broad Street,
Wolverhampton

Claims Department -

Mr White, Birmingham New Street

Fitters Shop and Gas Works -

Mr Lindop, Ellesmere Port

District Inspectors - Engineering Department
Tower Wharf, Chester -

Messrs James, Edge, Barnsley, Baker, Farmington (B.W.B.) and Venables (B.W.B.)

Norbury Junction -

Messrs Bowen Simpson, Palin, Lloyd Sen., Lloyd Jun. Boardman.

The first four of the above were transferred to Ellesmere at various times and Messrs Hughes, Hewitt and Howard (B.W.B) were sent to Norbury.

Welshpool -
Mr W Baker - closed 1922

The cabin of restored fly-boat Saturn. *The rounded top cupboard door is also a fold-down table*

9

WESTON POINT TO
WESTON LULLINGFIELDS

When I first visited Ellesmere Port, there was only Dock Street, and a few minor roads connecting with Merseyton Road, and a

The Ellesmere Port dock office, by the top basin, in the 1960s, after regular carrying had more or less ended

permanent railway that went from the docks up the main street to the station. However, from 1906 onwards, large numbers of houses were built around the Railway Station and Whitby. At the end of Ellesmere Port Docks, opposite the North Wall, the new Frost of Chester Flour Mill was built, together with a new arm and basin, on the same side as Imperial's and King's Flour Mills. This was convenient for the Ship Canal and river routes. The Jones Iron and Steel Works were transferred from Wolverhampton to Ellesmere Port, together with a large number of employees. In addition, there was a new cement works built on the sunny side, opposite and across the canal from Burnell's Iron Works. There were also new paint works and dye works near the cement works and the River Gowy.

The arrival of all these works made the canal very busy with flats, mostly horse-drawn as they were only half a mile from the docks. Jones had quite a fleet of steel flats built. This small town has been growing ever since, but the docks and the canal have stood still.

When we arrived at Ellesmere Port Docks after our trip to Kidderminster, there was a big fight going on between two boatmen at the end of Galley Row. They were two hefty chaps, both with their shirts off, and the fight lasted half an hour. They could have been champions, had they been trained. I watched while the Skipper went off to get our orders for our next trip which was to load a consignment of 100 tons of bone ash out of a flat. This was for Richard's Bone Works, Rednal near Oswestry. There were five boats on this trip. We had the first twenty ton, and were away. As we went through Northgate Locks, the Skipper was told to call at Mr Talbot's office.

He was offered a Pottery Fly Boat as one was coming vacant. However he turned the offer down, as he did not like the route. If it had been the Newtown Fly, he would have accepted it, as he regretted giving it up in the first place. We arrived at Barbridge on Tuesday night at eight o'clock, and collected our food and laundry.

Starting off at six o'clock, Wednesday, we turned right at Hurleston Junction, and went onto the Welsh Canal again. This time we were accompanied by Dick, my brother-in-law, whose boat had joined us at Ellesmere Port. It was a heavy day for the horses, and the going was slow as we had a heavy load and it was a shallow canal. There was a shortage of water owing to the dry weather, and also because we were meeting the current. We were carrying the maximum for this canal. We reached Hampton Bank on Wednesday night, and the horse deserved his rest. Here, there was a good stable which Mr Quest, the Lengthsman, had built himself from boat bottoms. There was also plenty of bedding which he collected from the embankments and stacked. The cost of stabling was 3d, making 6d for the two horses. There were four stalls, and all were full as there were two other commercial boats here on their way to Birmingham with cargoes of oil from Monsanto Chemical Works at Cefn, Ruabon.

We were off again next morning at a steady pace through the lovely woods, past the meres and through the tunnel at Ellesmere. Then we left the main Llangollen Canal, turned left and entered the Montgomery Canal at Frankton Locks. We worked down two double locks and two single locks, passing a private dock yard on the canalside, and a small cottage. At No. 4 Lock there was a small hut built over the weir on the towing path side. An old man of eighty named Starkey lived here. Inside was a clean bed and all cooking utensils, cups, saucers and plates. He had lived there for years and worked in the gardens of the local people. The Company allowed him to live there for 1/- per year.

At Lockgate Bridge, the Junction for the Weston Branch, we turned right and made our way across Perry Moor, under a lift-up bridge and alongside the River Perry. Passing under Keeper's Bridge, we arrived at our destination, Rednal. Turning the small bridge off, we entered the basin and works, and turned the bridge back again as it connected the towing-path. We removed our sheets, and off-loaded. We each used a pan shovel, and the works men wheeled the barrows into the works. This load was urgently wanted as they were preparing the agricultural land after the harvest. We managed to off-load one boat that day, which was Thursday. There was no stabling here, so we had to enquire at some of the farms, and then take the horse to Queen's Head, a mile and half away. This was a most desolate spot, with no houses or people to be seen, and few farms, only the main Paddington Railway Line at the end of the basin.

The following morning, we all worked together and managed to unload by noon. Dick, the foreman, told us that there were two loads waiting here, one for Weston Point, and one of manure for places up to Newtown. As we were the first boat we had the choice. My brother-in-law wanted to go Newtown way to visit his parents who lived at Ardleen, so we decided to go to Weston Point. We had a load of large empty Vitrol glass bottles, and had to bring them back when they were filled.

Rednal Bone Mill

We set off on Friday morning and arrived at Frankton. We handed in our Time and Way Bill and Back notes for our previous load to be signed, and collected our new Time and Way Bill with the present cargo entered. This was a red one. Mr T Price was the Clerk for Tolls here, and also porter and lock-keeper and in charge of transhipping. We went on to tie up at Grindley Brook for the night. Three men were engaged here – the two lengthsmen were J Dudley and F Challoner and Mr J Wood was the Toll Clerk and Porter. Mr Wood was also responsible for the boats cargoes from Cheshire Farmers' Mills, and for the feeder paddles, one of which was by the entrance to the lock, and one which drove the mill which was up a small arm. This one was closed on Saturday until Monday morning.

On Saturday morning we set off again down the nineteen locks, and arrived at Barbridge at one o'clock. We stabled the horse and had the afternoon at home as usual. We had our Time Bill signed, and also collected the river hauling rope and red lamp. On Sunday morning we proceeded to Middlewich and collected our permit from King's Lock Toll Office. We arrived at Broken Cross for Sunday night, together with quite a few boats from various parts, including the Cheese Fair boat from Manchester. The other four Cheese Boats had left Barbridge at two o'clock on Sunday morning as they were due at Castle Fields, Manchester at six o'clock Monday morning, and would be back again at Broken Cross on Tuesday night with a return cargo, mostly for places on their route.

Next morning we called at Dock Bridge, Anderton, for our permit for the River Weaver. We entered the Anderton Lift, and were shut in and lowered down to the Weaver Basin and Tranship Wharf, and onto the main stream. This was my first trip on this route, and I thought what a wonderful invention the lift was, and what an adventure to go down it. The same water was used all the time as there were no paddles, just a steel door to the tank. We came down with a boat from Wolverhampton, a John Perry, painted yellow, and we went butty with him to Weston Point.

We passed down Saltersford, Dutton and Sutton Locks. There was a towing path, but we had problems in opening the small gates that separated the fields in order to get the horse through. We had a long hauling line to help, but I had to put up with it until we reached Frodsham Swing Bridge. One good thing was that we could put speed on, and the weather was in our favour too. We met many ships and barges with cargoes for Anderton and Brunner Mond and Company.

We arrived at Weston Point early in the afternoon, but had to wait until next morning to deliver our cargo. The Perry boat was light, and he had to collect a cargo of "Blue Billy" for Wolverhampton. This was a blue powder that was used at Steel Works. I never learned the

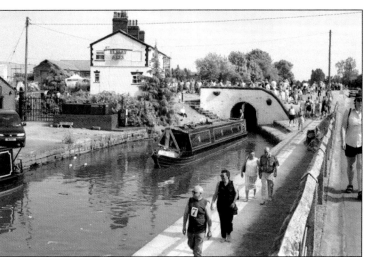

King's Lock, Middlewich, with eponymous pub, 2003. The photo is taken from where the Shropshire Union Middlewich Arm joins the Trent & Mersey Canal (North Staffs in this book)

correct name for it. The next morning our cargo was accepted by Castner-Kelner. We went to the foreman for our return cargo, but he told us it would not be ready, as no bottles were filled, and we would have to wait a day or more. We then had to ring Barbridge and explain the position, and were told not to wait, but to proceed to Frodsham Bridge and collect a cargo of 15 tons of bone manure for various places to Weston, near Baschurch on the Welsh Canal. Another boat would be sent for the bottles when they were ready.

Frodsham was only a mile away but the bone works were a difficult place to get to, as you had to go off the main river onto a loop, and use the shaft. Eventually we made the Mill and berthed for the night. The stable for the horse was another mile up the way towards Frodsham. We managed to part-load that evening, and next morning, Wednesday, we completed our cargo and sheeted up. My father told me to be careful on top of the planks when tying the top strings, as the last time he came, my brother George broke one, and fell into the river, and there was a strong current at this point.

However this did not happen to me, though I could swim and so could my father. We made for the main river, and were pleased to peg the horse on again. The current was against us on our return, and I was told it could be very difficult for a narrow-boat when the river was swollen in the winter, and they were not allowed to navigate it then, but had to go via Preston Brook.

We entered the first lock with a Salt Union flat which was going to Anderton loaded with goods for the canal, to be taken to the Potteries. He gave us a tow to Anderton, and this allowed me to walk with the horse, who gave a sigh of relief. My father would not allow me to steer on this river. We entered Anderton Lift again, and rose up to the canal. In the lift, we buttied a Salt Union Fly, *Foxland*. This was a three handed fly, Skipper G Morris, whose depot was at Marston, near Northwich. We collected our permits at Dock Bridge. As we passed Marston, I noticed the Dry Dock and Repair Yard belonging to the Salt Union Company, and a few boats under repairs. We kept in front to the Big Lock at Middlewich as we had a good horse and our boat could travel as fast as a fly boat if it came to a race, which it often did at that time of day.

The Anderton boat lift in the 1970s, before closure in 1983 and reopening in 2002 after extensive restoration work.

The Fly Boats from Runcorn, Preston Brook, Fellows Morton, the Anderton Company, Gandy's of Derby and the Shroppie Fly would mostly meet at King's Lock, and the Junction to the Shropshire Union. We let the fly go out of the Big Lock first as he had to travel all night to Etruria in the Potteries. We passed up the three single locks, known as "The New 'Uns", arrived at Wardle Lock and turned right. It was nine o'clock, and we stabled the horse for the night at King's Lock. Here we saw the two Shroppie Flys from Ellesmere Port, *Vesper* with her Skipper, J Morris, and *Cuba*, Skipper C Johnson. They entered the North Stafford Cut and followed the other fly boats. They would chase them, and most likely pass them before entering Cheshire Locks at Wheelock. This sometimes meant a fight. *Vesper*, the Pottery Fly had to deliver a few barrels of Guinness stout and a few goods at Wheelock, and left the *Cuba* and the other Flys to it.

We left Wardle Lock on Thursday morning at about seven thirty, and went about a mile to Stanthorne Lock. Here I took the nose tin off Dick, gave him a drink, and put on his muzzle so that he could go himself, i.e. baccering. He went well up this ten mile stretch as he was making for home. We had our breakfast in comfort, and near Winsford Railway Bridge, I stepped onto the path, and put the horse through. The main railway line from Crewe to Scotland passed over here and most of the horses were startled by passing trains and could fall into the canal. It was also a dangerous bridge for the boat as there was piling under the surface. We had to learn about all these sorts of obstructions. I stepped onto the boat again, and we washed the crocks, mopped the boat over, and had a wash ourselves. If we met any traffic we had the right of way, as the downhill traffic was responsible for the meeting of the horses, and we were going uphill. As we neared Minshull Lock, we passed over the River Weaver at Minshull Aqueduct. Having filled the horse's nose tin, Dad stepped off and placed it on his head, and then went on to get the lock ready. Dick went nice and steady, eating his feed, and we entered the lock as it was ready. The line automatically came off at the little iron foot bridge, and the boat went in. The driver drew a little on the paddle and the water held the boat off from the still; he then drew it

up completely as one gate was closing. When the next gate was closing he drew the other paddle. By doing this the boat was held close to the cill and would not run back and damage the helm. You had to work with the water, and this applied to all locks in different ways. We rose up and the tin was taken off the horse before we continued.

A recent view of Cholmondeston Lock, the last of four when going from Middlewich to Barbridge along the Middlewich Arm

We met a boat from Tattenhall Road Bone Works, carrying empty bottles for Weston Point. It was a Shroppie boat called *Canada*, the Skipper, F Wenlock. We passed the time of day as we entered Cholmondeston Straight. Here, there was an engineering boat loading clay. It was Ned Jones, alias Ned the Tailor. Our Skipper went ahead again to get Cholmondeston Lock ready. We were catching up with a Pottery boat loaded with 25 tons of basic slag from Shelton for Ellesmere Port. We passed through the lock, and after a mile or so, arrived at Barbridge. It was eleven thirty on Thursday morning, and we had taken just four hours from Middlewich.

We stabled the horse for a while, and went to collect the provender and necessaries from home. We also had our cargo entered on our Time and Way Bill, together with an advance of cash, and fresh orders. When the Skipper returned, he said he had decided to go as far as Hurleston Locks for the night, and walked back home along the road, when we had tied up above the four locks. There was a good stable there, and plenty of bedding for the horse. It was rented with the cottage. The lock-keeper, G Walsh, was also the reservoir attendant, and lengthsman, and had a mate, Fred Tinker. To my surprise, my grandad's boat was there with a load of coal for Berriew, on the Montgomery. He had been away from home for about three weeks, going from Ellesmere Port to Warwick with a cargo of wheat, a back cargo of flour to Crescent Wharf, Birmingham, and then to Holly Bank, Wolverhampton, for the coal. He was with his butty, John Wooley, whose load was for Aberbechan, near Newtown. The boats' names were *Brigand*, and *Swallow*. Both Skippers had gone to Barbridge for an advance, and my dad also went home for the night. I stayed on the boat, giving myself time for a chat with Bill, and John Wooley who always had a mouth organ.

When we left on Friday morning, our first call was at Burland Wharf with four tons of bone manure. The other two boats passed us here, and went on their way on their long journey into Wales. Our next stop was at Steer Bridge Wharf, Marbury, where we off-loaded another four tons. Both these warehouses were for the convenience of the local farmers, who collected their goods from there. We arrived at Grindley Brook Mill at four o'clock, berthed under the mill, and collected the nine ton of cattle food for the Weston Branch. We then tied up for the night. In the early hours of the morning, the Newtown Fly and the Llangollen Fly passed us. My elder brother was a hand on the Newtown Fly, and my Uncle Jack was the Skipper. One of them knocked on the cabin side and asked us if we were going to sleep all day! We exchanged a few words, and all went quiet again.

We started off again at eight o'clock, with plenty of time to get to Weston for Monday morning. The Whitchurch Fly was just turning off for Whitchurch. We went through the lovely thirteen miles to Ellesmere, and arrived and tied up at about four o'clock. This gave us time to buy the Sunday joint. We had collected all other necessaries from home.

During the evening, I took a stroll around the big mere, with the boys off the other boats. There was a good band from Crewe, playing by the Mere. I was delighted to see all the different birds who came swarming after the bits of food people threw for them. There were swans, geese, coots, moorhen, and widgeon diving and swimming in the water. Quite a number of holiday makers had gathered there, mostly on bicycles or horse and trap, but also a few cars. I returned to the boat, and found the men busy tidying themselves up, ready for the evening at the local pub. All were dressed in the boatman's fashion. The men had white corduroy trousers, with a blue waistcoat, and a blue and white, or black neckerchief. They wore blue socks, and strong shoes with a tongue above the laces. These were hand-made at Stone, and cost 15/- per pair. The women folk had lovely coloured frocks, and shawls around their shoulders. They never wore a hat. In the pub they would have a sing-song and music. They could certainly sing, both sentimental and comic songs, and also played the clappers, tin whistles, accordions and bells on straps. I was allowed in the pub in those days, and I certainly enjoyed it, and learned a few songs.

Sunday morning came, and we made a short day of it, going only five miles down Frankton Locks, and tying up again at Lock Gate Bridge, where the Junction turned left for Weston. My grandad and Wooley had passed the previous day. As it was early afternoon, I walked back to Frankton and spent some time at my Uncle's home. He was John Owen, alias Nixon and had the Newtown Fly *Fancy*. He was at home for the afternoon.

On Monday morning, we started off again down the six mile branch. We left two tons of meal at Hordley Basin and Wharf for the farmer. Then we went for a mile across the "Wilderness" as this spot was called. It was fairly deep, and there were plenty of fish, including pike, who made a good ruffle in the water. We arrived at

Weston Wharf buildings, Weston Lullingfields

Dandyford Wharf, and left a few more ton. Then we passed Hordley School, and arrived at Pedlar's Bridge which was rather a busy wharf where they received and signed for your cargo on behalf of the farmers. Two miles ahead, we came to Shade Oak Wharf, Warehouse and Coal Wharf, and lightened our cargo again, leaving bonemeal, thirds and meal. Old Ned Owen was off-loading coal here from his boat *Circe*, a Company boat from the Potteries. The last two miles were very winding like a W, and also very shallow, with plenty of weed. We arrived at Weston Wharf at two o'clock, passed under a very low bridge and entered the basin. There was a boat already there with a load of bricks from Ellesmere. We delivered the remainder of our cargo and turned the boat around when all was signed for.

Before we set off on our return journey, my Dad pointed out a hollow at the right end of the basin, where, at the end of the eighteenth century, a start had been made to cut the canal to Shrewsbury. When we were on our way, I spotted some mushrooms, and went over the hedge with a hand bowl to gather them. We reached the junction again, and went up the four Frankton Locks. Here we met with sad news. Sam Owen had been drowned in the early morning at No. 4 Lock, off Newtown Fly *Trentham*. He had been taken to Burland by another fly boat.

We went on to Ellesmere for the night, and I saw the STOP board out at the entrance to the short branch. The words "DOWNHILL BOAT CALL AT ELLESMERE" were printed underneath. Next morning we reported to Mr Pixton's office, and he told the Skipper that he was to take a load of timber for Chester Dock Repair Yard. This consisted of about six big oak and elm trees which were loaded in a short time by men from the Engineering Yard at Ellesmere. Mr Palin, the Inspector, had just been transferred here from Norbury. At eleven o'clock on Tuesday morning we were on our way with twelve tons, which allowed us to travel at a fair speed even though the pound was low because it was thirteen miles to the next lock at Grindley Brook. We passed through the tunnel, and went along by the meres, with a bloom of wild musk along the edge of the towing path. The lengthsman was busy mowing the grass, and it looked like a bowling green in places. There was a lovely perfume of cut grass.

We arrived at Wrenbury for the night, and next morning we proceeded to Barbridge, and stayed there for the afternoon. We spent the time tidying up the garden at home, and collected our necessaries. We then made our way to Tower Wharf, Chester, buttying old Tom the Wern down the big locks. He had the boat *Princess May*, which ran one trip a week to Brewood and Chillington Wharf. He and his wife were aged, and worked accordingly. They had a black horse, and a terrier called Susie, which was quick to bite.

We arrived at Chester Dock Yard, and berthed under a travelling crane, by the steam saw mill. While the timber gang off-loaded us, the painters puttied and painted the cabin top and the front bows. We had nothing to do with the off-loading here. I took a stroll down to the river locks, which connected with the canal by the dockyard. Down the two locks there were the Company's stables, and a large basin full of flats and boats waiting for repairs. There were two Company boats passing down the river lock on their way to Saltney to collect cargoes of manure for the Welsh Canal. There was also a boat clearing Crane Wharf of flints for the Potteries. This was the last load from there, and I have never seen one since. This had been the receiving dock before the canal to Ellesmere Port was built. From Tower Wharf General Offices you had a good view of the River Dee, the Welsh hills, and Shotton from whence a few flats brought loads of steel for Ellesmere Port and the Black Country. When I returned to the boat, the cargo had been discharged, and we left Chester at four o'clock and arrived at Ellesmere Port at seven. It was Thursday.

Grindley Brook staircase locks, October 1960, with part of the mill to the left

10

NEW BOAT - WARWICK AND WELSHPOOL.

At very short notice over a pint, and to my great surprise, we arranged to change boats with Tom Salmon that evening. We took over the boat *Milner*, and Tom went over to the *Times*. *Milner* was a much bigger boat, was paid tonnage and had a Company horse. This made old Dick redundant as Tom also had a Company horse.

Next morning we loaded 24 tons of wheat at the North Wall grain warehouse. This was for Warwick – one of our longest trips. We collected our load before dinner, came across the docks again, and went up the two locks to the canal. The Skipper settled for our previous trip of 180 miles to Weston Point, Ellesmere and Weston Salop. This came to £9 10s at mileage rate. We set off again, with a new horse called Jolly, and allowed Dick to walk behind, as we were taking him home to Barbridge. He would be turned into a field for a few weeks rest. We arrived home at midday on Saturday, and had a half day there.

On Sunday morning we were off again, collecting our provender at various stables on route, including Hack Green and Tyrley. We arrived at Norbury Junction on Sunday evening at about eight o'clock, and spent a jolly evening at "The Junction Inn". Mr Sands was the proprietor in those days. Monday morning was wet, but Jolly went by himself as traffic was

quiet after the Brumagem Fly had passed on Sunday. We collected a few feeds of provender at Autherley Junction, and also our permit, and then passed up the twenty one locks to Wolverhampton Depot. We called here for provender for the week. We had to leave Jolly here, and take the horse that was allocated for the Warwick route. I told the stableman I had not been to Warwick before and he said:
"Oh, Victor knows the way – he'll take yer."
And he was right. We made Tipton for the night.

On Tuesday morning, we went on our way through the Black Country, and entered the

Worcester Bar lock, in Gas Street Basin, where the Worcester and Birmingham Canal meets the Birmingham Canal Navigations. The lock has not been in use since both canals came into the same ownership..

Birmingham and Worcester Canal at Bar Lock, Gas Street, Birmingham. We had to get a permit before we navigated this canal. When we had passed through the shallow lock, the Skipper decided to stop for a meal, so we put Victor in the stable for a feed. Traffic was as thick as flies. There were quite a few donkeys in the stable. These took the boats to Diglis Basin, Worcester, and to Gloucester. There were also a number of privately owned hay boats here, looking for

Cadbury's wharves at Bourneville on the Worcester & Birmingham Canal

Clayton boat, who had been to Stratford with a load of glucose from Preston Brook.

At Lapworth Junction we turned right, and entered the Grand Junction Canal. It was quite a nice stretch to Hatton, and the water was deep. We had to get another permit at Hatton, and then passed down the twenty one locks. These were the old single locks. Then we arrived at Warwick Flour Mill. It was nine o'clock on Wednesday evening. Victor led me to the stable again, and I gave him a drink and a manger full of corn. At last we had our own meal and went to bed.

Next morning at eight o'clock, we were being unloaded by a hoist, one bag at a time, into the

customers to buy the hay.

We left again, and proceeded alongside the railway to Selly Oak. Then we passed Cadbury Brothers Chocolate Works at Bournville. A few of our Company boats were off-loading sugar from Ellesmere Port. One of them called out – "This ain't the Welsh Canal, Jack!" I smiled and said no, but I wouldn't mind if it was. Although there was a good smell of chocolate round here, the water in the canal was not clean like the Welsh, and I missed the scenery of hills and vales. When we came to King's Norton Junction, we turned left through the Guillotine Lock. Then we passed through Brandwood Tunnel. I had to take the horse over, while the Skipper shafted the boat through. Fortunately it was only a short one. At the end, we came to open countryside again, and rather a pleasant stretch. We tied up for the night at a country pub "The Bridge Inn". There was stabling here, and Victor knew where it was and led the way.

After a few miles next morning, we entered the first lock of Lapworth Nineteen. On our way down, we passed the entrance to the Stratford-on-Avon Canal, and met a Fellows, Morton and

*One of the original narrow locks at Hatton,
made redundant after the new wide locks
were built in the mid-1930s*

mill. This was completed by half past nine. Then we had orders from Crescent Wharf Birmingham, to load 20 tons of flour as a return load to Birmingham. After our second breakfast, we collected our load and our destination notes for the flour, and had our notes signed for the uphill load. At midday we were on our way again.

Looking up the Lapworth flight from Lock 14

At the bottom of Hatton, there were a few boats waiting for their turn up, and this delayed us for a while. There were a number of Fellows, Morton and Clayton butty boats. Fellows, Morton and Clayton were Agents for the Ship Canal. There was also a "Greasy Ocker", named *Turk*. These ran from Braunston to London and Birmingham. They went from Birmingham to Braunston with a horse and steam-power, left the horse at Braunston and continued to London under steam only. They were short boats with long engine holes, and only carried ten tons but they also towed a butty. Gipsy Jim had one. Eventually we managed to reach Lapworth Top Lock. The other boats had kept to the Grand Junction Canal, on their way to Fazeley Street, Birmingham. This was the depot for the Fellows Morton Company, who ran to London. We stabled at the lock-keeper's. It was a nice quiet

spot, and Victor was allowed to have an hour's grazing. Dad and the lock-keeper went off for a pint or two – it was 2d per pint then.

We were off at four o'clock on Friday morning. Everything was quiet, and we reached Crescent Wharf, Birmingham at about six o'clock that evening. We handed the horse over to Jack, the stableman, until we required him again. All horses were in his charge while at this depot. I had been here before with my granddad, and knew the ropes. Of course, my father had been here many times before. On Saturday morning we were told to be ready to unload on Monday morning. When my father heard this, he changed his clothes, took the food basket, and went to collect a quarter railway fare for Nantwich from New Street. He went home, and left me on the boat for the weekend.

There were quite a few boats here for company, and also other boys. I could have a quiet smoke while I was on my own, which I was not allowed to do when the Skipper was present, as he did not approve! I went to the theatre on the Saturday night with some other people off the boats. On Sunday I slept till midday, and then met the others for a game of jumping, and playing tip-cat. In the afternoon, the Mission people came to the wharf for the usual service, which all attended on their boats.

On Monday morning, I was ordered to No. 5 Wharf to off-load. I got the sheets off, and hung the sacks on the crane, four at a time. The boat was off-loaded by ten o'clock. I brushed it out, and rolled the side-sheets on the gunwale. I had to be careful, as the Skipper was very keen on tidiness, and this was the first time I had been left on my own. When we were working, my father was extremely careful of me. At night he would not let me go ahead to get a lock ready or meet any danger that might arise, but would put me to steer, and tell me not to move out of the doorway when steering. He was not afraid at night. I remember one evening when we were passing down "Hampton 21 locks", and a big bloke, rather a rough character, was walking along the path. He made an attempt to get on the boat to see what our cargo was, when we were in No. 8 Lock. The Skipper came back, and threatened him with a windlass, and would have used it if the bloke had not hurried away. This was the first time I experienced anything like this. The windlass is a useful instrument – it fits in your trouser pocket, and is convenient for drawing paddles, but it is also a good weapon in emergencies.

Ryders Green Locks

Father now arrived from home with the usual food and laundry, and reported to the office for orders. We were to proceed to Hednesford Colliery at Cannock, and take a load of coal for Abermule, in North Wales. We were soon on our way again passing down the eight locks at West Bromwich (Ryder's Green). We passed Braithwaite Steelworks, and the Patent Shaft, and Moxley, where we used to take candlefat and timber. Then we went up eight locks at Walsall, and round the Wirley [Wyrley and Essington]. We tied up at a pub called "The Jolly Collier" near Pelsall. The canal here was full of open coal boats, each with a fire bucket, and a frying pan. The boatmen cooked their bacon, while steering. Just before tying up, we met one of these, and as I lifted the line over, I accidentally dropped it onto the fire-bucket, and upset it. The boatman called me "a Welsh tup", and cursed me for half an hour and never used the same word twice, although I had apologised and stopped the horse. These men were difficult customers – if they were light, they always wanted to come on the towpath side, and expected us to move over, though our little boats would go nearer the side than theirs. They used to have the rope short to the horse, and the horse sniggering along, so you had to clear over. A rule is a rule, but their rule was theirs! We sometimes used to bump them out, and they often had a hole in them but they did not mind. If we got annoyed they would shout:
"What's' the matter with you, 'ave yer lost yer grandmother?"
We had a good time at the pub that evening with good company. One chap said to me "Have a drink, our kid".

We were away next morning, having made sure of our breakfast, as traffic was busy going the same way as us. We arrived at Hednesford after dinner, and commenced to load. The coal was carefully placed on the top of the wharf, built up tidy like a wall. When completed, we placed the sheets over to avoid any pilfering when we were stopped at night. Close by here there were some race-horse stables.

The following morning we set off, and turned right at the end of the Cannock Arm. We passed Hawkins at Cannock, and then went down the thirteen locks at Churchbridge. Here we entered the Hatherton Branch of the Staffordshire and Worcester Canal, and returned to Autherley Junction and the Shroppie. Harry, the stableman, told us to leave the horse Victor here, as he was to be returned to Wolverhampton. Our horse, Jolly, was ready for us, having been sent on with another boat. We tied up at Autherley for the night. Here we heard that the tugs from Autherley to Tyrley were to be transferred to Chester, and that horses were to take their place in the future.

We were lucky to get a tow next day for the 27 miles to Tyrley. Jolly walked at his ease, and I rode on his back most of the time. We reached Tyrley in five hours. The tug was the *Leader*, and there was quite a flush each side of the boats. At Tyrley, the tug tied up to collect his spares, and we had our Way Bill signed, and collected our provender. The locks were in our favour, and we also met some traffic as we passed down them. We tied up for Thursday night at Audlem. On Friday morning we collected our provender for two weeks, to take us to Aberbechan and back. We had to leave Jolly here as Tommy Masefield thought he was too free to go up the Welsh Canal with a heavy load. He fixed us up with Blossom, a mare who was more steady. We went on through Nantwich, and arrived at Hurleston Junction, where we turned left into the bottom lock, and ascended the four. Here we tied up for the day, and went home to Barbridge, which was about a mile along the road. We left the horse to be fed by George Welch, the lock-keeper.

When we arrived at home, my two young brothers, Alfred and Bob, asked Dad if they could join the boat, as they had a month's summer holidays. Mother and father decided that they could as there was plenty of room in the cabin of this big boat. In fact, it was a lovely cabin, but the boat was too big for my liking – you could not put on speed like you could with a fly boat. The following morning we collected our food and an advance of cash from Barbridge Office, and set off on our long trip.

We travelled at a slow pace. The boys helped to close the lock gates, made a great fuss of Blossom, and had a swim with a rope attached to the boat. We swam in the canal quite often as the weather was hot. However, the cut was not very full of water, being barely navigable. It was lovely to be back on it, after visiting the industrial areas. There was no industrial smoke on the Shroppie, once you had left Wolverhampton or Ellesmere Port, apart from the odd chimney here and there in a brickyard or mill. We passed through Swanley two locks, and Baddiley three, and came to the draw-bridge at Wrenbury. The two boys hung on the chain to raise it. This was great fun for them, as neither of them had been before. Here we passed alongside the River Weaver, which is only like a big brook, being fairly near its source. It passed under the canal at Marbury Lock, and then ran alongside it for about a mile. The towpath also changed to the other side here. On the opposite side, there was another brook which flowed into the Weaver near Marbury Lock.

We met a few boats along here. One was the Cheese Fly *Daisy*, going to Manchester from Ellesmere and Weston. The Skipper was Joe Jones. The next was the Cheese Fly from Whitchurch, whose Skipper was also called Joe Jones, but was not related to the first. He was making for Barbridge, and would be at Manchester Castlefields on Monday morning. The last boat was the Newtown Fly *Broxton*, the boat my father had recently given up. The Skipper was now Bill Stubbs, and his sons were mates. As we came up through Quoisley and

Willeymoor Locks, we met the Llangollen Fly. All these boats were making for Barbridge for Saturday night. Here they would meet, and have a sing-song and sometimes a fight in the "Jolly Tar" or "The King's Arms".

After passing up the six locks at Grindley Brook, we entered the long pound. The water was fairly deep here as the paddle which drove the mill was down, and the current was not so strong. This made it easier for the horse, but it only happened at the weekend, so the boatmen liked to work this long stretch at that time. We wished Jim and Mrs Wood good day at the top lock, and went on to tie up at Blackoe for the night. This was where the Llangollen Fly *Sirdar*, Skipper John Ellis changed horses. It was a very quiet spot, just a lengthsman's cottage and a four-stall stable with plenty of bedding. This was owned by the lengthsman, Ambrose Benkett, who also kept a cow, pigs and fowl. The cow was allowed to graze on the towing-path, and always kept out of the way of the horses. Quite a few lengthsmen on the Welsh Canal kept a cow, and were allowed to do so by the Company, as the animals soon learnt to move over when traffic appeared. We passed a quiet evening enjoying the countryside, watching the birds and rabbits, and having a chat at the lengthsman's cottage. There was no pub here for the Skipper to have his pint.

We left next morning at about seven o'clock, but we allowed the boys to stay in bed. The Newtown Fly, and the Llangollen Fly had gone past at about five o'clock on this Sunday morning. We allowed Blossom to baccer, and had our breakfast. The boys woke up, and were soon alert and eager not to miss anything.

Father cooked their breakfast, and then they made themselves tidy for Sunday. You used to meet quiet a lot of people taking walks on the canalside on a Sunday, especially near the towns. There were a number of draw-bridges

Former cheese fly-boat Saturn *at Frankton Junction in 1957. The four locks at the top end of the Montgomery Canal are to the left*

around Whixall, and the boys enjoyed opening them. As we entered Whixall Moss, the water became much deeper, and gave the horse an easier pull for a couple of miles to Bettisfield. Then we passed through the lovely scenery of forestry and meres, and turned left at Ellesmere through Tetchill and past Ellesmere College. At Frankton Junction we turned left again, and entered the Montgomery Canal. We tied up here at four o'clock to allow the boys to visit their two aunts and cousins. Both my mother's brother, and my father's sister lived here; the former was John Owen, who had the Newtown Fly and the latter's husband was John Jones who had the Llangollen Fly. Both of these had families. John Jones' eldest son had just joined the Navy for twenty one years, and was stationed at Portsmouth. This latter uncle had a religious nature, and occasionally said a prayer before a coffin left the home of any boatmen who had passed away, anywhere on his route.

Queens Head Wharf

had *Equerry*, a fly boat built for Newtown.

As we passed down the next three locks, we met a few light boats on their way either to Black Park Colliery, at Chirk for coal, or to the Glyn Valley Quarry, also at Chirk for stone, or to Queen's Head for sand. We passed Maesbury Wharf, and A. and A. Peate's Flour Mill, where a number of Company boats were waiting to be unloaded. I have already described the lovely scenery from here to Newtown. The grass was mowed, the hedges and trees were trimmed, and the locks were clean and tidy. The next locks were Carreghofa Two. The bloom around these locks was fantastic, with antirrhinums or snapdragons growing round the walls between the two locks and the Toll Office. Mr Beddows lived here, and told us that the flowers had grown there for years, and got thicker every year. Mr Tom Moody, the lengthsman, lived at the bottom lock cottage, and had a nice stable there. We passed Newbridge Wharf, the aqueduct and the ornamental bridge, and reached Burgeddin Locks. At Pool Quay we began to climb again towards Newtown. Mr G Lloyd had the lock ready for us, and we soon reached Welshpool. The boys were very interested in the two peacocks at Buttington, as they had never seen any before. We stabled the horse for the night at the Company Depot, and called to have our Way Bill signed by Frank Windsor, the night porter. We also collected a few letters and other oddments, as there was no fly boat on a Monday to take them.

We all had a jolly evening. Next morning we went down the four locks, and had a word with Tom Price and old Starkey at the bottom lock. We were travelling downhill from Frankton and this was much easier for Blossom, as the water was in our favour, and she could walk along with a slacker rope. We turned right and entered Perry Moor. Along this stretch there were rushes on the sides, where moorhens, peewhits and plovers made their nests. The two boys took their boots off, and collected a small basket of eggs, including some wild ducks'. They were taken from nests where the birds were not sitting. We passed through the boneworks at Rednal, and reached Queen's Head Wharf. Here was the crane which had killed a young woman in 1902. She was a lovely blonde girl, named Julia Hall, one of a family of four girls who lived at Barbridge, and only seventeen. She had been hanging sacks on the crane, when one fell off, and killed her instantly. She was on the boat *Caroline Mary* which her father, old Jack Hall, had new from Chester. It was the only boat I knew of to be launched with a bottle of wine. It finished up at Rednal, running bottles to Weston Point and re-named *Anita*. He also

We only had twelve miles to go to the end of our journey next morning, but it was very slow going owing to the twists and bends, and the low, narrow bridges. However it was very pretty travelling, and the people up here were most obliging, and thought a lot of the canal boats and horses. We passed through several locks, and arrived at Aberbechan at about three o'clock. We had a few hours left in which to off-load the cargo of coal. This all had to be weighed in a 2 cwt barrow on the scales, making it a long slow job. This was often the case when house coals were concerned, especially where there was no gauge plates fixed on the boat sides.

We worked till six o'clock, and after our meal we took a stroll along the Severn to Newtown. The boys wanted to see the end of the canal. We all walked at our leisure. Bob, the younger brother, had had an accident at home, falling through the bedroom window into the yard. This had affected his health for quite a while, but once he had had a boat trip and a change of scenery, he completely forgot his ailments and never complained once. My mother and father could hardly believe it, as he was quite a normal boy ever after. We returned from our walk at about ten o'clock, and decided to camp out on the canal bank. We took one of the sheets off the boat and made a tent, and cooked the wild eggs to eat with our cold bacon, and the lettuce we had been given on the way. We had also been given milk, though we usually used tinned milk when travelling.

On Tuesday morning, Dad woke us. He had made a fire on the bank, and I cooked the bacon which we enjoyed very much. We all put our old clothes on, and fixed ourselves up with shovels to start off-loading the coal. John Edwards gave us every encouragement saying to Bob "Sweet, Bob, lad", an expression which was used quiet a lot in Wales. John was a widower and had a son, George, and a daughter, Nessie. He also had a brother, Dick, on a Company boat. His other brother, Bill, could use a shovel well, although he had only one arm. The majority of the Shropshire Union boatmen came from Wales in those days. I knew many well; they came from places like Newtown, Welshpool, Llanymynech, and Pant, and also a few from Pontcysyllte, Cefn Garth and Llangollen. When people spoke of them they would say "Newtown George", although the man's name was Davies, "Llanymynech Jack", whose name was Jones, "Ned the Pant" whose name was Richards, and so on.

After we had delivered the coal, we turned the boat, and were off again. We took all the gangway down, and also the cratches, mast and stands, the water vessel and chimney, and placed them in the bottom of the boat. This was called "going down light" and helped us to go steady through the lower bridges, as this boat had a high cabin. The Newtown Fly and other smaller mileage boats were built especially for this canal, and the various fittings did not need to be taken down. When we entered Newhouse Lock, we gave the boat a wash-out as traffic was quiet. The two boys bathed in the canal, Blossom grazed and the Skipper and I washed and prepared for our next cargo. On this section, the rule was to call at the wharves to pick up. On the whole it was shop-keepers who attended to these wharves and warehouses, with the exception of Newtown, Berriew, Welshpool and Maesbury, which were all staffed by Company employees.

When we had completed our washing, we set off again, and Byles Lock, where we had a few words with Joe Thomas, the lock-keeper and his family. Then we came to Brynderwyn Lock and had a little chat with Mr Pryce, the postman, while the lock emptied. He had nothing for us to take on the boat. We passed under Glen Hafren Bridge, pretty but low, the next swing side bridge, and Braye's Bridge, which was also low. We called at the shop at Halfway House,

Brithdir Lock, 2004

Off again on Wednesday morning, we passed the small school at Belan. The young lady teacher, Gertrude, called out – "Good morning, Jack, how are you? Stop and talk to me a bit". I replied "I can't just now. See you again". It was quite a while before I saw her again in actual fact. We came up to Belan two locks, but Pryce-Webb, the lock-keeper, had nothing for us to take.

We next arrived at Welshpool Wharf. Jim Lloyd told us to take a load of macadam from Welshpool Standard Quarry for Swanley Wharf. The wharf was just through the bridge. This stone came by horse and cart in three hundred weight loads and was tipped into the boat.

While we were loading, a two-cabin boat *Manchuria* came up from Ellesmere Port with the remains of a cargo and unloaded at the wharf. The Skipper was William Owen, and he had no family. After unloading, he was engaged in the lock, loading a few large oak trees from the forestry, which had been placed on the lockside. This timber was for Naylor's of Warrington. They were rolled in steadily by a winch on each side of the lock, and there were stretchers across the boat's hold to ease the strain. They filled up level to the boat's side, and were placing the last one on top, when it unexpectedly rolled onto one side and sunk the boat in the lock. The fore-end of the boat was in the bottom of the lock by the bottom gates, and the cabin end stuck out of the water at the other end.

To raise the boat again, the three-legs were

but there was nothing to pick up. A mile and a half down Finney Straight, and we came to Garthmyl, and called on Mr Leo Owen at "The Nag's Head", but he had nothing for us either. Two miles further on, passing *The Revel*, we arrived at Berriew Wharf. The STOP board was out, so we berthed the boat, and told one of the boys to ring the bell fixed on the wharf. This drew the attention of the porter, Ned Windsor, who lived at the lock-house, a few hundred yards away. Ned came, and we collected twenty bundles of sacks to be returned to Liverpool. There was no pay for empty sacks.

We soon arrived at Brithdir Lock, and stopped for the night. We stabled the horse at the pub "The Horse Shoe Inn", which was convenient for the Skipper to have a pint or two. Dad knew all the locals up this section, and they wanted to know why he had given up the Fly, and what he had done with Charley, the horse. He knew he had made a mistake in this, with his sons growing up to act as crew. Tom Roberts was the lock-keeper here, but there was nothing in the small warehouse for us to take.

fixed over the lock and the tree was raised. The water levelled itself in the boat, and was then pumped out. The tree was then placed securely on top. Fortunately no damage was done. I went inside the cabin to look, and everything was dry, and the fire was burning in the stove. I have never seen a boat in that position before. As a joke after this event, the Skipper was called "The Manchurian Man". This was 1910, when Mr W Ireland was Agent at Welshpool and Mr W Baker Senior, the Inspector of the Engineering Department.

After collecting our load of 20 tons of stone, we set off. It was Thursday morning. We buttied William Owen to Swanley, and he left us on Friday morning. The four of us were quite busy unloading, but we had a little work left for Saturday morning, and then made our short journey home to Barbridge for the weekend.

Brithdir lockside warehouse, 2004

Belan Locks - a relatively timeless scene

11

A CHANGE TO *STEPHEN*, AND FIRST TRIP TO LLANGOLLEN

On his arrival at Barbridge, the Skipper was offered another boat, running mostly from Chester to Shropshire and North Wales. This was the boat *Stephen*, the old Llangollen Fly Boat, which my father had skippered previously, following his father's death at Bettisfield in 1892. It was now a mileage boat. Father accepted it, and I was pleased to get away from the big boat. We changed over during the weekend and tied the boat *Milner* up within sight of the office to await another Skipper. On Monday morning, father made his way to Ellesmere Port by train to settle up for our previous trip to Warwick and Aberbechan.

Cadbury Brothers works at Knighton, with several of the Cadbury fleet of boats which collected milk from wharves in Shropshire and Cheshire, for processing in the factory

We were not bound for Chester at this stage. We were ordered to the canal sidings at Calveley Station to collect a load of bungalows, along with five other boats. Dad left me and the two boys to proceed to Calveley. We took old Dick out of the field again, and delivered Blossom to the Company's stables at Bunbury.

The canal sidings were full of wagons with bungalows roped on. The men loaded us up. It was a light cargo, but high and bulky. These bungalows were for Cadbury Brothers, of Bournville, who were erecting a new works at Knighton, near Stafford, for the convenience of the canal. This Chocolate Works was built about 1910, and still exists today. After loading we returned to Barbridge. Father and mother were very pleased with my experience as Skipper for a day. I was about sixteen then.

My dad had had quite a good draw of cash, in all £11 which consisted of both mileage and tonnage – tonnage to Birmingham, mileage to Warwick, and Hednesford, mileage to Hurleston, and tonnage to Aberbechan and back to Swanley. Total mileage was 254, and lockage 246. The horse was owned by the Company so including two advances, making £5 in all, our pay was £16. This would be about £60 today [in 1969].

We were on our way again at four o'clock on Tuesday morning. We passed up twenty seven locks, Hack Green, Audlem, Adderley and Tyrley, and arrived at Knighton at two o'clock. This was about twenty three miles. Knighton Wharf was very small, consisting of a wooden platform and a warehouse for the local farmer which would hold about twenty sacks. It was near Shebden, where there were "short bridges", and the reservoir which feeds the canal. There was a party of men waiting to erect the bungalows, which were off-loaded in less than an hour.

We returned to Goldstone for the night, and stabled the horse at "The Wharf Tavern". This was a busy little place, with a coal wharf and warehouse. Bricks of land salt were also sold here at 2d a block. There were three hired boats tied up here, belonging to Price and Sons of Brierly Hill. The Skippers had a few pints together, and Dad decided to swop horses with one of them whose name was Ward. So poor old Dick had to go, and we took Jim. Dick was sixteen hands, and a little heavy for a light boat, while Jim was fifteen hands, and light-legged. This was a reasonable swop, as they both had a good home.

We hooked Jim on, on Wednesday morning, and made for home again, light. To our dismay, we heard there was a strike, but we managed to reach Barbridge. There were about fifty boats stopped here, from all routes, as it was a Junction. They were mostly loaded, with various kinds of cargoes, all for overseas. This was an unofficial stoppage, and lasted a fortnight. When the strike was over, the boatmen were all granted 2/6 per week special allowance. It involved all the workers on the Shroppie.

Just before the strike there were two boatmen, John Richards and Albert Wood, who came from the Welsh Canal. They had been on a "randy" (the beer), and had also drunk a bottle of whisky which they had purchased in Ellesmere. They left the horse baccering, and Albert steered, leaving John to sleep and sober up again. The sleeper had his feet in the cabin and his head in the entrance, where you stand to steer the boat. Eventually Albert tried to wake him saying:
"Isn't it very near time you got hold of this peg?" i.e. the tiller. However, he got no response – Jack was dead. This happened at Lyneal. Albert called a doctor and a policeman, and after the formalities were completed, they took Jack to Barbridge on a boat named *Ariel*. Jack lived at Barbridge, and as the strike was on, all the boatmen were able to follow the funeral to Acton church to show

respect. They wore their working attire. This was on a Friday in August 1910.

Also while the above dispute was in progress, the boat *Harold* was engaged on the Welsh Canal, working from Maesbury to Newtown, taking flour, meal etc. wherever it was required. This boat was skippered by a young man, George Hopwood from Whitchurch, and his mate, Bill Bristow. They were both about eighteen. When they reached Newtown and delivered their cargo, they suddenly decided to join the army. George joined the R.F.A., and was stationed at Preston, Lancs, and Bill joined the S.W.B. and was stationed at Brecon. They left the horse and boat in charge of Mr Matthews at the Newtown Depot, and it was later given to a new Skipper.

After the strike we returned to our routine, and were allocated to Cow Lane Bridge Wharf, Chester. However, our depot was Barbridge. There were six Chester boats, mostly for the Welsh Canal, Newtown and Llangollen. They were classed as two-handed fly boats.

Our first cargo was for Llangollen, Ellesmere, Chirk and the Glyn Valley. It was my first trip to Llangollen. We passed up the Welsh Canal, and entered Chirk by the Gledrid, and "The New Inn". I could see Chirk Castle in the distance, and also the village church, the viaduct, the aqueduct, the tunnel and the River Ceriog in the valley below. When we came up to Quinta Bridge, the Skipper told me we were passing over the place where a breach had occurred in 1908. During the weeks it took to repair, no water could get through to feed the Welsh Canal to Hurleston, and the Montgomery Canal below Frankton.

We arrived at Chirk Bank Wharf, which was cared for by Mr Jones, the Shop, who was paid tonnage. There was a large warehouse here to store goods etc, and also a corn mill, situated in the valley by the Ceriog. We unloaded 70 sacks of Indian corn here, and it was taken away in horse-lorries down a very steep bank. I noticed a half-legged horse, and asked the driver how old he was. He told me he was fifteen years old, and a veteran of the Boer War. He also showed me where he had been wounded through the neck. It was quite healed, and no trouble to him now. They called him Bullet.

We set off again, and sailed steadily over the aqueduct, alongside the viaduct. A couple of express trains passed over, and the passengers waved to us. The view from the aqueduct through the Glyn Valley was gorgeous. Fifty yards further on, we entered Chirk Tunnel. At this end was erected a steam pumping shed, which supplied Chirk Green Colliery with water. Old Jim, the pump man, had a few words with my dad, remarking that our boat "Stephen" had been my grandfather's old fly boat and had passed down from father to son. Jim, the horse, entered the tunnel, and had no objections as he had previously been through Harecastle, Dudley and Cosely and knew the

routine. He went by himself. We were light-loaded after our earlier delivery.

By the main line at Chirk Railway Station, there was a narrow gauge railway. It carried both passengers and freight up the main highway to the Glyn, calling at a few small stations en route.

We left the tunnel, and passed up the deep cutting. Dad pointed out a huge fir tree at the top of the cutting facing Chirk Castle. It was known as "The King". On the opposite side of the cutting, facing Chirk Railway Station, and nearing the end, there was a second known as "The Queen". We also passed a great stone, sunk partly in the towing-path and partly in the canal. Joking, the Skipper told me that every time this stone heard Chirk clock stroke one, it turned over. I took this seriously, and a while after, when passing the same place at one o'clock, I watched the stone, but it did not turn over. Dad said "It hasn't heard it yet".
I said "No, and it never will".
This stone was used as a getting on and off place for boatmen, when necessary. It was quite clean and so smooth you could slip in the canal if you were not careful. It is still there, but it is getting green now.

Just past here at Black Park, we stopped and placed a ton of flour and bran into the small wagons for the Glyn. These wagons were usually used for carrying stone from the Ceriog Granite Company to the canal. Old Bob was here, loading a boat with stone. The stone came off a high platform, down a chute, and made a lot of dust. Fifty yards ahead, there was a side-bridge for the towing path, and a short branch of

Chirk Tunnel, southern portal

canal went under the Railway Bridge, and divided into two small arms, one for Black Park Colliery, and the other for a factory which made paving stones for the towns, and also concrete slabs. There was also a land wharf, and a few old colliery cottages. This was a very busy place in those days, both with Company boats, and privately owned ones. There was one boat that collected a load of slack every day for Graessers, now called Monsanto. It was drawn by two donkeys, and the Skipper Williams, was called Welsh Jack. There were eight Company boats waiting to be loaded here today. Two were for Tattenhall Road Bone Works, two were loading paving stones for Joiner's Square on the Caldon Canal, and the last two were loading macadam for places en route.

On our way again, we passed through Whitehouses, a short tunnel, and came up to Irish Bridge, and a right hand bend. From this point, I had a lovely view of Ponty Aqueduct, the Cefn, the Garth, and the long railway viaduct, which were all above the river. In the valley, alongside the River Dee, I could see J C Edwards Brickyards, New Bridge, and a pub called "The Tally Ho", which was just in view. We passed the Vron Lime Kilns, which were very busy, loading boats with lime and stone. Then we went under the drawbridge, and along the top of the valley, with a cluster of fir trees on either side of the narrow canal.

We now came up to the aqueduct, but it was occupied by a boat coming to meet us, and we had to stop while he passed over. We could just meet at this end. It was old Bilston Tom, with a pair of donkeys, making his way to Bilston with 20 ton of stone for Deepfields on the B.C.N. We then entered the aqueduct. The Skipper led Jim by his head, while I walked behind to steady the rear, with my hand on the towing rope, leaving the boat to steer itself. Like me, Jim had never been over before, and I did not feel too comfortable. Jim had a look down and snorted, but settled to it halfway over. The Skipper told

me to go and steer the boat, and I did so, taking care not to move out of the doorway. I could see part of the canal bridge leading to Llangollen in the distance, and the tops of the trees just below me, and down below on the side of the River Dee, the white houses. What a height to look down upon, when steering!

There was only one place to walk, and that was the towpath, which was four foot wide, with strong rails four foot high to protect you. This aqueduct was built in 1805; its height is 125 feet, and its length, 1,000 feet. It is one of Telford's wonders. The railway viaduct is about a mile down the valley.

We left the aqueduct, and passed the dock-yard on the towing path side. On the offside was the entrance to the feeder to Llangollen. We had now arrived at Ponty Depot, where the Agent was Mr Roberts, the Clerk, Mr O Jones, and the Porter, Mr H Wood. Mr Roberts lived by the office. We had orders to pick up a few oddments from the warehouse at Acrefair, two hundred yards ahead. There was a railway siding in a small basin opposite, for loading coal. There was also a small canal pub "The Canal Tavern", whose proprietor was Harry Evans. Fights often sprung up here between the boatmen and the Welshmen. Near the office was a six horse stable with two stables reserved for the Fly. There were a dozen donkeys grazing on the wharf, some boats were loading stone for the Humber Arm. This was a storage depot for stone. The foreman at the dock-yard was Mr Stephen Roberts. This was a fair sized repair and building yard, with two dry docks, employing six boat-builders, one smith and one painter, all local men.

It was Wednesday night. We bow-hauled the boat to the feeder and had to pull up the draw-bridge, and pass under the narrow road bridge. The Skipper had decided to travel the last four miles to Llangollen that evening, although it was already six o'clock. We had to meet a strong

The overgrown end of the Humber Arm, with warehouse.
Note the canal bridge in the distance. August 1965.

Sun Bank Hotel nearby. There were seven or eight boats waiting here to load big stone burrs. These were the Humber Arm boats that I have spoken of previously. There was also a long stable occupied by donkeys, on the towing path side, above the railway.

We next went under Wenffrwd Bridge, which was known to the boatmen as "Birdcage Bridge", as there were birds in cages, hanging on the big house walls above it. There was also a lovely perfume of flowers, which grew on this high wall. On the towing path side was a let-off paddle. It was a very narrow and bendy turn on either side of the bridge, and one wondered how to get around it, especially on a dark night. However, it was pretty to look at, with clusters of blue-bells along the banks in the spring, and a huge pine tree between the towing path and the main road.

Further on, we passed the newly built black and white lengthsman's cottage. We were facing Crow Castle, well up on the mountains. We went under a draw-bridge, and entered the Rock Walls, where a heap of clay was kept in case of leakage. This was a narrow stretch, well above the road, railway and River Dee, which were positioned in steps on the hillside.

The Skipper told me that this section from Trevor to Llangollen had to be inspected every morning, including Sunday. The lengthsman was allowed a terrier to keep down the water rats.

We arrived at Llangollen Wharf at a quarter past eight. There was good stabling here. It was a Company Wharf, in the care of Captain Jones, who also had a business of pleasure rowing boats. He also had four long, light horse-drawn

current, but had only four ton left in the boat. The scenery up this stretch was lovely. My father could name every bridge and wharf – they all had Welsh names, of course. We passed Bryn Howell Hall, which had a small brick boat-house in the gardens. On the canal was a full-size, converted narrow-boat, built over to carry passengers, and painted blue and white. Its name was *Sheldrake*. Further along, we passed under a railway bridge. Here there was an old sunken boat. I asked the Skipper the name of it, and he said it was *The Woodman*. It was an old Ellesmere and Chester Canal Fly boat, and had been there forty years. His father could remember it working.

We passed Busby's Stone Wharf, with a boat loading stone from Trevor Rocks, which we could see in the distance. Half a mile ahead, we passed Sun Bank Wharf, situated between the canal and road. There was a tramway which ran across the road and up to the Rocks, and the boats, which were covered and could take fifty to sixty passengers. They usually took trips to the Horseshoe Falls at Berwyn. Our last four tons were for the Dee Mills, at Llangollen, which were within sight and easy reach of the canal.

I took a walk to the end of the canal at Llantysillio, to see the Chain Bridge, and the old paddle gear which took the water from the Dee into the canal. The Horseshoe Falls were beyond the paddle, and Berwyn Railway Station was on the other side of the Dee, about a hundred foot up. On the right, above the falls was a lovely small church, on the side of the Dee, and on the main road to the Horseshoe Pass. When I returned to the boat, I discussed what I had seen with my father. He had been up there once with the fly boat for slate slabs for Liverpool. He told me that the water came from the Arenig Hills, went into Bala Lake, and then passed through a sluice into the River Dee.

At seven o'clock on Thursday morning, Captain Jones and Issac Roberts, his son-in-law, came to collect our cargo into the Company Warehouse. They had to wind it out by hand-crane. Conversation was mostly about our old Llangollen Fly boat, *Stephen*, and the tragedy of my grandfather, who had been a Welshman. When talking amongst themselves, they would talk in Welsh, and they also counted the sacks in Welsh. I could not understand it, but my father could. After delivery, we turned the boat round in the winding-hole, just below the new Grammar School. The return journey was quite easy for Jim, as the water was in his favour. It was a matter of keeping the rope out of the water!

Llangollen Wharf, 1974

97

We arrived at Pontcysyllte at about ten o'clock. We had met the Llangollen Fly going up, at Trevor, and he would be returning shortly. This was the boat *Countess*, built to replace *Stephen*. Its Skipper was William Trow, and the working hands were his two sons, Bill and Joe. We took our orders from the office, and went on to Graessers, now Monsanto Chemical Works. Our load was caustic, in galvanised drums, for Calveley Station, where it would be transhipped to the railway. We completed our load, and were on our way again at about midday.

We made Ellesmere for the night, and Barbridge on Friday night. On Saturday morning, we proceeded to Calveley to off-load. Then we took the boat back to Barbridge until after dinner on Sunday. Then we returned to Chester, ready for Monday morning. The days were getting shorter, and Autumn had arrived. "Dark nights and deep locks", as the boatmen say. We prepared for the colder weather, by seeing to our clothes and bedding, and also the horse's rugs. A horse needs protection when standing at locks and wharves, where a stable is not always convenient.

Pontcysyllte Aqueduct, opened in 1805

12

LAST TRIPS WITH FATHER

To return to my story – I remember one trip we made to Berriew. On our return journey, we collected six tons of malt from the Malthouse, Waen Wen, near Llanymynech, for Jones, the Maltsters of Shrewsbury, who also owned this Malthouse. We arrived at Coachman's Bridge, Tetchill, for the night. Next morning we prepared to start off early, but found that the emergency planks had been placed in the grooves by the bridge. Part of the canal was empty, and the lengthsman was attending to it. This was Jack Edwards, who lived here. He had been called out during the night by a messenger from the Maintenance Yard at Ellesmere. The Inspector, Mr C Palin, had discovered the breach. He heard it from his bedroom, as the culvert had gone right by his back door. He raised the alarm, and all the men were called out. The emergency planks were fixed at the Red Bridge, near the yard. Every means were tried to repair the breach temporarily to allow the waiting traffic to proceed, but they failed.

Uphill traffic consisted of the Newtown Fly, the Llangollen Fly, the Manchester Cheese Fly, and many other boats from various places. Where traffic was urgent, it had to be transhipped at Oakmere Wharf nearby, and taken by the Railway's horse drays, to be delivered by rail. In our own case, as that of many boats, we had to be content to wait for a week. There was only one boat on dry land. That was *The Gleaner* from the Glyn Ceriog Granite Company, Skipper W Baines. There was not even one commercial boat in the basin at the wharf, as it was the weekend, and there was not much traffic as it was autumn.

The culvert that had breached was a water course, which also drained water from the dry dock situated in the Company's engineering

yard. It was repaired in a week with a four foot glazed pipe. A few pipes were left over after the operation, and are still there today. The old culvert had been ordinary red brick, and had been built when the canal was built. There were also two let-offs in the vicinity of the yard for emergencies.

Some of the boatmen, including my father, enjoyed the rest, and a week's lazing. A good fight also took place when one of the yardmen came to high words with one of the boatmen. Jack, a young boatman, challenged the best man in the yard to fight. This was Tom, an ex-service man. They were both in their mid-twenties. They stripped to the middle, and were engaged in the field opposite the canal yard. The fight lasted half an hour, and both men could hit heavy. The boatman won the fight, as Tom was not too well, and gave in, otherwise he would have been best man. He told Jack they would have another meeting, but they never did. Tom had to give up work a few years later owing to ill-health, but Jack is living today and has many fights to his account. He is now well into his eighties, and lives in the Black Country.

When we were able to go again, we went to Barbridge. We either had to off-load our six tons of malt, or collect more and take it directly to Shrewsbury. We decided to do the latter, and collected a few tons for Market Drayton. We loaded up again at Wolleston Mills, and Norbury Junction with goods for various places to Shrewsbury. While we were collecting our food, Mr Moore informed us that we could change into the boat *Ruth*, on our return. This had been a cheese fly, but was being replaced by a newly built boat, *The Equinox*, whose Skipper was Joseph Jones.

We delivered our cargo to Jones, the Malters, at Shrewsbury, and returned light to Wappenshall. Here, we had orders from Mr Whitehead of the Trench, to collect a load of coal from Humber Arm for Audlem Wharf. After loading and

Audlem. From left - lock cottage, lock 13, warehouse, wharf, stables and Bridge Inn (extreme right), pictured before 1915, when Kingbur Mill was built behind the shed

horse-drawn and with an urgent load of cheese.

We now set off on our way to Birmingham or "up in the smoke" as the boatmen would say. This trip was sixty miles and fifty locks from Barbridge to Birmingham. We met traffic of all kinds in the lovely countryside to Autherley Junction, but from Wolverhampton to Birmingham, we were meeting traffic from all over the country, every minute, both on the top and bottom summits. We arrived at Birmingham on Saturday evening, together with many others from Ellesmere Port. The Brummagem Fly was just leaving on his daily trip. Our weekend was free, and the Skipper went home on the train.

On Monday morning, I counted thirty two Shropshire Union boats waiting to be off-loaded at Crescent Wharf. Their cargoes were varied, and included timber. There were six boats

delivering at Audlem, we returned to Barbridge on a Wednesday to change onto the boat *Ruth*. Joe Jones changed onto our boat *Stephen*, and proceeded light to Chester boatyard to collect his new boat *The Equinox*. A boat built at the same time as *The Equinox* was *The Endeavour*, a pottery fly for Arthur Jones.

Ruth was loaded with a cargo of chair bottoms from Manchester for Crescent Wharf, Birmingham. We changed over in this way to avoid transhipping. In these circumstances, another boat would bring the cheese from Weston, Ellesmere and Bettisfield, and it would be transhipped to *The Equinox* at Barbridge. That boat would then take up its regular route. *Ruth* was a lovely shaped boat, and had a fair sized cabin, registered for a man, wife and three children. I was told that it had been the fastest boat to travel from Barbridge to Manchester when it did the fifty one miles in thirteen hours,

Griffiths Bros. corn mill at Chester, May 1970

loaded with soap from Levers at Port Sunlight. At this time there was a special warehouse built for soap only. All this traffic was attended to by Tuesday. There were five different wharves here, and plenty of men, as the boatmen were engaged whenever possible, at the rate of fourpence per hour. This was a fair price in those days, and very convenient for the boatmen when they were travelling. They averaged twelve hours a day. Our Skipper came back on Tuesday. He knew when to return, as he could telephone from Barbridge and find out what was happening to his boat at anytime, anywhere.

Our next orders were in conjunction with another boat. Our butty was *The Dog*, a pottery boat run by Bill Grimes and his missus. We had to proceed to Higgins Bottom Wharf in West Bromwich to collect a forty ton order for Liverpool. We started off on Wednesday morning, and we had to look out for this isolated spot, as neither of us had ever heard of it before, although we knew West Bromwich. We passed through the top of West Bromwich eight locks, and the Braithwaite Works, and found the canal full of rushes growing out from the edges, with a track up the centre. We enquired from different workmen, got our directions, and managed to berth at this works. There was a large black awning over the canal, which was a dead end here.

The cargo was short bars of steel for abroad. Both of us were loaded with twenty tons, which was rather an unusual weight for small boats. In addition to this, our boat still had to carry the cheese boards and fittings, until we could conveniently dispose of them at Barbridge. The two boats were deep in the water, but we had good side-sheets to prevent it coming over the side when we were going down locks.

We arrived back at Ellesmere Port on Friday, and transhipped to a Birkenhead flat. We then left our butty, Bill, who was to load china-clay for the Potteries, and went to Chester again. On

Saturday morning we collected a load of flour from Frost Flour Mills, for Manchester, and managed to make Barbridge for Saturday night, staying until after dinner on Sunday. We made Middlewich Big Lock on Sunday night.

On Monday, we passed the Anderton Boat Lift, and were hauled by tugs through the three tunnels, entering the Bridgewater Canal at Preston Brook. This time we were accompanied by a boat from Leicester, who was for Manchester Docks. We passed the *Duchess Countess* at Agden, and made Broadheath for the night. On Tuesday morning we met the three cheese boats, all with a cargo. There was J Partridge with *Saturn*, J Jones with *Equinox*, and David Parry with *Daisy*. *Saturn* was a new boat, but built before *Equinox*. We arrived at Castlefields to deliver our cargo, and wished our Leicester boat good day.

On Wednesday morning, we collected a cargo of sugar for Stoke-on-Trent. We left about midday, and made Preston Brook the same night. On Thursday morning, we hung onto the tug, and entered the North Stafford Canal together with a few other boats, including one from the Anderton Company, and two from Potters of Runcorn. Our boat was first on the tug, which loosed us off at Barnton. Now for a race to the Big Lock! We knew the others could not overtake us, as we had a lovely young mare named Rose, a Company's horse, half-legged and fifteen hands high. When we entered the Big Lock, the others were not in sight. We passed through Middlewich, and past the entrance to the Wardle Canal and the Shroppie. This time we had to go straight up the Cheshire Locks. We made Plant's Lock at Kidsgrove for the night.

When we arrived at Harecastle Tunnel, Dad legged the boat through from the cabin roof. His light was the usual home-made "duck" mentioned before. We had to put the fire out in the cabin before entering. I took the horse over, and did not have to wait long for the boat, as there was no traffic in the way. The last time I had come over this tunnel, there had been heavy traffic in front of us, and we could not pass them in the tunnel. It was midnight when I reached the other end, and I went to sleep on the horse's back under his rug. I was there when the Skipper and the boat emerged.

We arrived at Stoke-on-Trent at midday on Friday, having had a clear run from Manchester. The Pottery Fly, who had passed us at Kidsgrove during the night, had already delivered his cargo, and moved away so that we could berth our boat opposite the Police Station. We delivered our cargo, and made ourselves comfortable for the night. The Pottery Fly *Vesper*, Skipper James Morris, had completed its load of earthenware for Ellesmere Port. He stopped a couple of hours for a drink with father, and I went to the Hippodrome with one of the mates with whom I was friendly. We

returned to the boat at about eleven. The Fly boat started off for Ellesmere Port during the night, but the slow traffic was still. It was a four-handed fly boat, and used to pass down Cheshire Locks, and arrive at Ellesmere Port at about four o'clock next day. They would then off-load, and be ready for the following morning, having had a night in bed.

We had all our cargo signed for on Saturday morning, and had orders to proceed to Brownhills Colliery, Tunstall to collect a load of coal for Lyneal, near Ellesmere, Salop. We arrived at Tunstall Wharf, stabled the horse at the Company's Dept, and tied up until Monday morning. The Skipper went to Longport Station, and then home, via Crewe, leaving me in charge of the boat and horse. I had plenty of company, as there were lots of Shropshire Union boats having their weekend here, mostly loaded with flints and china clay. On the Sunday I had a few boys of my own age in the cabin playing

Harry Rathbone's horse-drawn boat Percy at the northern portals of the two Harecastle Tunnels. Telford's 'new' tunnel on the left, with Brindley's earlier tunnel on the extreme right. This seems to be a posed photo, with at least five children on the boat

different games such as Ludo and Snakes and Ladders. I also had a pair of boxing gloves. I was trying to teach the alphabet to those who could not read, and also how to tell the time. I was lucky to have been to school, and I passed my knowledge on whenever I could.

Monday morning came, and after I had fed the mare, Rose, I untied the boat and bow-hauled to the colliery which was not far away. I began loading the coal at nine o'clock, and was completed for midday. The Skipper arrived with the necessary food etc. and we were on our way again. We entered Harecastle Downhill Tunnel, and Rose took it quietly, although I could hear her feet passing over the planks, and

the water splashing over the low towing path. We left the tunnel, entered Cheshire Locks, and made Rhodeheath for the night. They called this place "Mortar Board". From there we made to Middlewich, and back on the Shroppie again to Barbridge.

This was my last trip with my father, as my younger brother Alfred had left school, and was to take my place. Father could not afford to keep us both, as there were still five more family at home going to school. However, he allowed us our choice, if we did not want to go on the canal.

Middleport Pottery, beside the Trent & Mersey Canal in Stoke-on-Trent

103

13

SECOND MATE ON THE LLANGOLLEN FLY, 1912

The Llangollen Fly had passed through Barbridge that evening, and was short of a mate. Next morning, after putting things in order for my brother, I collected some clothes and a few shillings from my father. I was given a privilege ticket from the office, and went to Nantwich Station, where I boarded the train to Ellesmere. When I reached the wharf, the boat had already left, so I walked along the towpath to Chirk, a distance of ten miles. Here I joined the Llangollen Fly, the boat *Sirdar*, and the Skipper, John Ellis. They were delivering part of a cargo of goods.

Pontcysyllte Aqueduct, arguably the most important canal structure in Britain, was completed in 1805 by William Jessop and Thomas Telford. Over 1000 feet long, it strides over the River Dee at 125 feet above water level

When they started off, I was told to go into the cabin and have a meal while they passed over the aqueduct, and through the tunnel. At the end of the tunnel, I commenced my work. I was driver. The horse was a Welsh cob, a round fat chestnut, named Mickey. We were now going through the deep cutting, and it was getting dark. It was moonlight at about seven o'clock, and I could see a few pheasants roosting in the trees. We came up to Black Park Stone Wharf. There were a couple of stone boats tied up, and a chute across the towing path. I had to unhook the horse, throw the line over the chute, take the horse around, peg him on again, and then lift the rope over the boats. The main Paddington line came close to the canal here, and Mickey

did not like the trains. However, I managed him. A mile ahead was the short Whitehouses Tunnel. Mickey required no light. I put his head over the rails to stop his collar rubbing the arch, and he hauled the boat steadily.

We came up to the Irish Bridge, the Vron Limekilns, and drawbridge, and entered Pontcysyllte Aqueduct. I held Mickey at his head as we met a few pedestrians, who had to keep in to the rails. They crossed at their own risk. At the end were the two dry docks and the repair yard on the towing path side, and the Agent's Office on the offside. The porter, Harry Wood, was waiting at the warehouse to collect our goods, which consisted of a few boxes of lump sugar, and some bags of bacon. This did not take long. We pulled the boat back to the entrance for Llangollen, and stayed there for the night.

We were off again at six next morning, just as it was coming daylight. I was steerer for this half-length to Llangollen which was about four miles. Mickey went by himself, and the two of us had a cup of tea and a "snap" of cake. We arrived at Llangollen at about eight o'clock, travelling fairly well against the current, as we only carried a few ton. The three of us were engaged in delivery, and in turning the boat around. On the way back, I was sleeper to Ponty, and so I had to cook the breakfast. The steerer took his first cup and his bacon outside, while the driver had his inside, and then they changed over to finish the meal. Mickey went along quite easily with the current in his favour, and the towing rope slack. The steerer washed

Jack Roberts and horse at Sun Trevor, Ellesmere Canal

up the crocks and tidied the cabin, while the sleeper rolled the night bed up and put the linen in the cupboard. Then he put the day-bed on the cross-bed, and had a nap to Ponty.

The Skipper told me that my wages would be 8/- per week, and my food. This was a three-handed fly boat, and did a trip and a half a week from Ellesmere Port to Llangollen. The two horses were owned by the Skipper, and were changed at Harry Pearce's lengthsman's cottage at Blackhoe, near Whitchurch. The distance was 72 miles each way, making a total of 216 miles each week. The Skipper was paid 6½d per mile each way, loaded or light. The first mate was paid 9/- per week – if you could lift 14 stone into the boat at one time, you got 1/- extra. There was plenty of food on this boat. Funnily enough we were all named John. The Skipper was John

Ellis, the first mate, his son, John Ellis, and the kid or second mate, myself, John Roberts.

When we arrived at Ponty Office, we were ordered to Graesser's Oil Works to collect a cargo of oil in drums for Calveley Canal Sidings. These were loaded with a small hand crane, worked by the boatmen. The drums were hung on by a chap from the works, stowed in the boat by the boatmen, checked by Harry Wood, the Company's porter, and invoiced at the office.

We were on our way again at two o'clock on Friday afternoon, and had a night out. I was driver again to Chirk attending to the horse through the tunnels, and over aqueducts; the Skipper was sleeper, and John steerer. We changed over about every four miles at what we called "Change Bridge". We worked down New Martin two locks, which were twenty one miles from the next flight. We passed Ellesmere at eight o'clock, and changed horses at Blackhoe at one o'clock on Saturday morning. We made Calveley at nine o'clock on Saturday morning, and transhipped to the railway.

After delivery, we took the boat back to Barbridge until after dinner on Sunday. When we started off again we had a butty, the Newtown Fly. This was the boat *Fairey*, Skipper John Owen. The Skippers were neighbours at Barbridge. At Bunbury Locks, we did not separate, but put the two boats in the lock together. The Newtown Fly left his horse at Bunbury, and took a Company's horse to Ellesmere Port and back. The Llangollen Fly did not do this. The Newtown Fly was four-handed, and his trip was 91 miles each way. One boat sent a lock-filler ahead at the first flight of locks, and the other sent one at the next flight. Working together, we passed through Chester and Northgate Locks, and made Ellesmere Port at about ten o'clock, for a good night in. The Brumagem Fly was close behind us, but he had to off-load and load again during Sunday night, and went on his way at two o'clock on Monday morning.

At six o'clock next day, both of us berthed our boats. We were usually loaded by eight o'clock and left together. The Pottery Flys, and other long distance fly boats, mostly left together. The Newtown and Llangollen Flys kept together as far as Bettisfield, which was the Llangollen Fly's first calling place. The Newtown Fly's first stop was at Maesbury, near Oswestry. We mostly met our opposite numbers during the night, every night. There were four fly boats to each place, one leaving each day from Ellesmere Port.

We left Ellesmere Port at about eight o'clock on Monday morning, delivering our cargoes at various places, to arrive at Llangollen by midnight on Tuesday. The Newtown Fly arrived at Newtown by eight o'clock on Wednesday morning. We left Llangollen on Wednesday, having collected our cargo from Ponty, delivered our cargo to either Ellesmere Port or Calveley, and berthed again for Friday morning. The same applied to the Newtown Fly, though he usually returned light. We used to meet each other at about Whitchurch, where we met the uphill fly boats during the night. Our horse to Ellesmere Port was a hunter type, called Rupert, who got along well. If we could reach Ellesmere Port by ten o'clock at night, we had a chance of delivering our cargo by midnight, and getting six hours sleep. If we met bad weather or other obstructions, we sometimes had to miss our sleep. The Newtown Fly rarely had a downhill cargo, which allowed him more leisure.

The fly boats expected a rough time on the Welsh Canal during the winter when snow was a burden. I have had the experience of going ahead of the boat with a pan-shovel, to clear the snow at the bridges for the horse to pass under.

This was when drifting occurred, and I had to miss my sleep. I also had to clear lift-up bridges, and locks where there was no night-keeper. We used to get along somehow, but freezing weather beat us often, and we had to give up in many desolate spots until the ice-boat arrived. We would have to cover the horse with a rug and sacks, and scald a feed of corn for him, or make him a drink of warm oatmeal. If we did not get released early, we had to make for the nearest shop, usually for bread. We also had to find a shelter for the horse, generally at a farm.

Working on the Shroppie in snow, 1967

The farmers were very obliging in those days, as we used to deliver their cattle food.

When I had been on the boat for a fortnight, I received my first pay of 16/-. This was good pay, as I was only sixteen. A man's wages on the length was only 17/6 to support a family, and he worked a sixty hour week. This applied to all labourers in those days. One trip of 144 miles, and 70 locks took 72 hours. Each man averaged 24 working hours, and six hours emergency brought this up to 30 hours. At a trip and a half a week, each man did 45 hours per week. If you were one man short, which was rare, you would have to work more hours, and the third man's money was shared between the two working.

Doing two men's work was more than enough! Once I remember the Skipper engaged a chap at Chester named Charlie Lloyd. After his meal, he was put to be driver from Calveley to the other side of Barbridge. I stepped onto the bank to go ahead and get the lock ready at Hurleston, and when I reached the horse I saw Charlie's whip tied onto its harness. Charlie had disappeared. I told the Skipper, and went on to the lock, leaving the horse to go on his own, as most of them would. When we entered the Welsh Canal, we had to continue on our own. Leaving the horse to go on his own, we took it in turns to have a nap between locks. On this particular occasion, I was steering between Marbury and Quoisley, and dropped asleep, steering. The boat went into the bank, and I awoke with a start and pulled myself together. Fortunately the Skipper never heard anything! We reported the matter of his disappearance but, I have never seen or heard of Charlie Lloyd since.

We were a little weary, but we carried on. We were able to have the next night in bed at Pontcysyllte, as it was the weekend, and once we had delivered our goods on the Saturday, we had to be ready for our return journey on Monday morning. On Saturday night, the Skipper and I went to the "Wharf Tavern" for a couple of hours. This pub was built in the seventeenth century. It was only small, but very warm and cosy, with old oak beams, and an old-fashioned fire-grate. On the mantelpiece was a "Pinter", which you could use to warm your pint on the fire. There were quite a few boatmen and their wives in, mostly Welsh. Both they and the local people could sing well. One young woman sang "A Lonely Flower", a lovely sentimental song. I have never heard it before or since.

The old "Wharf Tavern" is no longer a pub, but

it is still occupied. It was near a railway siding, and the canal basin which was used for loading coal from Ruabon, and bricks from the great brickyard of J C Edwards of Acrefair. All the cottages on the wharf were owned by the Shroppie, and built of grey stone. On Sunday about twenty donkeys and a mule grazed on the wharf, which was about a hundred yards long, and grassed. Mickey had to stay indoors, as it was rather too cold for a horse. We could not have a pint on Sunday here, as it was in Wales. Near the aqueduct, down a steep bank and close to the River Dee, was the boat people's shop run by Mrs Jeffreys. It sold general food supplies, boat lines, whips, muzzles, harness and clothes especially for the boat folk. She did an excellent trade. I went to that shop many times in those days, and visited it a few weeks ago. I found the shop and its name, but there are no occupants now.

One night when I was with John Ellis on the *Sirdar*, we were told not to go over the aqueduct because of the bad weather. We went into the pub at eleven o'clock, and John had one or two, though he did not usually drink much. We waited until four or five o'clock, and then he said:-
"Never mind the boss. I've not been beaten boating yet, and I'm not going to be beat now". He got the horse, and he took him over, and I followed on behind. The wind was terrific, it blew me in the rails, and it blew the sheets off the boat. We were loaded with pipes, and it shifted the top ones about. I can tell you, I was glad when I got over that! However, when we got to Chirk cutting, there was a big fir tree right across the cut. John had to stop then. I said:-
"You've been beat at boating now, Mr Ellis, you can't move that".

He certainly could not – he had to wait for them to come from Ellesmere. So we lost a day there, but we soon made it up again.

On Sunday night, the Saturday Fly from

Ellesmere Port appeared to deliver his goods, and went on to Llangollen for Monday morning. This was the boat *Aden*, Skipper Jacky Morris, mate Harry Morris, and kid, Bill Chissup. Jacky was a short little chap, and always wore clogs. He had an Irish Terrier dog called Jack. The two were always together, even in the pubs and travelling at night. Jacky's nickname was "Forty Year Ago", as all his stories started in this manner. His favourite hobby was playing the tin whistle, and I went to his boat that night to hear him.

On Monday morning, we were ordered to load glazed pipe for Liverpool. We berthed to collect our cargo, and were on our way by ten o'clock. We were lucky to get an early start, and made good use of it as there were only two of us. We had a few words with the lengthsmen, as we were early. The first was Bill Davies, and the second, Jim Edwards at Chirk. We entered the first lock at New Martin. Here there was a Toll Office where the collectors were Mr and Mrs W Clay, both getting on in years. At the bottom lock lived Tom Windsor, who loved a pint of beer, and walked to the pub "The Boot" at Whittington every day after work. We changed

horses at Blackhoe, and pegged Rupert to the line. He was fresh and frisky. We had a word with Harry Pearce, the lengthsman, who cared for the horse. He was usually in bed when we changed horses during the night. It was only eight o'clock now, but it was getting dark. When we reached Grindley Brook, the Skipper asked me if I would like to tie up for a few hours. I said I would prefer to go straight through to Ellesmere Port, and finish early on Tuesday morning. This we did, and when we arrived John, his son, joined us again.

The Skipper looked forward to Chester Cup Day, and one Wednesday morning in May 1912 he approached the dock foreman, William Cash, and asked if he could get away as early as possible. We were soon off, together with the Newtown Fly, and arrived in Chester, where we stopped to see the racing. I forget the name of the winner, but I backed two horses, one "Girl of the West" and the other "Penny Bridle", and both won at ten to one. That was my first bet, and I returned to the boat very pleased with myself. We continued on our way together up the big locks. Our mate, John, and George Owen, hand on the Newtown Fly, decided to change over with the permission of the Skippers. John preferred a four-handed fly, so George became my mate.

About this time, there was a breach on the canal bank near the Vron Lime Kilns. The emergency planks were placed at Cross Street, and brought us to a halt. Our cargo had to be delivered by horse dray, and was transhipped at the Irish Bridge Wharf and railway siding. This old siding no longer exists.

Toll House family at New Martin (now known as New Marton) Lock. The sign says "William Clay, Toll Collector"

Aston at the top of Northgate Locks, Chester, July 1963

4 wharf, and who should appear but Jacky Morris, the other Llangollen Fly. He had been at Ellesmere Port when the canal breached, and had loaded with goods for Brumagem, like us. I notice the dog, Jack lying on top of the stern under the tiller, which was his usual place. He was very still. I asked Jacky what was wrong with the dog. He hesitated in answering, and then I saw tears. He said the dog did not like the Black Country, and it had broken his heart to leave the Welsh Canal. During the night he passed away.

Jacky found a box and placed old Jack inside with clean straw, and dusted with disinfectant. He said he would dig a grave for him when we got back on the Shroppie, on our own route.

We made the best of our way back, picking up a load wherever we could on route, while there was sufficient water to navigate. The feed of water from Llangollen had already stopped owing to the breach.

When we reached Barbridge, we were ordered to proceed down the Middlewich Branch to Cholmondeston to relieve a boat of his cargo as he was leaking badly. He was loaded with 18 tons of soda from Winnington, Sandbach, which was then Brunner Mond's, for Crescent Wharf, Birmingham. There was little damage to the cargo, and transhipping was carried out successfully. We called at Barbridge for our Way Bill and food, and next day we were on our way to "the smoke". The Skipper and the horse had never been to Birmingham before, but both George and I had been many times. We made Wheaton Aston the first day, and Birmingham the second afternoon.

The Skipper had never seen such an amount of traffic. We had to meet it every minute, as it came from other branches. I told him that when we reached Tipton, there would be a towing path on each side, and only one way traffic to worry about. Calling at gauging stops was a menace to him! We delivered our cargo at No.

After this had occurred, Bill Taylor, an old boatman who was foreman at Crescent Wharf, called our Skippers to the office. The Shipping Clerk asked them if they would like to butty to Ellesmere Port. Without hesitation, they said they would, and explained the position. He told them he had two urgent loads for Liverpool, and as they were both fly boats, he thought they could be at Ellesmere Port for the midday tide on Friday. It was now Wednesday. They said they could manage this. Our Skipper was told to proceed to Phillips, at Monument Lane, and load his boat, while Jacky had his boat unloaded, and then joined us. We were loaded with six tons of bedstead cases etc. on each boat. It was a very bulky cargo.

We both left at eight o'clock on Wednesday evening, which meant a night out. It was dark as we went down Wolverhampton Locks. We only had one horse to each boat, and we had eighty four miles and sixty nine locks to go. The following evening as we were passing Beeston Castle, Jacky decided to have the funeral. We dug a grave about four foot deep in Foxy Wood, and buried the old Irish Terrier. I could find that spot today – it is just off the towing path. He had been a faithful dog. I remember my father and Jacky went on a randy in Chester once, and both got merry. They came back to the boat for a sleep, and Jacky was lying on the cross-bed and dared my father to pull him off. Father attempted to do so, forgetting that the dog was under the bed-cupboard. It came from under, and ripped the seat out of his pants!

Another dog I remember was one named "Nip". He belonged to a couple, David and Ann, and

Jack Roberts steering hostelboat Aston *in June 1964*

their daughter Liz. The father died leaving the two women to work the boat *Hope*, which was engaged in hauling stone from Crickheath to the Porth y Waen Lime and Stone Company. They had a mule named Jimmy. Nip was a fair sized cross-bred terrier. If they told him there was a policeman about, he would hide out of sight in the cabin or in the deck. I have seen this for myself. He would act without being told. Liz, the daughter, used to ride on the mule's back in

a pair of trousers, and he would kick his legs up but he could not move her.

We arrived at Ellesmere Port on Friday morning at four o'clock, and transhipped our cargo into a ship at the docks. The breach had now been mended, and we returned to our Llangollen route again on Saturday morning. It was June, 1912, and lovely weather. We loaded early, while the Skipper settled for his pay. Our mate, Jacky, had to stay until the Monday Fly. We buttied a Pottery Fly boat, *Sedan*, Skipper Sam Bell, all the way to Barbridge. Here we collected our basket of provisions, and met the Newtown Fly who was behind us. We buttied as far as Bettisfield, where we parted company on the Sunday. Delivering our goods as usual, we made Pontcysyllte on Sunday night, and Llangollen on Monday, and were back in Ellesmere Port for Wednesday night.

Rupert, the horse, had suffered an accident to his fetlock, and we were forced to sell him. We got permission to engage a Company's horse, and went to the big stable to tell the horse-keeper, George Cowup. He fixed us up with a lovely mare, Lola, a five year old, and fifteen hands high. She was frisky and wild, but calmed down after a few miles. We changed horses at Blackhoe, as usual, and took Mickey, our own horse. As there was a vacancy on the Newtown Fly when we started off, I decided to give the Skipper a fortnight's notice, and change my job.

14

FLY BOATING TO NEWTOWN, THE POTTERIES AND BIRMINGHAM

When my notice expired, I joined the Newtown Fly, the *Princess May*. The Skipper was my uncle, Moses Owen, my mother's brother. At times, we buttied my old Skipper, John Ellis. This was a four-handed fly, and my mates were Bill Statham, and Bill Morris from Gobowen. Bill Morris was an Army Special Reservist, and had to report for training for one month a year. The three of us were all young men, and the Skipper was forty, a big chap of fifteen stone, and six foot high. We left Ellesmere Port, with our butty, John Jones, on the Llangollen Fly.

When we parted company with the Llangollen Fly, we turned off down Frankton Locks. We changed horses at Aston, leaving Molly and taking Tinker. Our first calling place was Maesbury with six hogsheads of stout, sugar and bacon. We also collected a few oddments for Welshpool. It was midday, Sunday, and there was little traffic moving, although we did meet the other fly, the boat *Trentham*, Skipper Edward Owen, no relation to our Skipper. Our next delivery was for Walls Bridge, Llanymynech, and then we went on down Carreghofa two locks. Here we changed over, two out and two in, and had a meal. All was quiet. Bill Statham and I were workers, and our next delivery was to Canal House, Four Crosses. The parrot was still here,

over Mrs Lloyd's door, and he started swearing at us for working on Sunday. While Mrs Lloyd was checking our goods, I went quietly and had a few words with Polly – I will not repeat what she said!

Our next delivery was at the Orchard, with two sacks of sugar, two boxes of oranges, two bags of bacon and a few boxes of salmon and fruit. Mr Davies gave us a bottle of beer each. We went down Burgeddin two locks, and up Pool Quay four, having a chat with Mr G Lloyd at Crowther Hall Lock, and Mr Lloyd at Top Lock.

Carreghofa - Lock and Toll Office

We met quite a lot of people having an evening walk, or going to the lovely small church by the canal. Some gave Tinker a pat. All of them knew the horses and the name of the boat. This was a lovely stretch, passing through hills and forestry. We called at Buttington to deliver a few sacks of cattle cake, and a large case of cattle

111

Berriew Aqueduct

medicine. I had to go to the farmer who attended the small warehouse, to get the note signed. Our next and last Sunday delivery was for Welshpool. We stabled Tinker while we off-loaded, and Bill called out one of the sleepers to assist. I went to inform the porter, Jim Lloyd, of our arrival. He was the nightman this time. We had to unload about six tons of goods, and load the same amount for further on. We could not get a pint as we were in Wales, but there was one pub, "The Pheasant", where you could get one if you had travelled four miles. None of us were interested, so we pulled into the lock and had a meal. Then we pegged Tinker on, and proceeded on our last fourteen miles. It was midnight, but lovely weather.

Bill Statham and I were sleepers, so we dropped on the bed. Deliveries were made at Belan and Brithdir. When we arrived at Berriew Wharf, I was called out to assist, as there were a few ton to deliver. When we set off again, I returned to bed while further deliveries were made at Garthmyl and Brynderwyn.

The next big delivery was at Aberbechan, but this time Bill was called up. This was the last one. While passing through Freestone Lock, we

both got up and got breakfast ready. Then we tidied the cabin and had a wash. When we arrived at Newtown Basin, the Skipper took the horse around to the stable, while the three of us hauled the boat from Factory Bridge, and shafted across the basin. It was eight o'clock on Monday morning and we had left Ellesmere Port on Saturday morning. We had handled forty tons of goods in that period, both loading and off-loading.

After delivering our cargo we decided to stay for the day. Opposite our wharf was the Cambrian Flannel Factory, where quite a number of girls were employed. At midday break they came to the boat for a chat. The three of us arranged a meeting place for the evening. They were all lovely Welsh girls, and my girl was Lizzie Price. We met on Halfpenny Bridge, and took a stroll round the town and countryside. The Montgomeryshire people were very sociable indeed, and one did not hear them speaking Welsh very much between themselves.

Garthmyl malting house

Tuesday morning at six o'clock, we were on our way again. I was driver and Bill, steerer. We changed over at Finney Straight. We collected traffic where the STOP boards were out, though we had to call at Berriew as it was a Company Depot. We rang the bell and waited a few moments, but nobody came, so we went on our way. Ted Windsor lived at the lock, and we had to pass his cottage. We passed Belan School, and the children ran to wish us good-morning. Gertrude came over to the bridge, and I stopped for a few moments and had a short chat. She wanted to know how long I would be working on the Fly. I said I did not know, but asked her to meet me at Welshpool the next Friday night. She said she would. Then I had to run after the boat. Bill asked;

"Who's her?"

I said "That's Gertie".

"A nice kid, ain't she?"

"Oh yes", I said.

Bill was very quiet and shy. He said:

"This is your first trip with this boat. You're soon getting to know the skirt. You had one last night at Newtown and was busy talking to Mr Price's two daughters this morning while the lock was emptying at Brynderwyn. Put me a word in next time with that young 'un, will you Jack?"

I said "Yes, I will Bill".

When we passed through White House Bridge, I called the sleepers up, and we arrived at Welshpool, where we called at the wharf. Frank Windsor said there was nothing to put on, so we continued on our way. After a meal, and tidying the cabin, we both dropped on the day-bed. Bill could not read or write, so he asked me if I would write a letter for him, to the girl at Brynderwyn, who had taken his fancy. He said:

"There's two ov'um, one each."

I said "Don't bother, Bill, we shall be up again early on Saturday morning". We are both sleepers up that top end, so we can have a talk, and we might also have some goods to deliver there". We both decided to sleep.

We changed over at the usual change places, and met the other fly boat *Fancy*, Skipper John Owen, another uncle, and one of the mates, my brother George. We exchanged a few words when we met, and our Skipper jokingly told George that I had been after his girl at Newtown on Monday night. He shouted:

"Have you?"

I said "I don't know her yet."

He warned me "Be careful, Johnny".

They were the Monday boat from Ellesmere Port. After a night out, we arrived at Chester, and stopped to collect our basket of food. The Skipper lived at Chester, near Hoole Lane Lock. We passed down Northgate Locks, and Nancy went by herself to Ellesmere Port.

On Thursday morning, after a good night's rest, we set off again, and arrived back at Welshpool

Brynderwyn Warehouse, seen from the road, August 1965

early on Friday evening. Gertie met me there, and we put Tinker in the stable. She gave him a little pat, and then we took a short walk through the town. I had to leave her, but she had a bicycle, and rode off up Berriew Road. I told her we would be passing the school about midnight, so she said "Crack your whip – I shall hear you!"

Early next morning, we arrived at Brynderwyn, where there were a few goods to deliver. We were sleepers, and I said to Bill, - "come on, get out, we're there".

The girls were both out, smiling at the gate, while their father, the postman, received the goods. I introduced Bill, and told them my name was Jack, and tried to arrange to meet them in the afternoon in Newtown. They said they both worked in Newtown, and their names were Nelly and Megan. They knew we had both been out with the girls last Monday, as they both worked at the factory, and knew the others. I told them I was not serious at Newtown, and would prefer Megan.

We had met my brother earlier on, and he told me his girl's name was Mabel. When we arrived in Newtown, a lovely young girl came across to the wharf, looked at me and said:
"I'm not offended at your letter, Georgie."
I told her I was not George, but his brother Jack. She said "Oh, sorry, I can't tell the difference – you are like him".
I must admit we were like twins, although he was two years older than me. She thought George had joined this boat and made a very quick return, as she had seen him only two days before.

When we got back to Ellesmere Port, we heard bad news. Bill, who had taken over my job on the Llangollen Fly, had got himself entangled in the towing line, and dragged along the towpath a few hundred yards. He had fallen in and out of the canal and hit a telegraph pole. He had been taken to Chester Hospital in a critical condition, and was detained a few weeks. This had happened at Wharton Lock. The mare, Lola, was nervous and had been frightened. Bill could have been killed, but they met another boatman who managed to stop the horse and liberate Bill. He had experienced great difficulty, as there were two horses, but he managed to tie Lola to the fence.

I worked on the Newtown Fly for another three months, and enjoyed it very much, although there were obstacles and bad weather, and sometimes we had to work two-handed. Then the General Manager agreed that I should join a Pottery Fly, *Endeavour*. The Skipper was Arthur Jones, a single man, who had taken over after the death of his father, and supported his mother and the rest of the family who were still attending school. He lived at Ellesmere Port. This was a four-handed fly boat. John France, an elderly man, and Jim Shackleton worked together, and I was the kid again. It was August 1912, and I commenced on Monday morning.

We were a Stoke-on-Trent boat, and collected our goods at the top Long Warehouse. The Skipper's mother handed me the basket of goods, which I placed in the stern cupboard. We set off at eight o'clock, accompanied by Alfred Wally, his sons and his boat *Equerry*, a fly boat bound for Tunstall and Burslem. We pegged the horse to. It was a mare, named Alice, who went a good rate by herself and would also meet traffic. When we came to Northgate Locks, I was called out to go ahead and prepare them. They were big locks, and there was a lock-keeper at each lock. The Skipper and I were sleepers to the top lock at Christleton, and Jack and Jim were workers. When we came to the top lock, I was steerer. After a good meal, the two mates lay down for a sleep. It was an eight mile stretch, and Alice was baccering well, while the Skipper and I had a chat. The horse on the boat behind us was keeping alongside our cabin.

At Brookhole Bridge, I changed over to driver. When we entered Wharton Lock, I stepped off the boat to attend to the horse and draw the paddles. Our butty had sent a lock-wheeler ahead to get the locks ready, so we did not have to call our sleepers up. These were big locks, and took two boats. If you were on your own, you would have to lock-wheel every time. We passed up the last five locks to Bunbury, where we had to single out as there were two boats in the lock already, and two cannot meet two, although one can meet two [see page 65]. These were double locks, called a staircase. The sleepers came out when we got on our way again, and had another meal. I had to change sides and put the horse past Calveley sidings. Then I stepped on the boat again, and ate a thick sandwich, and drank a basin of tea. We had no cups on a fly boat, only basins with flowers on, mostly bought by your girl friend, if you had one. At Bridge 103 we changed over, as all fly boats did. Arthur, the Skipper, and I were sleepers to Wardle Lock, Middlewich. I stepped off the boat and ran ahead to collect my laundry from home. It was in a small hand-made bag. I explained to my mother where I was working, and she gave me advice as always, "be careful, and don't fall in the cut".

At Barbridge Junction, we entered the Middlewich Branch, and while we were both resting, the two workers changed horses at Minshull Vernon stables. When I changed over at Middlewich we had a black horse called Bill. We entered the North Stafford Cut at King's Lock. There were three more fly boats in front of us so we had to wait our turn. While we were waiting, the Skipper discussed our position, and said we wanted to pass them before Wheelock. We went up King's Lock, and Joe Lowe's Lock, Kinnerton Arms. We managed to overtake the first boat up this mile pound. It was an Anderton Company fly boat, known as a "knob stick" which was a bigger boat with a heavier load. Then we passed up the three locks at Booth Lane, and overtook the Salt Union fly. He was about our weight, but his boat was not such a good swimmer, and his horse was not equal to ours.

We now had to overtake the Fellows Morton, called a Josher Fly. This was a new motor boat, and the first mechanised fly boat to run from Preston Brook to Albion Wharf, Wolverhampton. They went daily. However, we failed to overtake it, along the four mile pound, known as Wheelock Pound.

Minshull Vernon fly-boat stables on the Middlewich Arm in 1999, shortly before conversion to a dwelling

About midnight we entered Cheshire Locks, the flight of twenty one locks, in twos side by side or "abreast" as the boatmen used to say. At the second lock we both entered, one on each side

We had each arranged to have a lock-wheeler ahead to insure that the lock should not be against us. I heard the two Skippers having a few words, and it ended up with a fight in the space between the two locks. They were both medium sized men, and they fought a good clean fight, with shirts off and windlasses on the ground. There was not much to choose between

Minshull Vernon stables and house in the 1960s, with an unidentified fully laden boat. There was no road access to the house, with everything having to come by boat.

them, but Jack gave our Skipper best. We were now first and drew a paddle at each lock, in favour of Jack coming behind. I must admit we were in the wrong, as it is in the rules and regulations that you must not pass another boat in locks. In this case, if the lock-keeper, Sam Lowe, had been present, our Skipper would have had to appear at Sandbach Court. This often happened in those days. Our other fly boat was not involved, as he had to deliver goods at Wheelock, Rhodeheath, Red Bull, Tunstall and Burslem.

We passed up the rest of the locks, arrived at Plant's Lock and entered Harecastle old tunnel. I was the last steerer, and I made a bed of a sack of provender, and legged the boat through, while the Skipper took the horse over the top. Jim and old Jack had a nap. There was no steerer, as the tiller was taken from the helm. I had a "duck" for my light. We had a clear run. While passing through, I saw a couple of almost white rats appear on the gangway, so I picked up the mop to hit them, and they dropped in the canal. These rats very often appeared while boats were passing through. They jumped off the turn-rail on the old tunnel that connected the two main tunnels. In the old days, coal boats were loaded straight from the pits, in tunnels connected to the main tunnel. The rats were apparently after food, but the boatmen regarded them as a bad omen. There were no ventilation holes in the old tunnel, so no fire was allowed. Heavier boats than ours needed two leggers.

In my grandfather's day there was only one tunnel. There are two now, but only the new one is in service. There had been a murder in the old tunnel many years before. A Duke's Fly boat was passing through Wolverhampton, when a woman asked for a ride to Manchester. The Skipper agreed to take her. I understand she was attractive, and he fell in love with her. The two hands and the Skipper quarrelled while the fourth hand was taking the horse over the top. The murder took place in the tunnel, and the two mates were later found out and, according to history, executed. A while after there was a song composed. I have heard several boatmen sing it, but can only remember a few lines:-

"Roshannah was her name
From Wolverhampton she came,
The Captain fell in love with her;
I'm sure it is not lie –
It was in Harecastle Tunnel
That she was doomed to die".

I can just about remember a boatman named Wood being drowned in this tunnel off a Pottery Fly. I knew his son well. He skippered a Pottery Fly named *Phoebe* and was one of our neighbours at Barbridge in about 1911. He passed away in 1924, and was engaged on the last Middlewich Fly from Ellesmere Port.

Before leaving the tunnel, I called Jim and John up to arrange a meal and put the fire ready to light up. At the end, we changed workers again, and the Skipper and I were sleepers to Stoke. However, I was called out at Etruria Wharf to assist in delivering ten tons of goods. Then I assisted in taking the boat back, and entering Stoke Top Lock. I was lock-wheeler down these five busy locks. We arrived at the Stoke entrance to the Newcastle-under-Lyme Canal, where our wharf was situated opposite the Police Station. Here we discharged the remainder of our cargo. We were off-loaded at dinnertime on Tuesday. Jock, the horse, had a rest in the stables. We had changed horses at Tunstall, leaving Bill, and would change over that night on our way back. After dinner we commenced loading again. The goods arrived in drays from various parts of the city, and included barrels and crates of earthenware for Liverpool. We had collected it all by six o'clock. We were full up, but had only about six tons of bulky traffic.

After our evening meal, we decided to have a few hours recreation. Some went for a pint at the "Glebe" pub, and I decided to see a variety show at the Hippodrome. We returned about

The Newcastle-under-Lyme Canal leading off the Trent & Mersey Canal in Stoke, March 1974

eleven o'clock, and started off again for Ellesmere Port. All the slow traffic was tied up for the night. I was the driver, and pegged Jock to the rope. Old Jack had had a few pints, and was asleep, while Jim was the lock-wheeler, and the Skipper steerer. We left Jock at Tunstall, and pegged Bill on. This horse knew the ropes, and worked well.

When we arrived at Harecastle downhill tunnel, the driver fixed the bulkhead lamp on the deck, and took the rope up short from the cabin end. He rode on the deck to be near the horse, and the light showed it the towing path. Halfway through the tunnel the arch was very low, and you could hear the top crates rubbing the side. The towing path was also low and covered with water, and planks were placed over it to allow the horse to travel. It was a temporary affair, but quite safe. I could hear Bill proddling through the water and walking on the thick planks. At the end, the rope was put to normal again, and we changed over to the opposite side.

All four men were now engaged down Cheshire Locks. We averaged two minutes to pass down a lock, if all the paddle gear was in order. About halfway down, at Rhodeheath, we started to meet the uphill fly boats. There were Shroppie Flys, and also a Gandy Fly from Preston Brook to Derby. Our mate, Whalley, was well ahead and had been tied up at Middlewich and home for a few hours. We joined together again, and arrived at Ellesmere Port at four o'clock on Wednesday afternoon. We went down into the bottom dock and delivered some of our cargo at the Crate Warehouse, and transhipped the rest into a flat. We then went up to the top berth again, and berthed for six o'clock Thursday morning, when we should start again. First however, we had a good rest.

Our next trip, we had to deliver at places from Wheelock to Burslem, Rhodeheath and Red Bull, and be back at Ellesmere Port on Saturday. Then we had Sunday to rest. Then we did not change horses at Tunstall, only at Minshull Vernon. There were four fly boats a day from

Wheelock Stables, Trent & Mersey Canal, 2002

Ellesmere Port to the Potteries. This was our normal routine. However, obstacles did occur, like foggy weather at Liverpool, and Eastham Lock. Sometimes we were only three-handed, and have been known to go two-handed. This made the trip all work, and you slept when you could. The docks were open for both day and night shifts. The distance from Ellesmere Port to Stoke-on-Trent was 54 miles each way,

totalling 108 miles per trip, 100 locks. That was 216 miles and 200 locks per week.

I stayed on the Pottery Fly boat for three months, and then I decided to have a go with the Brumagem Fly, if there was a vacancy the first time we met at Ellesmere Port. I asked the Skipper, Bill Jarvis, and he said there would be one the next Saturday. Ernest Pool was leaving, and starting as Captain on the timber length. This was usual, in all cases – you started off with an old boat, but serviceable.

I made my way to Birmingham for Saturday. It was November, and winter was on the way. We left at four o'clock in the afternoon with a very expensive cargo. There were twelve tons of cases of a variety of goods for abroad. My first order was to harness up the horse at the well-kept stable, and meet the boat at Tindal or Farmers Bridge. The other three pulled the boat to that point, while I took the horse around the Crescent.

I was driver to Tipton, and I pegged the horse, Joe, onto the line and we were away at four miles an hour. Joe knew the way, but I had to walk because of the side-bridges, and boats moored along the side. I had to lift the rope over to avoid it fouling. We passed Winson Green, near HM Prison, and came to West Bromwich gauging and weighing stop. I could now ride for a mile as all was quiet, and there was a towing path on each side. At Smethwick, I stepped off again, and stopped the boat to be gauged and have our toll ticket examined. Here a Collie dog took your ticket to the toll clerk, and brought it back again. There was not much delay. I had to walk the remainder of my half-length to Tipton. There were a number of brick boats moored along here, near to Barnett's Blue Brickworks, and also the Junction to Stourbridge.

We passed alongside the main railway line, and Dudley Port Station, two docks, one on each side of the canal, the entrance to other parts, and Tipton Railway Station. This was Dudley Port Valley.

We arrived at Tipton Locks, known as the Factory Three, and passed up to the top lock. I changed jobs with the Skipper who had been steerer. I steered to the top of Wolverhampton twenty one. The two other hands were resting on the daybeds. From Tipton there was only one towing path, which changed over to pass through Cosely Tunnel, and changed back at the other end. There were lights fixed in the roof of this tunnel. We passed through the Deepfields, and Alfred Hickman's Springvale Furnaces. The canal water was hot and steaming, and in the foggy weather, I had to guess to steer. I could see the sides a little, and relied on the shape of the boat. The driver could hardly find the way, and his job was to keep the towing-rope up over moored boats and side-bridges. If he wanted to attract the Steerer's attention, he would crack his whip, and lighted matches were used for signals. As we passed the steel works, the noise was terrific, as there were two works together here. I think we travelled by instinct. When we were about to meet another boat the driver would shout "Keep out, there's one coming". Sometimes you would meet with a bump, and foul language!

When we arrived at Wolverhampton, we stopped for a few minutes in the top lock. The Skipper went to Broad Street Offices, and was timed on his Way Bill by the night Shipping Clerk. We did not change horses here except in an emergency. We started off again at eight o'clock, and it was getting dark. It was proper November weather, and you can guess the difficulty travelling. We now changed over, and

the Skipper and I were sleepers, but I had to lock-wheel down these twenty one locks, whether they were in our favour or not. Usually we passed down in about an hour. At the bottom lock, Aldersley Junction, we left the B.C.N. and entered the S.W.C. [Staffordshire & Worcestershire Canal] for half a mile.

When we entered the Shroppie at Autherley Junction, we changed horses. Joe went in the stable, and Sweep was ready harnessed to peg to the boat. There were two nightmen here, the S.W.C. Toll Clerk, E Parr, and the S.U.C. horsekeeper and timekeeper, Harry. We had a meal, and left Autherley. It was about ten o'clock and quite foggy still. The Skipper and I took our rest to Wheaton Aston. I heard the two workers change over at No. 6 Bridge, and our meeting a few boats. In two hours we were at Wheaton Aston Lock, and I heard the clock at the church in distant Lapley, strike midnight.

We changed over again, and the Skipper was driver and I was steerer. We swapped jobs at Gnosall. We had to walk with the horse through this deep cutting and tunnel, and we could only just find our way as it was very dark and foggy, but we managed without a light. We passed through Norbury Junction, Grubstreet Cutting, Shebdon and Knighton. Then we called up Joe and Ted, and we all had a meal and gave the horse a feed in his nose-tin, which he ate while travelling.

All was in order, so the two of us took off our boots and coats and lay down for a rest. Our next change was at No. 15 Lock, Audlem, but one of us was called out at Tyrley to lock-wheel. We changed horses again here. We passed Market Drayton and Adderley Locks, but no-one was called out if the locks were ready. Then we came up to Audlem Locks, and the Skipper was called out whether they were ready or not. It was just breaking day here, and I had managed to sleep the whole length. The church clock struck nine. It was Sunday morning, and we had travelled in the dark from Birmingham. After passing down the fifteen locks, we changed over again, had a meal and tidied the cabin. Joe and Ted took a rest. At Hack Green Locks, we had the time entered on the Way Bill. The horsekeeper, Tom Masefield, was a day-man, and very conscientious. He would sometimes report himself for minor misdemeanours, and signed dead on the minute. However, he was very good at his job, and examined the horse thoroughly. After passing down the two locks, we started to meet the uphill traffic from Ellesmere Port. There was quite a fleet. I had to meet the other horses, and lift the rope over as we kept going.

We passed Nantwich, and came to Barbridge, where one of my young sisters came to the boat and handed me my laundry for the week. At Bridge 102, we changed over again, and Joe and Ted came out. The Skipper took a rest, but I was preparing to lock-wheel as we neared Bunbury big locks. Here we left Sweep and took Vixen, a strawberry roan mare, a little wicked at times but an excellent worker. We were joined by the Newtown Fly and we took the ten locks together. We had time for a chat with the other hands while travelling.

After passing down the first six locks, we came to the eight mile level. Vixen went on her own, and the other fly went on ahead as it was light, but they waited for us at the next lock, Christleton. At this lock, traffic was stopped from ten in the morning to six in the evening to avoid its passing through Chester during Sunday. However, all was clear and we went in the lock with the Newtown Fly, and buttied down to Northgate Locks.

We arrived at Ellesmere Port at about eleven o'clock, took off our sheets and off-loaded our cargo into a flat. We sometimes loaded up at the same time from another flat on the other side. We were on our way again at three o'clock on Monday morning, and arrived at Birmingham again at ten o'clock on Tuesday morning. The Brumagem Fly was thus engaged regularly, and was usually punctual to these times, though occasionally it varied. I was engaged on this fly for a few months.

The Jolly Tar pub and stables at Barbridge, October 1960
(since demolished and replaced by another pub of the same name)

15

WORKING THE TRENCH FLY AND THE TRENCH INCLINE.

Later on I joined a Trench Fly, the boat *Bee*, and the Skipper John Owen. The other mate was Bill Paxton. The horses, Ginger and Prince, were owned by the Skipper, and were changed at Barbridge. This was a three-handed fly, one of the smallest boats on the canal for commercial trade. It was built especially for the nine Trench Locks, being seventy foot long like the other boats, but having only a six foot beam, and a very low cabin.

We left Ellesmere Port on Monday morning, and were always the last fly out, as we had the bottom cargo from the flat. Often we did not leave until midday. Our first calling places were Nantwich, Audlem and Market Drayton, all during the night. We arrived at Newport on Tuesday afternoon, and then called at Edgmond and Wappenshall.

There we passed up the nine Trench Locks, which had guillotine gates. We turned the boat around and entered helm first, having previously removed all the fittings, including the chimney. It was very dangerous in the dark, if you were not fully loaded, and you must not forget to drop in the cabin as you passed under the guillotine gates. A man once lost his head at No. 8 Lock, by forgetting this. The gates at the bottom had to be wound up and fixed in slides in the lock wall.

We arrived at Trench on Wednesday morning, and delivered the remains of our cargo. Then we loaded up again with sixteen ton of iron or copper wire for Liverpool. Mr Whitehead was the agent at Trench. He had been a railway man previously, and was now in charge of Newport, and all traffic to Shrewsbury. There were three

men engaged here, George Mason, Jack Rogers, and Jim, and they were always busy. We left Trench Top Lock at midday on Wednesday, and arrived at Ellesmere Port on Thursday night at about six o'clock. We off-loaded into a flat or warehouse until about eight or nine o'clock, and then had a pint and a night in bed. I was engaged on this fly for two months.

There were twelve Trench boats, including four fly boats, which ran one each day from either end. Our routine was a trip and a half a week, with a full cargo each way. There were 64 miles and 73 locks each way. This amounted to 192 miles and 219 locks each week. The pay was 6½d per mile each way to the Skipper. He paid the hands 9/- per week, all found, and also bought and fed the two horses. This does not sound much today, but it was a fair job in those days, and amounted to £9 16s per week.

My next job was with the Shrewsbury Fly. This was two-handed, and made only one trip a week, leaving Ellesmere Port every Tuesday. The Skipper, Thomas Sutton, lived at Coole Pilot [Pilate], near Hack Green. The boat was called *Rhoda*. There was only one horse, a blue roan, fifteen hands high and half-legged. The distance was 72 miles and 68 locks each way. The pay was 6½d a mile each way, loaded or light, and my wages were 10/- per week. We had every Sunday at home.

When we left Ellesmere Port, our first calling place was Newport. We turned right at Wappenshall, and went down Eyton two locks, which had guillotine gates, but were much higher and wider than the Trench, and would take any boat. Our calling places with goods were Long Lane, Longden, Rodington, Withington, Berwick, Uffington, Sundorn Wharf and Castlefields, Shrewsbury. Of course, we had to leg through the tunnel at Berwick every week.

After a few weeks on this boat, I thought I

would join the Whitchurch Fly, which did two trips a week from Ellesmere Port to Whitchurch and back. This was another two-handed fly, and the horses were owned by the Company. The Skipper, Harry Green, was paid 1/3 per ton, and could take 20 tons. If it was bulky traffic, the pay was for 18 ton full up. Return cargo was only paid at 1/- per ton, but there was not much, only a few ton of cheese sometimes. There were three Whitchurch Flys, one per day. They loaded at Ellesmere Port one morning and delivered at Whitchurch the next. It was a very busy wharf, and a big warehouse, mostly for agriculture, but also quite a quantity of goods for the local shops, and some cheese for Manchester and for export at Ellesmere Port. Mr Wyn was the agent and the two porters were Harry Talbot and Tom Porter.

I did not stay on the Whitchurch Fly very long, as there was a lot of heavy work, both in navigation and in winding out the cargo by hand-crane, as there were only two of us. The only place at Whitchurch where there was a jigger supplied to off-load your cargo was at Wright's Mill, which was private.

There were also three Cheese Fly Boats which collected once a week. The boat *Peel* collected from Ellesmere and Whitchurch for Liverpool, and the boat *Ruth* collected from Weston, Ellesmere, Whitchurch and Wrenbury for Manchester. The boat *Tit* was called the Fair Boat, as it met the mid-week cheese fairs at Whitchurch, Nantwich and Market Drayton, on alternative weeks. It mostly went to Manchester and to Griffiths of Broken Cross, near Northwich. In later years, I was to experience all these routes.

About this time, the Company decided to make all the Fly boats redundant for economic reasons. Their place was to be taken by weekly boats, which were much bigger boats, and could take more weight. Two hands were engaged and the Company found the horses in every

case. This applied to Newtown, Llangollen, Wolverhampton, Birmingham and Trench. All these routes were arranged and engaged accordingly. Later on the Company had six new boats built for work on these routes. They were built at their dock-yards at Chester and

Fly-boat Cuckmere, *children and pet at Whitchurch Basin, at the end of the Whitchurch Arm*

Pontcysyllte – twenty tonners for the Welsh Canal, and thirty tonners for Trench and Wappenshall. At Wappenshall, two small Trench boats were stationed to haul the material down the Trench Locks, and tranship to the bigger boats which could not get down the locks. The boats built for Wolverhampton and

Birmingham were thirty tonners, built by private firms at Polesworth and Braunston. Later still, quite a few more were built for Market Drayton, and twenty tonners for the Manchester Cheese Boats.

One boat a day left from Ellesmere Port for Llangollen, Newtown and Trench. However, the removal of the four-handed fly boats from Newtown and Llangollen was a mistake indeed. The result was too long a delay in delivering the goods, as it took two days or more owing to the increased weight and decreased man-power. All the small fly boats were dispersed to various parts, some for the Pottery Length, and others for railway boats in the Black Country.

When the fly boats were stopped, most of the hands engaged were given the chance of being Skipper. My brother took over the previous Newtown Fly *Broxton*, together with one of the mates. His route was anywhere on the Shroppie. I was engaged on one of the South Staffordshire weekly boats, *Valentine*, that went from Ellesmere Port to Wolverhampton. We mostly had a cargo of sugar and Guinness Stout, and took 26 tons 15 cwt uphill.

The rate was 1/9 per ton uphill cargo, and 1/- per ton downhill cargo. Our weight varied, but we were paid for 20 ton full up, for bulky traffic, and if it were over, we were paid more. We did a trip a week, and on an average were paid £3 10s per week. Tom Rush, the Skipper, paid me 11/- per week. We mostly had two days off-loading and loading our return cargo, and we never returned light.

We used to leave Ellesmere Port at eleven o'clock and hung onto the tug to Chester. Then we had a horse to Autherley Junction. Our first stop for a rest was at Cocks Bank [Cox Bank, Audlem flight lock 3], where we arrived at five or six in the morning, and stopped for six hours. At dinner-time, we started off again, working through the night, and resting in daylight. Our

next stop would be Wolverhampton or Birmingham. We left our regular horse at Autherley Junction, and took a reserve horse to the end of our journey.

This job was a fair one, but it was not for me, as it was a very big boat and too slow. I did it for about three months, and then decided to try another route. I applied for a job on a Stourlifter, running from Wolverhampton to Kidderminster, but there were no vacancies. These were L.M.S. boats and were paid weekly. So I worked my passage to Ellesmere Port, and joined my brother and his mate until I found a job. He had changed from *Broxton*, and was engaged on the boat *Spot*, a Trench boat running to Shrewsbury and various places on this branch. These boats had been made redundant along with the other flys, but had been put into service again, owing to increased trade.

After one trip, we returned to Ellesmere Port with a load of copper wire from the Shropshire Iron Works at Trench. After delivering our cargo, my brother came to me and asked me if I would like to start as Skipper. I hesitated and then decided to have a go. I was only seventeen. We both went to the office to get permission. This was granted by Mr Stockton, the wages clerk, who had control at Ellesmere Port in those days. He said: "You're young - be careful." George said I could have everything in the cabin, bedding, food and brass fittings for the bargain price of 15/-. I also took over the mate, Bill Statham, and the horse.

You had to be reliable to have a fly boat, as this was a boatman's promotion. You did not need to be a scholar [i.e. able to write] as long as you could get your boat there on time. The porters did all the clerical work, and all you had to do was put a cross to your name. You did not have to be able to read either, but it was best to be able to count, as boatmen were often blamed for what was stolen by the dockers or sailors. They were responsible for their loads. Sometimes the dockers or sailors would remove goods and replace them with stones or wood of the same weight. You had to be on the look-out for these things, because if anything was missing, you had to pay for it. I nearly got caught at Crescent Wharf once, when they found that the meat in a tin of corned beef had been replaced by a block of wood. I was cleared because it was found to be mahogany, which was not available in this country. It caused a big fuss!

Sagitta, *an ex-Grand Union Canal Carrying Company "small Northwich" boat, at Norbury Junction, in the entrance of the former canal to Newport, closed in 1944 (opposite the canal maintenance yard).*

My first cargo was 16 tons of wheat for Bullocks, at Donnington Wood Mill, above Trench. We started off at four o'clock on Tuesday morning, and buttied another Trench boat, Tom Wilday and his wife, with a cargo for Newport and Rodington. Both of us had good boats and horses that went well on their own. I had Mary, a chestnut, and he had Lucy, a grey. We passed up Northgate Locks, and arrived at Barbridge where I called at home for my laundry and a few cakes from mother. We reached Tyrley at midnight, after a long day, and took the two horses to the stable. They were fed by the horse-keeper, Alfred Talbot. From about this time all horses were Company owned.

We started off next morning at seven o'clock. I walked through Tyrley cutting with the mare, as this was a dangerous mile and a half for both horse and man, owing to falls of rock and marl. At the end, I stepped on board to steer while Bill fried the bacon and tomatoes. He then brought his plate and basin of tea out and steered, while I went in and got my first helping inside. Then I got my second bite, and took it out to steer, while Bill came inside to complete his meal. After breakfast, Bill washed the crocks and then tided the cabin as he was steerer, and the driver steered. He then lay down for a nap. This was the routine on the boat, providing the horse would go on his own. In an hour we reached Knighton, and I called Bill out. He was driver from this point, and took a feed of corn to hang on the mare's head. At the next bridge, Shebden, he took the feed tin off, and gave her a drink while the boat swam slowly on. He then fixed the muzzle on so that she could not stop to graze, and away she went on her own. Bill then stepped back on board, and relieved me while I had a nap.

As we neared Norbury Junction, I was called out again. Here we turned right, and entered the Newport Branch, and prepared to pass down the seventeen locks. Our friend Tom was close behind us. The locks were against us and Bill had to fill them. As the driver opened the gate, the boat entered the lock; then he lifted the rope over, dropped the paddles, and swung the rope out of the lock to prevent its being cut by the boat. He then drew a few notches of paddle, and went ahead to the next lock. The steerer stopped the boat with a thicker rope, pulled the top gate to, and lowered the off-side paddle when the helm was clear of the sill. He then put the rope on, ready for the next lock. Then he went down to the bottom end, raised the two paddles, and when the water levelled, opened the two bottom gates by stepping from one gate to the other. He pulled the rope clear and started the horse. All horses knew their jobs, and performed accurately after a few trips. This routine applied to all locks, both uphill and downhill. We also had to meet traffic without any delay. At this point we were moving downhill, and were responsible for the meeting of the horses.

After passing down these seventeen locks, I closed the top gate at No. 17, and stepped onto the boat to brew the tea, and prepare our dinner of cold boiled beef, while Bill opened the bottom gates, and started the mare going. Bill then got on board, washed his hands, and sat down inside. I came out to steer, with my first basin of tea, and a beef sandwich about an inch thick. Afterwards Bill came out to steer, and completed his meal, and I went inside to wash the crocks and tidy the cabin. By the time the meal was over, we were at Meirtown, and I was the next driver. I stepped onto the bank with the windlass in my pocket, and trotted ahead of the boat to make Mosspool lock ready. I raised the paddles, and went ahead to prepare the next lock, No. 19. No. 20 was Newport Lock. When we entered it, we stopped a few minutes to go to the shop near the wharf. There were six boats waiting to be loaded and off-loaded, so our butty, Tom, who was coming behind, would have to wait his turn. There were three men here when it was busy, Joe Tonkinson, the clerk and porter and Charlie Oakley and Tom Moore, the lock-keepers. The two lock-keepers were engaged every night in those days, owing to the busy traffic.

We next passed down locks 21 and 22, a mile pound and then No. 23, Edgmond Lock, the widest single lock on the Shroppie. Then we put Mary to baccer, and I stepped on the boat to steer until the change bridge, a mile ahead. Bill took a short rest. At Crabtree Bridge, No. 20, we changed over, and Bill came to the tiller

while I dropped in the cabin for about half an hour. There were no locks for four miles, but I had to come out while Bill attended to the horse and line when the towpath changed sides.

Next came Kinnersley Aqueduct, where Bill stepped on again, and I had another half an hour's nap. Bill called me as we entered Wappenshall, and then got onto the bank at the

Wappenshall Junction - Trench locks in the distance. July 1965

junction where we turned left for Trench, helm first. We had to wait a few minutes to empty the lock, and wind the lock gate into the frame. The boatmen called these "Pictures". I took the chimney down, and moved the water vessel, and also connected the tiller to two small ropes which were fitted one each side of the cabin doors. We had to leave the tiller in to keep the helm straight, in case it should contact the sill [cill]. I climbed up the lock walls, and lowered the gate down, while Bill raised the top paddles. He then went ahead to prepare the next lock, with the big windlass to wind the gate up, and a small one in his pocket to raise the paddle which was fixed to the gate. When the lock was half empty, you could force the gate up a little if you wished, which made it quicker. There was a winch fixed securely on the lockside, with a chain over the top of the frame on a big wheel which connected the chain to the gate, and on the winch was a chain brake, for use when lowering. You could only raise the gate about five feet above water level to allow the boat to pass under. This was why the boats only had a six foot beam, and very low cabins. The locks were eighty one feet in length, having been designed for tubs, not boats. Owing to busy trade, the Company experimented with these small craft, after the locks had been built.

One of the guillotine gates at Trench Locks, known by boatmen as "pictures"

These nine locks were very dangerous, especially at night. You had to get your head down quickly or you could lose it, particularly if the boat was moving at a fair speed. When lowering the gate with the brake, you had to step on it quick, or it would bounce up again, leaving a foot gap, and the lock would not fill up. Boatmen who were working with their wives, which meant double work and time, never trusted them at these locks. I once saw a boatman's wife's head severed, when the windlass flew off the winch. This boatman was a hard case and very careless, and mostly had too much beer.

We arrived at Trench at about eight o'clock, and stabled the horse. We had managed to have our tea on the way, so, after a wash, we went to "The Barley Mow" for a pint and a chat with Mr Woodfin and the locals who worked in the furnaces at the Shropshire Iron Works, and on the canalside and the railway sidings connected with it. After a good night's rest, we prepared to deliver our cargo. This had to be transhipped into eight tubs, twenty five bags of wheat into each tub. We used a small hand-crane, one hanging on, one at the crane, and one loading the tubs. When completed, we harnessed up the horse and hauled them to the bottom of the incline, about a quarter of a mile. Here the trolleys were ready in the canal, having been lowered down the incline. We floated the tubs onto the trolleys, four at a time, and then gave a signal to the engineman, Bill Jones, about four hundred yards up at the top. They were hauled up on a wire rope, at the same time as other trolleys were lowered on the opposite side. At the top, the tubs were put back into the canal again, and hauled about a mile to Bullock's Mill. This was the Coalport Canal, but it was more like a brook, the maximum width of its locks being 5' 2".

I attended the horse, while George Mason guided the tubs with a pole. They were held together by chains, and were each about twenty foot long, with square sides and no helm. We delivered the first four and went back for the others, which were ready and waiting. While we were off-loading the tubs, the horse took his feed. All we had to do here was to hang the sacks of wheat on the hoist one at a time, and the mill man used the hoist. In about two hours, we were on our way back again with the tubs down the incline and down the wharf. My mate, Bill, with Jack Rogers and Jim, were loading our boat with steel and copper wire for Liverpool and abroad. We also had a large crate of Coalport China and Barrels. This was the last I ever saw go from here. About this time, the Basic Slag Works were transferred to the

Trench inclined plane

Humber Arm, as being more convenient for despatch to the main canal.

I heard that our friend Tom and his wife were on their way up the locks to collect a load, so I walked down to meet them and lend a hand as he was working with a woman. He had been delivering his load at Newport, Longden, Rodington, and Withington, which meant long days. It was Thursday night, and on Friday morning we all worked together and loaded the second boat up. We collected our Way Bills, which were both red ones, and meant fly, and took off again down the locks. They were ready, but we still had the gates to wind up.

We passed down the nine guillotine locks, climbed up the other twenty eight, and arrived at Norbury Junction at seven thirty. Here we spent the night, and had a sing-song in the "Junction Inn", which was full of other boatmen from different routes. On Saturday morning we set off again, and arrived at Barbridge for a merry evening in "The Jolly Tar", and a night at home. There were boats from all parts here, and it was difficult to find stabling.

On Sunday morning we went down the big locks together, and reached Christleton at about two o'clock. Here we were stopped with the other traffic until six o'clock, when the lock-keeper took the padlock and chain off, and allowed us through. This practice was a nuisance to boatmen, who had to work late on Sunday night to make Ellesmere Port to deliver his cargo at midnight. Taking our turn, we passed down the locks, and eventually made Ellesmere Port.

We were called out early on Monday morning, and transhipped our cargo into a ship for abroad. Both us Trench boats and other boats from various parts transhipped into the same ship. When everything was signed for, I proceeded to Mr Stockton's office. To my surprise, he ordered me to change boats with

Jack Stubbs. I wanted to know the reason, and he told me that Jack was an older hand and I was the younger and had taken over from my brother. I thought of giving up, but Bill told me to give the new boat a trial. It was the boat *Fritz*, a Trench boat like *Spot*, but not in such good condition. I did change in the end, but there was nearly a fight.

However, I was pleased to receive my first trip's pay as Skipper, and paid Bill, my mate. This was a mileage boat with a Company's horse. The distance from Ellesmere Port to Trench was 64 miles each way, and 3½d per mile each way loaded with over six tons made £1 17s 4d plus 2/6 special allowance per week for ropes, totalled £1 19s 10d. If you retuned light, the mileage would be 2½d per mile. You could do more than one trip a week, and very rarely returned light from Trench. My mate's pay was 10/- per week and food. This was a most regular route, and never slack. The pay was good, allowing you £1 per trip after food was found. However there was plenty of work owing to the locks. There were 65 each way, which meant 110 per 108 mile trip – more locks than miles. You were not always bound for Trench with your uphill cargo of wheat, copper bars and goods, but could call at Shrewsbury, Uffington, Berwick, Withington, Longden, Longlane, Brewood, Wheaton Aston, Gnosall, and sometimes Birmingham and Wolverhampton, before returning light to the Trench or Humber Arm for downhill traffic. It was a very busy industrial place in those days and only this certain type of boat could get there. I have been engaged a week at a time, hauling traffic down the nine locks, and transhipping at Wappenshall to the bigger commercial craft. In this case I was paid by the ton, as the distance was only two miles.

Trench inclined plane

A view down the plane in 1966

The engine house

16

STEPHEN AGAIN, LONG TRIPS, AND MARRIAGE.

I only worked the *Fritz* for a short while, and then I changed over with another chap to the boat *Stephen* which had been a Llangollen Fly. My grandfather, E Roberts, had been Skipper of this boat, and after he drowned at Bettisfield my father, Alfred Roberts, took over for a few years. Now in 1912 it was myself, Jack Roberts. However I was engaged, not as a fly boat, but as a North Boat, running mostly to North Wales or wherever required. During this period I was engaged on my two longest trips. One time I went from Ellesmere Port to Derby with a cargo of leather. Usually on this route, cargo was transhipped at Preston Brook. My second trip was from Ellesmere Port to Coventry with 18 tons of sugar. Both of these were good mileage trips. I had a special horse from Wolverhampton who was kept for the Coventry route only, and left on return. He was a lovely mottled grey, called Puffer, and never made a mistake.

After a few months, I was passing Tower Wharf, Chester, when I met Mr George Talbot on the towing path. "Jackie", he said "There's a new boat for you at the dock repair yard. Would you like to change over? She's a Trench boat called *Patriot*. You're young, and so is your mate, and our Trench trade is getting very busy again." Of course I said yes, and he gave me a note which I handed to the boat-builder foreman, John Owen, giving me permission to change over. Everything was new and painted up, and the cabin was lovely. I made my way to Ellesmere Port and had to have the new boat tested with weights at the Indexing Dock. Usually they had to be tested for a night, but in this case I was straight in and out again.

On Saturday morning I was called out at six o'clock and loaded with 16 tons of copper in an hour. It was for the Shropshire Iron Works at Trench again. I knew what this meant. It was an urgent cargo and expensive, and demanded a quick journey. I settled up for my previous trip, got my provisions, and was on my way by half past nine, having our second breakfast going along. When we arrived at Northgate Locks, I pulled the boat through by hand, while the mate called at the stables for provender and the horse had a feed. Inspector Talbot met me at the top lock and handed me a note to give to the horse-keepers, to the effect that I should change horses at Bunbury, Hack Green or Tyrley. We had two brothers, Dick and Joe Hammond, with the boat *Colonel* for our butty. We called at Barbridge for our laundry and baking, and had half an hour's chat with mum, who expected us to stay the night, being unaware of the circumstances. We paid for our necessaries, and set off for a night out. We arrived at Trench on Sunday night at six o'clock, while the local people were on their way to church. We were well ahead of time as we had been told to be there for nine o'clock on Monday morning. We were off-loaded by ten on Monday morning, and the copper went into the works nearby. We loaded up again with steel bars for Liverpool.

My boat had to call at the G.K.N. at Hadley Park, which is Sankeys now. This was above No. 2 lock. We had to raise a drawbridge and enter the basin to collect the remaining part of our load, which was nails for abroad. After collecting the cargo, we went down the locks with our butty, and moored at Wappenshall. We looked back up the locks where the guillotine gates were lifted up like pictures in a frame. They were attractive to look at, but not to handle. We were both urgent again, having red Time Bills, but were not tied to a tide time.

We made Audlem next day, and changed back to our regular horse, leaving Marshall, which was an excellent horse. This was a change stable in 1913. Next day we passed Barbridge, calling at home as usual, and arrived at Ellesmere Port about eight o'clock. It was Wednesday, and we had only left on Saturday. On Thursday morning we were ordered out into the docks to off-load into a ship which occupied the full length of the dock, known as the Raddle Wharf. Then John Sheffield, the dock's foreman, ordered me to King's Flour Mill to collect a mixture of cattle food, bran and thirds for Gnosall, Wheaton Aston, Brewood and Chillington Wharf. We parted company with our butty, and while Bill was loading, I went to have my last load signed for, collect my pay and order provisions. We moored up after loading, and decided to stay the night and go to the Hippodrome which had just been erected at Ellesmere Port. We left on Friday morning together with a Pottery boat *Cecil* worked by John Palin and his wife. We made Barbridge and had a Saturday night at home. John Palin

The Boat Inn, Gnosall, September 1961

left us at the Junction. He was bound for Stone with a load of grain for Stubbs Mill. We both had plenty of time to deliver on Monday morning, and worked accordingly.

Leaving Barbridge on Sunday morning, we arrived at Gnosall in the evening, and had a few pints and recreation with several other boatmen. On Monday morning we delivered our goods,

a couple of bags of bacon, sugar and butter in tubs for Mr Bancroft at the shop near the canal bridge and wharf. The "Navigation Inn" was on the opposite side. We had our notes signed, and went on to call at Bridge 31 to deliver for a busy farmer, who also stored for other farmers in a fairly large warehouse built by the Canal Company. Our next call was for another farmer at High Onn. Then we went to Wheaton Aston, where Mr Clay and his daughter were engaged by the Company as toll clerks. Next was Brewood, where there was a private wharf and a large coal business. Our last call was at Chillington Wharf. On the wall of this warehouse were printed the words "GOODS CAREFULLY HANDLED", which are still visible, though well-worn. There was also a coal wharf and a house, rented from the Company by private people.

During this trip we met a Staffordshire boat near Audlem Locks, where the aqueduct takes the canal over the River Weaver. There was a girl walking on the tow-path, picking flowers. She was dressed in a red frock, and a white pinafore and bonnet. I had met her once before in Wolverhampton. I passed the time of day, and had a short conversation with her while the boats passed. She was engaged in private service at Wolverhampton and was having a fortnight's holiday on the boat with her parents.

After delivering our load, we returned to Norbury Junction, where I had to call at Mr Johnson's office. I was ordered to load a few tons to take down the Newport branch, and then proceed to the Trench light, and collect a cargo for Liverpool. We delivered our cargo at Newport and went up the Trench again. The gates were up in our favour this time. We were soon loaded up and were away in three hours, collecting our Time and Way Bill. We stopped for the night at

Wappenshall. The lock-keeper at Leagomery, Mr W Owen, and Mr Salmon at Wappenshall both remarked how quick we had been. We had the company of our other mates at Wappenshall, so about eight o'clock we decided to walk and have a drink at "The Malt Shovel Inn" at Leagomery.

When you were on your own, Wappenshall was a desolate place to be. It was like a wilderness,

Wappenshall Junction, July 1965

and in the winter you would not see or hear anyone, only the windows and doors of the large warehouse going "bing bang" all night, a fox howling or an owl "two-hooting". All the boatmen thought it was haunted and talked about a man who walked with no head. I was never afraid at night, but you were inclined to be nervous if you saw something unusual when you went to feed the horse at night. In those days there were quite a lot of poachers about. Bill and I did not mind meeting a couple of men, as we were both young and useful if need be.

We set off again at four o'clock on Friday morning, hoping to reach Barbridge that night.

It was a long day, 42 miles and 50 locks, and we would only do it if the way was clear, and we were not held up with traffic. We had a clear way to Norbury Junction, which we reached at nine o'clock. At midday we reached Tyrley, and I decided to leave Mary for a rest if there was a good change horse. I asked Alf Talbot, the horse-keeper, if I could have a look around. We knew all the relief horses all over the systems, and their characters. I found a little mare, named Lottie, No. 301, a chocolate coloured horse with four white legs and a white face. The horse-keeper told me it was time I gave Mary a rest. "That's three trips you've done this last fortnight". We did not like to leave a good horse that knew the route, and could be trusted to go alone in the dark or in daylight.

All the locks were in our favour, and at No. 5 we placed the muzzle on Lottie's head, and then stepped on the boat to have our meal. As we finished we were nearing Adderley Locks. We only had 16 tons as it was a very small boat, and this made a difference to Lottie as she was used to bigger boats on this section, loaded with 25-30 tons. We passed down the locks, and moored at Barbridge at nine o'clock for a short night.

Off again at seven on Saturday morning, we entered the locks at Bunbury together with a boat from Seddons at Middlewich with a load of brick salt for Cow Lane Wharf, Chester. We passed down the big locks to Chester and parted company again.

Then we passed single down Northgate Locks, and met two Pottery boats in the locks. It was Bill Bell and Bill Grimes. The last nine miles were quiet, except for the tug *Luna*, hauling flats to Chester. We arrived at seven o'clock.

Here I saw again the girl I had met at Audlem the previous Saturday. Her father told me they had been delayed in delivering their downhill cargo from the Midlands, and were now loaded up with aluminium for Birmingham, but were staying till Monday morning. I thought this would give me a chance to have her company and for us to get to know each other better. I made myself presentable and took her to the Hippodrome on Saturday evening. On Sunday afternoon we took a walk along the Ship Canal side to Eastham Lock. It was all green fields in those days, with yellow broom brushes along the embankment. On Monday morning I went to wish her goodbye, and arranged to write letters occasionally, and to meet whenever possible at Wolverhampton. Her parents had only recently moved there from Kinver on the Kidderminster canal. Her father, Henry Stokes, had been engaged on the three-handed Railway Fly Boats from Wolverhampton to Stourport and back with cargoes of vinegar. He had now changed over to a Hampton Boat, a weekly boat running to Ellesmere Port, and usually worked with his son, Charley.

We transhipped our cargo into the same ship as our previous load. This ship was almost full, and ready to sail. I reported to the traffic foreman, George Doan, for my next cargo, but he told me that traffic was quiet for my route and there was only raddle for the Humber Arm, Donnington. I did not like this for a goods boat as it was dirty, but it was still good traffic. I asked if there was any choice, so we went into the office, and he looked at the invoices and said was the boat fit for a load of sugar for Dudley. I said yes, it was a new boat, but I could only take 16 tons. He knew all about that, and told me to bring her up the locks and go in the cross-berths. I did this without hesitation, and we were soon loaded up and ready for off on Tuesday morning.

After getting everything signed for, and settling for my pay, we set off. I knew we would catch up with my girl before we reached Wolverhampton, as they were loaded with 25 tons. We passed a few words as we overtook them, and I arranged to meet them coming up the 21 locks, in the evening, after we had arrived at Wolverhampton. I managed to do this, and we visited the Empire Theatre from nine to eleven o'clock. On parting, we arranged to meet at the girl's home when I was on my way back from Dudley. She was working in the town after her holiday.

Humber Arm: bridge over the canal and the railway engine shed

At six next morning, we were off again, and arrived at Tyrley where we left the horse, and took Mary again. She had had a good week's rest. We made Barbridge for Saturday evening and moored till Sunday. Both of us lived at Barbridge and had been to school together, though Bill was older than I. We had a good evening in "The Jolly Tar" which was full of boat people. All our food and laundry had been put ready for us, and we went on our way to Ellesmere Port, after breakfast. We had to wait at Christleton Locks, but fortunately we were first to enter, and left twenty or more boats behind, taking their turn. We made Ellesmere Port by ten, berthing the boats at the Raddle Wharf ready for Monday morning, when we discharged our loads into a foreign ship with a coloured crew.

When the cargo had been signed for, I went to the office for my pay. Mr Stockton looked at my times of departure from Ellesmere Port, arrival at Dudley, departure and arrival at Trench, and return to Ellesmere Port, calculated the distance, and told me I had travelled 186 miles. He asked how many times I had change horses. There were 202 locks both ways. The pay came to £5 12s for the week at a rate of 3½d per mile each way, and including special allowances. This was excellent pay, but it involved long days – twelve hours a day for two men. However, we were quite happy if we had a good horse who would go by himself, so that we could get a nap in between locks and traffic. After receiving my pay, I had to pay Bill. He had 30/- and was very excited. Of course, I also had all the food to find.

Before taking another order to load, I applied verbally for a change of route, which meant another boat. I wanted to travel the route where my girl lived as often as possible, and could not do this with a Trench boat, as they were kept specially for Trench locks. My application was granted, and I changed over into the boat *Eric*, an ex-Pottery Fly, which had been replaced by a new boat *Rembrandt*. It is still afloat now, converted into a pleasure craft, re-named *Shroppie Fly* and moored at Brewood. My first trip with this boat was with a load of candle fat for Darlaston, near Moxley, in the Black Country; this allowed me to visit my girl-friend again.

Eric was graded as a North Wales boat, but it could travel anywhere, and you had a choice. My mate Bill decided to leave me and joined a Pottery Fly, so I had to engage another one. This was Billy Mulloy, who was about sixteen and had no parents. He stayed with me until I was married. I am not going into detail of my trips during 1913, but I travelled to all parts of the canal. I also decided to get married to the girl I had first met at Audlem, twelve months previously. The ceremony took place at Ellesmere Port on 10th April 1914, where my parents had recently gone to live.

17

CANAL LIFE, MYTHS AND MISUNDERSTANDINGS

My first trip with the wife for mate was to Aston, Birmingham, loaded with timber. She was very useful, as she had had a little experience with her parents, but I had to be careful not to forget myself when we were working in the locks, and be certain where she was, especially at night. After delivering our load at Aston, I made my way to Crescent Wharf for orders. I had to proceed to Phillips for a load of bed-stead cases for Liverpool. It was a Wednesday in April. I made Ellesmere Port on Friday night, and delivered my load into a ship. I was just in time to draw my pay on Saturday morning.

During the weekend, I decided not to go to the Black Country any more, and to take the North Wales route whenever I could. It was a more pleasant route, clean with fewer locks and less traffic. So, on Monday morning, after the fly boats had left, I was given a load for Welshpool and places to Newtown. I was still paid by the mile, and still had the horse, Mary, who knew the way as well as I did. The wife had never been up the Welsh Cut before, and remarked on the lovely scenery, the clean canal water, the grassy towing path, the mountains of Montgomeryshire, and the friendliness of the people.

I had known plenty of young ladies when I was engaged on the Newtown Fly, and was approached many times with an "Ello" and "How long had I entered matrimony?" I was still only nineteen. The wife remarked that she had obviously not been my first girl, and was inclined to be a little cold at times. We entered Welshpool, after calling at a few places, and saw Breidon Hills, and the Abbey Bank at Buttington, where the two peacocks still walked. The wife had never seen a peacock before, nor such scenery. All the lock-keepers and their families were surprised that I had married, and pulled my leg of course. We put Mary into the stable in the yard, and both went for a wash. Then we had a chat with the porters, Jim Lloyd and Frank Windsor, and took a stroll to "The Swan Inn" to have a drink with Mrs. Price, the landlady, whom I had not seen for two years.

On our return, the fly, or rather the weekly boat, had arrived. He had left Ellesmere Port before me, but had been delayed delivering and collecting traffic on route, and was loaded heavier than me. It was my uncle, John Owen, who had been Skipper on the previous four-handed fly. The porters were engaged until midnight off-loading the fly, as they had priority at wharves. I thought I would have to tranship my traffic for places past Welshpool, onto the fly, which was the custom to economise on my mileage, but, to my surprise, I delivered my Welshpool traffic, and then picked up all that was left from the fly.

On Thursday morning, we were on our way to Newtown, and delivered at Belan, Berriew, Garthmyl, Brynderwyn and Abermule. We were carrying all manner of bag stuff, and even some coffin boards. We met the fly, *Arcturus*, on his return journey, and arrived at Newtown in the early evening. The wife led the horse around the road, while I poled across the basin, near "The Waggoner's Inn". She found the way, and all was well.

We found that Frank Windsor had been sent over from Welshpool that day to take over from Mr Taylor as part-time agent and porter. I saw that the Cambrian Wool Factory had been burned down during my absence. This meant that I should not have any girls to visit me across at the wharf. Most of them had voluntarily transferred to Huddersfield. My Brother's girl-friend, Mabel Jones, who lived at Sun Bank,

Newtown, had gone there. She came from Huddersfield to Ellesmere Port to be bridesmaid at our wedding. We paid our half-penny to cross over the river, and had a stroll round the town. We passed the old pump house on the way back, and had a word with Mr and Mrs Gough, who were the attendants. This pump was used to raise the water from the Severn to feed the first three miles of the canal. At Freestone Lock, the river and canal came to the same level, and the water came through a pipe there and fed the canal down to Pool Quay. The water flow from Frankton and Newtown met at Wern Mill. The over-flow first drove the mill, and then found its way back to the Severn.

On our return journey, we had a word with John Edwards and his daughter Nessy, at Aberbechan. She was seventeen then, and lives in that same cottage today. I sometimes visit her, and another old friend, Mrs Lewes, who was Elsie Morgan fifty years ago. They like to have a chat about the old days. At Byles Lock

Byles Lock

we had a word with Joe Thomas and his wife, and at Brynderwyn, a chat with Mr Price and his two daughters. They did not smile as they used to do – I had been very attentive to Megan once. At Glenafron, I had to stop and take down all the gangway and cratch, and also the water

vessel and chimney. This boat had not been fitted for this route, so I took the measurements of the bridge's height etc., and did a little carpentry of my own for future occasions.

When we reached Welshpool, I was ordered to load Macadam from Welshpool Standard for Swanley. I agreed to this, though I did not like it. As I was a mileage boat, I only got the same rates as if I were light, 2½ per mile, and no fly time bill. This was the usual arrangement. If I had been a tonnage boat, I would have been allowed 1/- per ton, but the Company avoided this as often as they could. I did not argue, as the agent at Welshpool was a difficult man to get on with.

On Friday afternoon we were loaded by horse and cart from the Rock. We stayed the night, and were on our way on Saturday morning, moving at a slow rate through the lovely countryside, occasionally meeting traffic, including a few donkey boats. At Llanymynech, we stopped to do the week-end shopping for meat etc. However, we purchased potatoes, lettuce and other vegetables from the lock-keepers on the way, who also sold eggs at 6d a dozen.

We passed through the Pant, Porth-y-Waen, Maesbury, Queen's Head, and arrived at Frankton Junction for the night. We spent the evening with my aunt and uncle but had to stay in the house as there was no pub for a drink. In my father's memory, the house below the lock there was a pub "The Canal Tavern", but it was closed because too many people got drunk and fell in the canal. On Sunday morning we set off, and reached

Baddiley Locks near Nantwich. There was a good stable here, and we tied up early in company with two of our friends on commercial boats going the opposite way. After tea we walked to "The Farmer's Arms", a mile away. Mrs Nelson, a widow, was mistress there. She was sister to the lock-keeper, where our boats were moored. We had a few country songs like "The farmers boy" and "Barley Mow" sung by the locals, and a few canal songs by the boatmen. You were not allowed to sing a comic song on a Sunday anywhere in those days.

On Monday morning we made our way to Swanley Wharf to deliver our cargo of Macadam stone. This meant getting out the shovel. There was no other help, so the wife had to join in. You could pay someone 2/6 per ruck to help, but you could hardly afford this. I told the wife to go at her leisure, and we started at ten o'clock, and had it all out by two. This was a 20 ton load, and two young men could off-load this in three hours at a good wharf. If you had to wheel-barrow it, it took two hours longer. We pegged to again, and went down Hurleston Locks, and arrived at Barbridge Depot, where I had everything signed for on a white way bill.

I was worried about my wife working with me and I had my worst experience while working a boat with her. It was at New Martin No. 1 Lock. She was opening the top lock gate, when the horse started too soon. She was going down the foot-holes in the lockside, and missed her footing as she jumped onto the boat which was moving too quickly. She hung onto the hatches side, with half her body in the canal. I was with the horse, and when I heard her screaming I let him go and ran back. The boat was still moving, and well near the middle, but I jumped and landed on it, and got hold of her hands to pull her up. It was a struggle, but I managed to get her to safety. I think I must have had double strength in the excitement of the emergency. If I had not forgotten myself, this would not have happened – I had been talking to Mr Clay, the

toll clerk, at the time. It is easy to forget sometimes. The wife was quite unnerved afterwards, and I had learned my lesson – keep your mind on your mate night and day on the canal.

During our first year's married life, I was ordered at Barbridge to proceed to Northwich to collect 20 tons of soda for Birmingham. On our way down the Middlewich Branch, near Stanthorn Lock, I put my windlass in my pocket, and ran ahead of the boat to get the lock ready, leaving my wife to steer, and the horse coming nicely after me. I got the lock ready for the boat to enter, and Mrs Roberts closed the gate, while I was raising the paddles. When I looked around to see if she was alright, I noticed she was crying, and had got on the boat. I went back to the cabin end, and asked what was the matter. She said she had lost her wedding ring in the canal, near the bridge near the weir. I told her not to upset herself, I would buy her another, but she went on crying and said it was bad luck. We went down Wardle Locks and entered the North Staffs Canal, through Middlewich, where there was plenty of traffic, and boats loading salt at Henry Seddons Works. We came to the Big Lock, and paired up with a Gandy Fly from Derby. We allowed him to go first, as Mrs Roberts was in the Big Lock Stores, buying food. This shop sold everything for boat people, and there was also a public house and stabling. For a couple of miles through the woods, the horse was allowed to go by himself as traffic was quiet for a while, and we had a meal. I had bought the wife a lovely shawl in a coloured fabric at the Big Lock Stores, and she admired it, but she could not forget the loss of her wedding ring.

After we had had a rest and washed the crocks, we met more traffic from Runcorn, Preston Brook and Manchester. We knew the times of the tugs through the tunnels and expected to meet them. They were all horse-drawn in those days. After meeting one, you could relax until the next came along. So we arrived at the

Wardle Junction, entrance from the Trent & Mersey Canal (North Staffs in this book) to the Wardle Canal, with its one lock, and end on junction immediately afterwards with the Middlewich Arm of the Shropshire Union Canal

Anderton Lift, and passed down with another boat to enter the River Weaver. This was the end of my journey, and I put the horse in the stable and tied up for the night.

Next morning we went across the river. I had to use the pole or shaft to berth for my cargo of soda. Everybody had to come off the boat while loading was carried out. We went into the kitchen which was provided by I.C.I. until the cargo was complete. The boat was loaded by ten o'clock, and we went back across the river to the lift. This boat was a small one, and 20 tons were quite enough, leaving only six inches dry side. There was a fair wind, so we had to pull the side-sheets up before starting off. We passed up the lift again, and I harnessed the horse and walked him to the top, ready to peg him on the boat.

We came to Dock Bridge, where there was a toll office, and the boat was gauged with a staff for the weight of the cargo. While this was being done, I noticed the boat was deeper in the water, so I raised the sheet, and saw water on the bottom of the false floor, and the soda getting wet. I had to stop for a while to pump. There were two pumps, a deck pump and a side pump. I used the deck pump, and I could see that the water was coloured and foaming, so I knew the cargo was damaged. All I could do was to get to Barbridge Junction, the Shroppie Depot, which was eight hours work.

After pumping dry, we started off again. We passed the industrial sites, and came to the Broken Cross, a pub on the canal bank, near Wincham. Here we allowed the horse to go himself, while I pumped again and the wife steered. The boat was still leaking, but I could just about cope. After pumping dry again, I went back to the cabin end to steer, and wait my chance to run the boat onto the side where there was plenty of silt settled. I stopped the horse and ran the boat onto the silt in a wide place, which caused quite an eruption of silt to bubble round the boat. After this, I had to get Bill, the horse, on again, and haul her back, which made him blow a bit.

Big Lock at Middlewich in April 1971, with a very industrial skyline. In earlier times, wide boats could reach Middlewich from the Manchester area, hence the dimensions of this lock.

We went on and entered the Big Lock with a Salt Union Fly. While the boat was rising, I tried the pump again, but there was little water in, and it would go for about an hour. There was a boat waiting to come down the lock, and I asked if the next three locks were ready. These were known as Middlewich New'uns. We were ready to start out of the lock, and the fly wanted to go first, but I went first, and told the wife to keep her straight. She knew what I meant. I had five tons more weight than the fly, but I knew he could not pass me, as my boat was a Shroppie, and Bill was a good horse. The fly tried to pass, but he got well behind. It was only half a mile from lock to lock, but these next were single locks. I entered the lock and drew the paddles up, while the wife shut the bottom gates, and we went up the three in this way. The fly boat chap came up to prepare the lock after us, and used a bit of sarcasm. I was not in a very good mood myself, owing to the boat leaking, so I told him we would go where the bull gets his dinner. I knew the chap well, and knew he could fight, but I could also fight in those days, and was ready for a meeting. However, the Skipper came up and told the mate to shut up, so it was left.

We came to Wardle Junction, and turned up the Shroppie again, while the fly boat continued on his way to the Potteries. The boat was still leaking, but not so badly. I knew the silt would be washing away again and I would have to renew the treatment. I tied up for the night, and ran the boat onto the clay silt. There was plenty of it at this point. It was seven o'clock, and I took Bill to the stable for the night. We had had some long days. The wife and I had our tea, and during the meal she said: "I told you it was unlucky", referring to her wedding ring. I had thought the same myself, in a way, but to ease the situation, I told her it was only superstition. After an hour, I decided to go for a pint at King's Lock, and pay my stabling at the same time. It was fourpence in those days. I took the wife with me, and we returned at ten o'clock. I told her to go to bed, while I attended to the pump again. When it was dry, I returned to the cabin, and lay down on the side-bed, only taking my coat and boots off. I knew I would have to attend to the pump about every two hours.

At six next morning, I fed the horse and prepared breakfast for myself and the wife. We started off again, and passed up Stanthorne Lock. I decided to stop where the wife had lost her ring, and she pointed out the spot. I took my clothes off, and found an old frying pan, and dropped in the water. I scooped along with the pan, and felt with my feet. I tried for an hour with no success, and eventually gave up. I knew it was a difficult task, but I had had a good try. We arrived at Barbridge at about eleven o'clock, and reported the leakage to the office. After discussing the matter, we examined the cargo in the bottom near the mast, and we could see that some of the sacks of soda were wet and melting. I had to tranship to another boat, a Staffordshire boat *Arenig*, Skipper Arthur Drinkwater. The damage was only to five sacks of the cargo. Then I had to proceed to Chester Dock for an inspection.

I must say that life on the waterways is good, healthy, clean, jolly and interesting, if you make it so. If one is in ill-health or suffering from nerves, depression or any other ailments, then experience of life of the canals is a good way of getting rid of such things. From my experience, and the life of boat people in general, illness is rare on the canals, and the majority live to a good old age. Every minute, there is something to attract you – passing through locks, the changing countryside, cattle, birds, fish, a call at the local when you feel like it – stop when you like – eat when you like – sleep when you like. If you have a pleasure boat, do not lay it up in September, but go into November, and see the autumn countryside, and the snow on the mountains, but stop when ice forms on the canal. And there is little danger if you learn the correct way to work the locks. I have worked, and stepped across lock gates in the dark. It is like a trade – you must learn it well. The old fly boats averaged two minutes passing down a single lock, and five minutes for a big lock. For instance, meeting traffic, but no other obstructions, we could come up or down the

fifteen locks at Audlem in under an hour.

I refer now to actual living on boats. The raising of families became more frequent when the canal boats were registered as dwellings by Act of Parliament in 1894. All boats were registered then. However, the Shropshire Union had quite a number of houses built on various parts of the canal for the convenience of boat people. The majority were occupied, but quite a few preferred living on the boats. This meant that husband and wife could be together, as a boatman's life was mostly travelling away from home otherwise. I did not have the experience of living on a boat as a child, as my parents insisted on our having an ordinary home, and being schooled from the age of five.

When the boat was away, and my mother wanted money, she could get an advance from the office. There were forty or fifty boatmen living at Barbridge in those days, and they all had this same privilege, which applied all over the Shropshire Union. It also applied during frosts, sickness and suchlike events, and allowed you money to purchase a horse. You paid everything back in instalments. During difficult periods, the men would usually be found other work, and the rate was four pence an hour then. The longest frost I remember was while I was at school, in about 1902. It lasted fourteen weeks.

We hear a lot these days in book, magazines and papers about the old boatmen's life, and family life on the boats. A lot of these stories are not true. For instance, they did not lead a Romany life. I do not know where they got that idea from. On the whole boatmen were clean and tidy, and took pride in the appearance of their boats. Of course, there were exceptions, but their faults were soon pointed out to them.

Another story tells how a couple would leave the boat at one bridge, get married, and meet the boat again at the next bridge. This again is nonsense. During my life on the canals, I could not name a dozen girls who were pregnant before marriage. Parents were most strict in such matters. Religion was never forgotten, and boatmen mostly built their own churches. When applying for employment as a boatman, a couple would have to produce their marriage certificate, if they were unknown to the Company. If the family were on the Company's records already, this was not necessary, as their background would then be known.

Education was never neglected. The children on the boats were given a school card, and would have to attend school at various places en route, while waiting to be off-loaded or loaded. This could be a few days sometimes, but would be for longer periods if there were an obstruction on the canal, like frost or repairs. The school card had to be signed by the school-master, and was inspected regularly by the Agent of the Depot. At Ellesmere Port, Jimmy Price would approach the boats daily, as they entered. If there were any school-dodgers, the father would be called to the office to explain. These were the Shropshire Union rules.

You could also be approached anywhere by the Inspector of Council Registration Authority, and asked to produce the Cabin Registered Certificate. Then your family was counted. If you were over-crowded you would be stopped until this was corrected. I saw this happen many times. The boats were registered as follows:- in a fly boat after-cabin there could be either four men, or three women, or a man, his wife and two children under twelve years of age, or in some cases three children according to the space available. In the fore-cabin there could be one adult, male or female. When these inspections occurred, the inspectors could use their discretion with regard to the cleanliness of the occupants, or whether repairs, paint or more ventilation were needed on the boat. The name and registration number of your boat had to be clearly visible. If anything were wrong, it would be reported to the General Manager at Tower Wharf, Chester. This applied to all boats registered as dwellings by the Canal Boats Act of 1894.

Another story put about, is that when a donkey died, the boatman would throw it down into the river from Pontcysyllte Aqueduct. This is nonsense. The boatmen were not ignorant in such cases. When a donkey did die, it was buried on the canal bank or sent to the knacker's yard. What would the River Authority have said if a dead donkey were thrown in? If a donkey had a foal, the baby would be put in the boat, and lifted out to be fed at intervals. However, donkeys were only used on boats carrying stone.

When a donkey died, either from old age, or an accident, they were often buried at Plas Isaf Bridge on the Llangollen Canal. Old Brown once told me that he and Bilston Tom went to bury a donkey once, when they were lugging stone. They dug a big hole, but they did not dig it deep enough, so, when they put the donkey in, on his back, his legs were sticking out above the ground. Old Bilston Tom went and fetched his mattock, and cut them off at the knees. That soon fitted him in!

Boatmen were always very careful of their horses, and saw that they were right before they saw to themselves. My relations told me that my grandfather insisted on having a good horse. He purchased one from the coal pits at Ruabon, as it was too tall for the mines, and brought him home to Pontcysyllte. He hooked him on the boat, but had to lead him for about three days, as he was blind, but he could see his way through Chirk and Whitehouses Tunnels. He was very intelligent, and would shoulder the lock gates open. He would also drink tea out of a tin tea bottle. If a little of the roof fell on him when he was going through a tunnel, he would get away smartly. An old collier told me that down the pit this was a sure sign of a fall, and you should keep clear. This horse's name was Toby.

I would like to mention here that boatmen had a language of their own at work. For instance for "raise a paddle", they would say "draw a paddle", and for "lower a paddle", "drop it". They did not say "right" or "left", but "out", meaning "out to the offside", and "in", meaning "in to the towing path side". After changing sides at a roving bridge, the same terms applied though the side had changed. The powered commercial boats also used these terms "in" and "out". The downhill boat was always responsible when boats were horse-drawn and meeting.

To drop a paddle, the boatman removed the windlass (not key), pulled the catch up, placed his hand tightly on the bar and pressed, dropping the paddle lightly in the frame under water. He would not have time to use the windlass to wind it down, as this would have been a hindrance. The windlass was only used to draw a paddle. It was mostly carried in his pocket or over his left shoulder, with the eye under his braces. A woman carried hers in the belt around her waist. A boat pole was called a shaft, and it was placed on the boat with the hook end nearest the steerer. This meant that if there were an emergency, one would not have to turn it around.

Lock gates and paddles at Hack Green top lock, near Nantwich

18

FIRST WORLD WAR

The First World War had begun by now, and I had considered joining the army, although we had been notified by the Company that we were all exempt. However, I did not mention it to the wife. We went on to Ellesmere Port where we were loaded with candle-fat for Darlaston, near Walsall. I did not like this, but had no alternative. The wife went shopping and I settled up. This last trip came to £2 10s 6d, but if I had had a red way bill, I would have had £2 17s 6d.

We left Ellesmere Port on Wednesday morning. I intended to deliver this cargo on Saturday morning, as I did not want to be stuck there for the weekend. We had to put in long hours as it was 80 miles and there were plenty of locks to pass through. We managed to get there as it was lovely weather, and we got back to Wolverhampton for the weekend so that the wife could spend a while at her home. At nine o'clock on Monday morning I reported to Broad Street Depot with my back notes signed for my cargo, to have my Time and Way bill signed. Mr Jones, the shipping clerk, remarked that I was a North Wales boat. The Company Depots knew who everyone was.

I had orders to proceed to Springdale Furnaces, Bilston, to collect a load of basic slag for the Severn Valley Company at Abermule, on the Montgomery. We did this quite quickly, as it was only three miles away, and it only took an hour to load the boat. We were back at Wolverhampton by two o'clock. Having collected our provender, we passed down the 21 locks, through Aldersley to Autherley and back onto the Shroppie again. We left the Black Country smoke behind, and made Wheaton Aston for the night. I had a pint at the "Hartley Arms" with an old boatman. It had been a quiet journey as it was a Monday.

On Tuesday morning, the Brumagem Fly *Tariff* passed us before we had started, on his way to Crescent Wharf, Birmingham. We passed down the thirty three mile stretch, and twenty seven locks to Hack Green, where I collected my week's provender for the Welsh Canal. These were the last stables before the entrance to the Welsh Canal. The horse-keeper, Thomas Masefield, looked through the traffic book, where records of all boat time and traffic were kept, and told me that my horse required a rest. He said:
"You only went through here last Tuesday."
"Alright Tom" I said "It will 'avter be."
So I harnessed up Daisy, a mottled grey, and a very steady horse for the Welsh Canal, which was not very deep. Mary had been rather too free for a heavy load of 18 tons. However, he

Dee Basin drydock and warehouse, Chester, with stables just visible on left, May 1970

promised he would keep Mary until I came again, if it was possible.

Owing to the delay in changing horses, we only got as far as Hurleston Junction, and tied up for the night on the Welsh Cut. I went on next day to Abermule, delivered my cargo, and returned to Chester. I had to leave my boat there for painting and repairs.

While this was being done, I was given a temporary job on the docks, and in the stables. One day I was told to take two horses to the blacksmith's shop to have new shoes fitted. I liked this task very much, and placed a bridle on one horse so that I could ride it, and a head-stall on the other for leading. This was at the Dee Basin Stables, and the blacksmith's was at Northgate Locks, a few hundred yards away. While I was trotting up the cobbled bank, I met two officers of a mounted corps. One remarked to the other: "It's chaps like him we want", meaning myself.

I delivered the horses, and took two others back. However, I had started to think about things in a quiet way, and I joked with Bill Ellis, Bill Johnson and the other horse-keepers - "I think I'll join the artillery one day". When I returned to my boat at six o'clock, I learned that one of the painters had joined the Artillery. This gave me some encouragement, although I had not discussed the matter with the wife.

On 6th January 1915, I was engaged in scooping water out of boats with a bucket. The boats were full owing to rain and leakage. All at once, I decided to join the army, so I dropped the bucket, and went up to Chester Barracks, in Skipgate Street. I walked straight in, and was taken to the Medical Officer, and passed. To my surprise, the orderly who escorted me to the doctor was Tom Brooks, a schoolmate of mine. He was a little younger than me, and in the Cheshire Regiment of the Regular Army. He had returned from the battle of Mons at the beginning of the war. I thought this was a strange coincidence. I returned to my boat, and the wife wanted to know where I had been. I told her I had joined the army, and had to report next morning. Of course, this news brought tears.

Next morning, I reported at Chester Castle to be sworn in. I was not aware that I had to do this, or I might have changed my mind! Next, I had to attend the Quartermaster's Stores for my suit, shoes, bandoliers and spurs. I was a soldier - a gunner in the Field Artillery. Taking my civilians back with me, I returned to the Dock, and was met by the Inspector. He said: "What made you join? We want men to work the boats and serve the country." I had to go before the Manager. When I entered the office, he

Private Jack Roberts on 16 January 1915, ten days after joining the Royal Field Artillery, aged 19

congratulated me on volunteering to fight for my country. However he was concerned because my services were also required to transport food and all traffic to do with war weapons etc., and I had joined the army without permission. If I had applied to go, I would have been allowed part of my pay which I would now have to forego. I was rather upset about this.

My pay in the Army was 9/6 per week, plus 3/6 allowance for my wife, making 13/- per week altogether. This was just enough to feed and clothe one, but it was a very poor existence for a householder who had to pay rent. However, I left my wife to live with my sister at Barbridge.

After a few week's training at Chester in foot-drill, and a little at a riding school on Chester Race Course, a few hundred of us left Chester Castle with a band to play us to Chester General Station. We were bound for Cambridge, and arrived late in the evening. We were billeted in private houses. Myself and a chap named Ivan Totty were sent to 54, Union Lane, fairly close to our horse-lines and gun park. It was a homely lodging with an elderly couple, Mr and Mrs Rayner. Next morning, we both reported for duty. The Sergeant called the roll and told us we were in the Third Battery. This consisted mainly of chaps from Crewe, and was a Territorial Battery in peace-time.

After the first day, I began to feel like a soldier, a Gunner in the Royal Field Artillery. I was trained as a driver but we had to be capable of taking over different duties. We had rifle drill, bayonet fighting practice, and cleaned harness. Our guns were old fifteen pounders, drawn by four horses. In a few weeks, we marched to Bedford and were stationed there for a few months for more training. I had my first five days leave from there.

On my return, we were moved to Salisbury Plain, where the guns were all new eighteen pounders. We were a six gun battery, with six horses to a gun. After a few days, we moved over "the herring pond" from Southampton to Le Havre. In the course of a week we met our opponents, the Germans or Jerries. I will not go into detail of my front line experience - enough has already been written and read about that subject. May I just say I am happy to be here. After about two and a half years, during my third leave to England, I was on Chester Station, waiting for my train to Ellesmere Port. I was approached by my old canal inspector, Mr Talbot, and we both got on the train to Hooton. We had a chat, and he asked me if I would like to go back on the canal. I thought he was joking but he said he was serious, so I said I would. We parted, and I went on to Ellesmere Port where the wife was staying.

I returned to active service, but after a few weeks was on my way back to England. I arrived at Huntingdon and was engaged in training horses for the front line. I was in a private billet with a youth called Bert Starkey, who had been recalled to the services because of his age. He had been in the Dorset Regiment. Our billet was like home. It was with a young married couple, with no family. I forget their surname, but he was called Archibald and he built Limber Wagons for the government. I often wondered why I had been sent here, as I had been given no reason. However, one morning the Staff Sergeant came to me, and wanted to know if I had any civilian clothes. I said I had not, nor had I any at home, as I had sold them all when I joined up. He said that I might be home in a few weeks, if I did not have to wait for some civilian clothes. I said I would do my best to get some, though it would only be some oddments from a second-hand clothing shop, as I had no money left out of my 6/- per week, and it was no use sending home for any.

During that afternoon, I was orderly at the Battery Office, and met a young man who had been called to the service. We got into conversation, as one does in the army, and he told me that he had been to the Quartermaster's Stores for his clothes and equipment, and would have to wait a few days for them. I told him of my position - how I was waiting for civilian clothes, and was then going home for transport service. He looked to be a very clean young man, and about my size, so we suggested we should change clothes. He agreed, and we contacted the Quartermaster Sergeant for permission. My khaki suit was a good one, as I had had it from the tailor's. His suit was of blue serge, a little worn, but respectable to travel in. I had to sew a split between the legs with a needle and cotton but it was not a long job. Once I was fixed up, I reported to the office, and was given my railway ticket to Chester. Staff Sergeant Williams had been a Shroppie Union Clerk before joining up, and he asked when they would call him out of the army. But it was boatmen only, at that time.

I called at Wolverhampton and had the weekend at the wife's home. On Monday morning we caught the first train to Chester and reported at Tower Wharf. I had a short interview with the chief clerk, Mr Thompson, who was pleased to see me, and sent me on to Inspector Talbot to be fixed up with a boat. He said they had arranged to have *Sir William Robertson* ready for service for me. I had not seen this boat before, as it had been built during my absence. It was alright, but it had two cabins, fore and aft, and mostly worked on the Welsh Canal. I refused it because of the two cabins. The Inspector smiles - he knew it was not a fly boat type. Then he pointed across the canal to my old boat *Patriot*, that was running to the Trench and Shrewsbury as before. I collected the stores. and went to the stable to choose a horse. It was a chestnut, 16 hands high, with four white socks. It had been the Manager's hackney, taking him to Ellesmere Port and back.

19

BACK ON THE CUT, UNTIL THE END OF S.U. CARRYING, 1921.

We set off, and reached Ellesmere Port at about eight o'clock that night, ready for a cargo next morning. During the evening, I had plenty of friends helping to put the boat in order. Some of the boatmen wanted to know why I had come out of the Army, where had I been, what front I had been to, and whether I had been wounded or gassed. I just told them I was happy to be home. Next morning I was berthed by six o'clock, and loaded with 16 tons of white flour to be stored at Shrewsbury. My load was completed by eight o'clock, before breakfast. After we had sheeted the boat up, and eaten, the wife went to do the shopping. I had to go to Mr Stockton, the cashier, for an advance of money, and the food was sent to the boat with an errand boy.

horses. We arrived at Shrewsbury on Wednesday evening, although the last fourteen miles were very heavy going. We had to leave one boat behind and put the two horses on the other. We delivered our cargoes at Castlefields Basin, and stored the loads in the Great Western Joint Goods Yard, near His Majesty's Prison.

We left Shrewsbury on Thursday afternoon, and arrived at Wappenshall, where Frank Owen, the porter, ordered us to proceed up the nine Trench Locks to collect two loads of copper for Liverpool. We were both loaded by midday Friday, with a Red Time Bill, which meant

The original canal basin in Shrewsbury, pictured in 1971

We were on our way just after nine o'clock, following closely on the fly boats. Our butty was Albert Williams, a single chap, with a Trench boat named *Colonel*. He was for Shrewsbury too, with a load of corned beef which was also to be stored. When we reached Chester, I had to leave my horse and take another. My next was a chocolate colour named Marshall. Albert had a grey named Lucy. They were both good horses, and would go on their own or "baccer t'it" as the boatmen called it. Practically all these horses were trained to do this. If they could not, they were used as change

urgent. We managed to reach Newport that same night, in time for a pint and a good talk with other boatmen in "The Wharf Tavern". Next morning we went up the seventeen locks to Norbury Junction, entered the main canal, and went down the next twenty seven locks, making Barbridge at about eight o'clock on Saturday night. We arrived at Ellesmere Port on Sunday night. We met plenty of traffic for all parts of the country, carrying war materials, shells and food.

On Monday morning we both transhipped into a flat, and thence into a ship for Liverpool and abroad. I had the loads signed for, and went to the office for my pay. My mileage came to £2 12s, and I learned that I also got a grant of 36/-, a war allowance on the cost of living. This was my first pay on my return, and amounted to £4 8s. After deducting my previous advance of £3, I had £1 8s to draw. At this rate, it was not long before I could manage without an advance.

From then on, I was involved in practically the same route, week after week. However, a few weeks later I was allowed another boat, *Hogarth*. It was nearly new, and the smallest commercial fly boat to be built on any canal in the country. It was built in 1915 for Trench Locks, and its registered load was 16 tons. The boat still exists, and is sound and working as a maintenance boat at Worcester, near Diglis Basin. I saw her four years ago, and knew her, although she had lost her name, and I discussed her previous working route with the chaps working on her.

After working *Hogarth* for a few months, I was a little more in pocket, as the route was regular and never short of work. However it was a little too much for the wife. My next move was to get an easier route, so I applied for another boat, named *African*, which was mostly engaged on the Welsh Canal, but had to go anywhere if required. This boat was at Pontcysyllte Dockyard, so I had to load for the Llangollen route, and change over there. After changing over, I was ordered to load chemicals from Monsanto, Ruabon, for Liverpool. Mr Roberts was agent here for Denbighshire, and part of the Shropshire, and Oswald Postles was the porter. The previous porter, Harry Wood, had been killed in action.

We left Pontcysyllte at midday on a Saturday, and had to be at Ellesmere Port for the Monday afternoon tide. This did not give us too much time, and meant long days. We arrived at Ellesmere on Saturday night with our butty,

Dick Jones, my brother-in-law. We both worked with our wives. After a good evening with quite a lot of other boatmen, we set off at four o'clock on Sunday morning, and made "The Royal Oak", Tiverton, at the foot of Beeston Castle, for another jolly evening with Shroppie boatmen. We left at six on Monday morning, and made Ellesmere Port by two o'clock, tide-time. We transhipped into a foreign cargo boat. We were both pleased to get rid of this cargo as chemicals sometimes tended to explode when bumped, and there was also a very healthy "perfume" from the drums.

We made ready for our next cargoes, and were also in time to settle up for the last trip. My boat was a tonnage boat. If I was light, I received no pay, only my war bonus. I was paid 4d per ton for up to 4 miles, 6d per ton for up to 10 miles, 9d per ton for up to 15 miles, 1/- per ton for up to 20 miles, and 1/9 per ton for up to 35 miles. Longer mileage varied. The longest mileage was paid at 4/- per ton. It was 91 miles from Ellesmere Port to Newtown, and I was paid 1/- per ton back again light, if it was under 20 miles. This was the limit on downhill traffic. If we went on another canal, we would be paid mileage. The South Stafford boats were paid up to a maximum of 1/9 per ton to Birmingham, and 3½d per mile if they entered another canal. The exception was on the North Stafford Canal, now the Trent and Mersey, where they were paid 5d per mile.

I was engaged on tonnage boats until 1920. I had the *Albania*, the *Duma* and then *Daisy* in that time, and I travelled all over the country. It was during this period that my wife and I decided that we would rent a house, if we ever got the chance. This came all at once. I was passing a house at Swanley Bridge near Nantwich on the Welsh Canal, and noticed that it was empty. I stopped the boat and went to see the landlord, Mr W Jaques. He granted me the tenancy, and I paid 2/6 per week rent. It was a two-bedroomed house with a garden, and also a stable for the horse. It was very convenient for a boatman as it was near the canal and stone wharf.

After a few weeks, I decided to set a mate on and leave the wife at home, as she was not very robust. Working with her meant I had to do all

The Ellesmere (Llangollen) Canal from Swanley Bridge in 1966. Around 1920, Jack Roberts lived in a rented house here

the heavy work at the wharf, and also attend to the lock-work at night. Having a mate meant that I had to get more work to pay him and keep the home going, so I worked like a fly boat, and picked up a load as often as I could. I would work all night sometimes, in order to have a weekend at home, if I was on the Welsh Canal. However, if I was away in Birmingham or Wolverhampton, I could get a ticket and travel home by train.

This sort of life lasted for about six months, and then an opportunity came to have a fly boat, taking cheese from Cheshire, Shropshire and Staffordshire. I had a lovely clean boat named *Blockade*. It was fitted up in sections for the cheese, with a square hole on the front catch, covered with bars to keep the rats away, and to allow fresh air to circulate while travelling. The sheets were specially dressed to keep out the

heat. I called at Whitchurch and Market Drayton on alternate Wednesdays, and Nantwich on the third Thursday, collecting cheese for Manchester, Castlefields. Much of it was for export. I managed to get home for half a day every third Sunday on the Whitchurch run. My back cargoes were general goods, which had to be transhipped at Barbridge Junction, if they were not for my route. They were then collected by other boats and taken to their destination.

I did about 190 miles per week, and was paid 4d per mile each way. This was good pay in those days, and I also had a bonus. The Company owned the horses, and they saw to it that we had a reliable one, as the cheese cargoes were very urgent. It was a two-handed fly, and I had several mates with me during that period. I even had to engage the wife again in one instance. The best mate I had was called Harry Hanley, but known as Brown. He always pretended to be whistling when he wanted to speak to me, as he was very deaf himself. He was extremely reliable, although his deafness made things awkward at night, when we were meeting boats. If I was driving the horse, I used to strike a match to a signal.

Hauling cheese to Manchester was very busy during the summer months when there was a good supply of milk on the farms. For the three winter months we mostly had to go anywhere we were sent. One of the last loads of cheese I took to Manchester was during 1921, and on that occasion I brought another load of cheese back in round wooden boxes. It was from abroad for Birmingham.

About this time, the 48 hour week was introduced to boatmen, and also 6/8 in the pound was deducted from their tonnage and mileage, which made quite a hole in the week's pay. We were allowed to work a 56 hour week, and got 6/- for attending the horse at weekends, if we were in private stables in the country. In most cases the boatmen would work 56 hours, and then found that they had to stop on Thursday. This meant that the cargoes did not reach their destinations on time, and delays were caused.

The very last time I loaded cheese for Manchester was in June 1921. On my return, I delivered at Market Drayton, and then went back to Nantwich to collect my usual cheese. After completing my load, I went on to Barbridge, and arrived on the Thursday evening. My boss, Mr Moore, reckoned my time up, and said I had worked over 56 hours. He told me to take my load to Calveley Station, a mile and a half further on, and discharge it into the railway trucks. To avoid losing my mileage to Manchester, I offered to take it without overtime pay. This he would not allow. So my last time had come. I could only tie up again until Monday, and take the horse to Bunbury stables for the Company's Horse-keeper to attend to. After that, all cheese was to be transhipped to the railway and road.

After a few weeks of going anywhere, notices began to appear all over the system, saying that the Company would cease to be Carriers after a certain date. All their boats, flats and ships were collected and moored at different parts of the country for disposal. Quite a few were sold to Fellows Morton, the Anderton Company, the Mersey Weaver, A. and A. Peate of Maesbury Hall Mills, and to a few new firms, which did not exist for long. The docks at Ellesmere Port were taken over by the Manchester Ship Canal Company. At times, we had thought they would take over the Shropshire Union Canal, but this was not so. All other existing carrying companies carried on as usual for a few years, to Ellesmere Port, but gradually faded away, owing to the growth of road and rail transport.

If Mr Witham, the general manager of Tower Wharf, had continued to organise the Shropshire Union, I am sure he would have got the better of road competition in time. I understood he was asked to try it for another five years, but was not interested. If he had accepted, I think the Shropshire Union Company would have existed today, and kept quite a lot of traffic off the roads, and then British Waterways could have taken over from them. If this had happened, the canal would have been kept silted out, as it is nowadays for pleasure. I am sure it could have remained commercial and defied road and rail transport. The Shropshire Union Company could collect today, and deliver tomorrow, or in some cases the same day, by their registered fly boats. As

Mrs Elizabeth Roberts with youngest daughter Linda in their garden at Grindley Brook, approx. 1955

it is much deeper today, it could deliver more quickly. There will never be another firm like the Shropshire Union.

I delivered my boat at Chester for the last time, and was then engaged at Nantwich, in charge of the boats that were being sold to various firms. I had to keep them afloat for a few weeks, until they had all disappeared. At that time I lived at Burland, close to Nantwich. My next orders from the manager at Tower Wharf were to report to Inspector Madely, at the Railway Engineering Department, Gresty Road, Crewe. I was a railway man.

The Shropshire Union Canal Company's boatbuilding yard at Chester,
latterly known as Taylor's boatyard, after a subsequent owner,
shown here in May 1970

20

15 YEARS ON THE RAILWAYS, BEFORE BACK TO BOATING.

After my medical, I was sent to Ellesmere Port to a Permanent Way Gang, who were engaged in laying a new siding connecting Shell-Mex to the main Helsby and Hooton Line, and also to the Ship Canal Railway. This was quite a long job, and lasted about twelve months. During this time I lost the first finger on my right hand.

I next moved to Crewe, where I was placed in a Relaying Gang x 2, which numbered sixty eight. My first place of work was at Bidston, Liscard and Poulton, and the old Wirral Railway. I lodged at "Seacombe", Florence Road, and travelled home every Saturday to collect my food, returning the same night. After completing the Wirral Railway, we came to Runcorn Bridge and relayed the permanent way there, and also at Ditton Bank.

One Monday morning we arrived, but did not commence work. We were involved in the General Strike of 1926. I stayed at Runcorn on the Monday night to have a look round the canal. There was no sign of a settlement on Tuesday morning, so I took my bicycle and had the pleasure of pedalling to Burland, Nantwich, where I was living at the time. I stayed at home, and reported to the N.U.R. Branch at Nantwich almost every day, until the settlement. We were placed on a five-day week for a few weeks after this.

After completing the Runcorn job, we moved to Gnosall, near Stafford. I got lodgings at "The Boat Inn" by the canal, which was run by Mr and Mrs J Hill, whom I had known before. There were four of us lodging at the pub, and we had a good time there at nights in the bar With the boatmen, who I knew well. Every night we had singing round the piano.

I will not go into more detail regarding my work on the railway. I travelled and worked from Crewe to Rugby, Shrewsbury, Stockport and Runcorn. This was the district in those days. I was engaged on the permanent way for fifteen years and ended up as a lengthman at Nantwich.

My next move was to apply to go back to the canal. I arrived at Norbury Junction, and worked under Inspector G Lloyd senior as a maintenance boatman. I had to find my own horse, and travelled from place to place with every kind of material, repairing locks, tunnels and aqueducts, and taking the new lock gates which were fitted all over the Shropshire Union Section. I managed to bring my boat home to Nantwich at weekends, and sometimes had a week or two in that area. I later moved house to the Basin End, Nantwich.

I found quite a change in the canal, after my fifteen year's absence. All the pride in appearance had diminished and the traffic was different as it was now a toll canal. All the old fly boats had gone, and also the men from the various warehouses and depots. These buildings were almost all locked up and rusting. Some of the old stables had been demolished. Traffic was still busy at Autherley Junction, and the stables there were still open for horses. They were mostly oil boats run by Mr Thomas Clayton of Oldbury. However these stables missed the attentions of Jack Musson, Bill Lovekin and Harry, all Shroppie men who had been retired when it became a toll canal. The toll clerk had been replaced by a man from the North Stafford Section, Samuel Lomas from King's Lock, Middlewich. The canal was now L.M.S. Shropshire Union Section.

The engineering side of the canal came under the Engineer, Mr Turnbull, at Gresty Road Railway Yard at Crewe. However there were quite a few Shroppie men left, including the

Manager at Tower Wharf, Chester, and a few clerks who travelled about, collecting rents and fishing rights, and taking the men's wages. The Manager was Mr H Talbot, the Inspectors for the Shroppie Traffic Department were Mr Lea, Mr Goddard, Mr Hughes and Mr Barnsley. In the Engineering Department were Mr G Lloyd at Norbury, Mr Baker senior at Welshpool, Mr P Bowen at Ellesmere and Mr W Baker junior at Chester.

While I was engaged on the Norbury District I had the experience of taking loads of clay to several breaches. Quite a few breaches occurred during the Second World War, including those at Wheaton Aston, High Onn, Gnosall, Autherley and Audlem. These forced traffic to go via the Potteries, causing delay and expense. I also took material, bricks, mortar and clay down to Shrewsbury to prevent breaches occurring. There was very little traffic on this branch then, only a few loads of coal for Longden and Withington in privately owned boats, which were eventually stopped for good. I had rather a rough time reaching Shrewsbury, owing to the deterioration of Eyton Locks, the drawbridges, and weeds and also the tunnel at Berwick. However we managed to keep the old canal open for a while.

Jack Roberts' boat tied up at Ellesmere canal maintenance yard, and his horse Dolly grazing on the towpath opposite

I have told you of my first trip to Shrewsbury in 1907, when I saw the debris of the train disaster. In August 1944 I made my last trip. That is 25 years ago now, and one of my sons was born on my return home. There has not been a boat down since. The weir on Butry Valley had breached, near Kingsley Aqueduct

and Edgmond. Later on, I tried to go to Newport to collect some material from the station. I went onto the canal at Norbury, and entered the seventeen locks, but at the third lock I could not open the gates due to vandalism. During the war, large drums of concrete had been erected in each lock as obstructions. These had been taken out and broken up, but a large amount had been thrown into the locks, and made them impassable. I had to give up and return to Norbury.

After six years at Norbury, I was transferred to the Chester District, under the Assistant Engineer, Mr Harbottle, and Inspector W. Baker. My depot was Barbridge, and I would get home to Nantwich nearly every night on the bicycle. I had my good old mate, Harry Hanley, alias Brown, whom I could trust to look after the horse and boat. We had worked together on the cheese fly. He knew the ropes, though he was even more deaf now.

A few months previous to my transfer, I had lost my first wife, at the age of forty six. We had three daughters in fifteen years, with five years between each one, and all born in the first week of October. We had lost two of them at about eighteen months, but I reared the middle one, who is now doing well, and is married with a small family. I had been married to the first wife for twenty eight years. I decided I ought to marry again, for the sake of my young daughter, as I had to be away from home on occasion. In a few months I married a woman younger than myself, a widow with two children, a boy and a girl who were company for my daughter. We still lived at Nantwich.

I was only on the Chester District for about three years, and my routes were Ellesmere Port, Chester, Middlewich and Whitchurch. My work was all maintenance, and the only difference was that there were quite a few big locks, including Chester Northgate Locks, which were quite interesting.

Hauling the large lock gates from Ellesmere, where they were made, was a difficult task on a narrow boat, owing to the precarious balance. There was only just enough space to navigate under the low bridges, and fixing them required good practical experience. I never saw one put in wrong. These locks were very dangerous for commercial traffic at night, and there were lock-keepers on duty for twenty-four hours there. You had to mind how you raised the enormous paddles and do it a few notches at a time.

My next move was to transfer to the Ellesmere District, owing to redundancy. A motor boat was put to do the work of two horse boats, although this was not really possible. However my transfer was to be, and I was ordered to take my boat and horse to Ellesmere. It was the same sort of work, but the canal was very quiet. There was no traffic, only myself, although pleasure traffic was beginning to come, and I welcomed its appearance. But in places the canal was full of segs and weeds, and I spent many Sundays

helping to clear them. The pleasure craft increased every year.

When British Waterways had agreed to my transfer, I looked for another house on the Llangollen Canal. I moved to Chirk Bank, near the Aqueduct, viaduct and tunnel. It was in Shropshire, but on the borders of Denbighshire. We settled in here, and the children attended Weston Rhyn School. However Mrs Roberts did not like the situation, because of the trees on the high bank between the railway and the canal. We got no sunshine at the front, and very little at the back. The house was well above the River Ceriog, and the tops of the trees that grew by the river below and between the railway and the canal, were level with the bottom of the garden. Waterways built me a good stable near the house, and I could moor the boat near the

"Waterways built me a good stable near the house"
Chirk, March 2001

front door. I managed to get home nearly every weekend, and often during the week as well. I sometimes cycled from Llangollen, or anywhere within reasonable distance, but I had to be back at my boat for the starting time - half past seven in the morning. I worked till a quarter past four in the afternoon. In my wages, I was given an allowance for the horse and the mate, whom I engaged myself.

During this period, I was engaged in cleaning out the Chirk Aqueduct. We had to empty it by placing the stop planks at each end, and withdrawing the round plug in the bottom. There was a chain attached to this, and we had to find it with a boat hook, as it was always laid on the bottom to avoid interference. It was quite interesting to see how this tank was made, and joined together. After completing this job, I had to boat the silt down to Whixall Moss, which was the dumping section. My next job was to assist in taking down the old wooden guards from the tunnel. This was a very tough job and had to be carried out by lamplight. It took a couple of days to complete, and we did not fix new ones.

My next big job was in about 1957, on the aqueduct at Pontcysyllte. This was an experience. We fixed the stop planks at either end, and let the water off into the River Dee, 100 feet below. It was quite exciting to see. The plug was attached to a bar, and was fixed on the towing path and locked up with an unusual lock and key. The plug did not empty all the water out of the bottom of the huge tank, owing to the sections. To get it completely dry, a gang of men were engaged at each end, to force the water towards the plug hole with hard brushes. The plug was nearer the Trevor end, in order to be over the river. After it had been dried out, the tank was inspected by the Engineer, Mr Marsh. The entrance to the Vron end was found to be leaking through the brickwork which connected with the tank. This had to be grouted with a few tons of cement to make it dry. While the bricklayers were engaged in this, a gang of us cleaned the sections out with shovels, and put the silt over the sides but not in the river. After this we washed and scraped the sides of the tank and tarred it with brushes. I noticed the different shapes of the thick plates, and near the entrance there were a few plates with letters and figures cut into them. The bolts were about six inches long, and the nuts were eight inches square. These connected the sections. One of these nuts was a little rusty, and the Engineer had it screwed off to examine. It was put back again, as the screws on the bolt were as bright as silver. I can only remember the outside of the aqueduct being tarred once in my time, in about 1926 when a special gang of steeple-jacks in private business were engaged to do the job.

About now the L.M.S. decided that my working conditions were to be altered. I was allowed a Company's horse, and a mate who was provided and paid by the Company. I had to sell my own horse. The new horse came from Birmingham. It was named Sandy, and knew the hauling well. I was paid a set rate for the care and feeding of the horse for a seven day week. This was much better than finding my own, because of the insurance costs.

In due course, the canal section came under British Waterways. I moved house to Grindley Brook, after living in Chirk for about five years. Four years later I reached retirement age, and was asked to retire accordingly. My boat and horse had been made redundant, and I had worked as a lengthsman, which had reduced my pay quite considerably. It was a mere existence as I had a large family, with three still at school. However, I was able to take odd jobs here and there, sometimes on a farm.

21

PLEASURE CRAFT

Two years after my retirement; I decided to move to a council house in Whitchurch, as the school at Grindley Brook had been closed. One morning I received a letter from Manchester, asking me if I would take a passenger boat around the waterways. It was a horse-drawn narrow boat. I accepted the job, and was engaged for four years, during the summer months.

We would leave Stretford, Manchester, at about three o'clock on Saturday afternoon, and make our way to Llangollen to arrive there at about three o'clock on Friday afternoon. This allowed the passengers time to look around, before they left the boat on Saturday morning. The following week's passengers would arrive in the afternoon, and meanwhile the boat had to be cleaned, prepared and re-provisioned. The trips were popular and had to be booked well before the season started. The boat was often booked by parties of young people, youth clubs, scouts, foreign students and probation boys.

We had accommodation for twenty passengers, but later this was reduced to twelve, to allow extra facilities. It was run on the same idea as youth hostels, in order to keep the costs down. The passengers were accommodated in two dormitories, one for men and one for women. There was also a common room for use during the day, and for meals and a galley. The crew, which consisted of myself, a mate and a cook, used the traditional cabin, and the fore-cabin. The passengers learned to work the boat if they wished, and also helped with such chores as washing-up and potato-peeling.

On leaving Llangollen, our next destination was Tettenhall near Wolverhampton. On the way, the boat would stop at any interesting places during the day, and at villages and towns overnight. Passengers were then able to sight-see or spend the evening in a country pub, as they wished. From Tettenhall, we would proceed to Coventry, and so on round the country. We visited Oxford, Leamington, Stratford-on-Avon, Stourport, Chester, Marple and the Peak Forest. We always had plenty of interesting passengers, but the Shropshire Union and the Llangollen Canal got the most bookings.

It was in 1960 that I saw the Renfrew breach. It was the biggest breach I ever saw. I think you could have got the Queen Mary in it for width! I saw it leaking, when I came down with the *Margaret*, and intended to report it, but I did not see anybody. We were lucky to get past before it went. It would have taken the boat right

Hostelboat Margaret *and horse Mary at New Marton Lock No. 1, September 1961*

down to the fields below. When a tow-path goes, it goes with a bang, like a gun.

This boat was run by Hostelcraft Limited. Its name was *Margaret* and the horse's name was Mary. She was a Clydesdale, and much petted by the passengers. The charge was about £8 per week. It was not exotic, but good food and accommodation was provided. The idea of the horse-drawn hostel boat is still alive. There is now one that starts from Slough, and goes on different routes, but the conditions of space and comfort have improved, and the price has increased in proportion.

At this time, there was another hostel-boat, named *Firebrand*, running from Guildford in Surrey to Birmingham. It was a bigger boat, like a small flat, with a beam of about 10 foot. This could only navigate the locks as far as Hatton. It also ran on the Thames from Abingdon to Lechlade and back.

I was once asked to take this craft on temporarily for a fortnight. I had to find my way from Brentford to Abingdon. If I had had any previous experience on the Thames, I would certainly have never entertained the job with a horse-drawn craft, as there was no towing-path, only fields which were fenced to the river edge. All these fences had to be moved and replaced, and where they could not be moved, we had to take the horse along the old back lanes, across the fields and along main roads to by-pass them. When this happened the boat had to be hauled by man-power, often against the current. Sometimes there were alder trees, too high to pass the rope over, and also pleasure craft, some with high masts, moored in many places. As we neared Lechlade, we came to a place where we had to take the horse over the lock-gates. We had to take his harness off, as there was little space, and the paddles stuck out. Fortunately George, the horse, was not thick-set, and he was very quiet and would go anywhere. If he had been a big one, I am sure there would have been

an accident, and he would have fallen in and drowned in the deep lock. I was certainly pleased to be relieved of that job. However, ignoring the inconveniences with a horse-drawn craft, I found the Thames very interesting and pretty. The locks and the lock-keepers' gardens were quite picturesque, and the lock-keepers were mostly obliging. I took the train back to Whitchurch, to return to the *Margaret*. I was glad to be back where I belonged, on the canal.

It was my last session skippering the boat, as from September 1964 I had to remain at home, owing to my wife's ill health. I had two girls and two boys at home and they were all working, except for the youngest girl who was eleven. I took a job as a casual at the old canal wharf for a few months - the branch had been filled in years previously. After that, I was engaged in light work at a garage for two years. The three boys had left home and got married, leaving me with the two girls to look after Mother. The sad day came on 12th May 1966, when Mrs Roberts passed away, aged 56 years.

I still look after the home, and the youngest girl, who is sixteen, and is engaged in a local office. My elder daughter is twenty, and has just entered matrimony. I have given up working owing to my age.

I still visit the canal whenever I can, and attend the boat rallies which occur at various times and places. I am also a member of the Shropshire Union Canal Society, and I am very keen to see the Montgomery Canal restored. My very best days on the canal were when I was engaged on the Newtown Fly Boat, *The Princess May*.

I made many friends taking passengers around the waterways, and I still visit them whenever possible. They come from all over the country, Bristol, Oswestry, Newbury, Bury, Manchester and Newcastle-upon-Tyne to name but a few. In addition, I know of eight couples who have entered matrimony after meeting on the boat during their holidays afloat.

So I close my story of practical life on the Shroppie, and other canals. I have just enjoyed a walk from Frankton Junction to Crickheath and Llanymynech on the Montgomery Canal. It was rough going along the disused towing-path. This canal has been closed for thirty years, but my latest experience was being one of the many volunteers on 18/19th October 1969, helping to clean it out at Welshpool, as a first step before restoration. My first trip to Welshpool was in 1901 at the age of seven. I hope I have not made my last.

John Roberts
alias Jack Naylor

September 14th, 1969

The unveiling of a replacement milepost on the Montgomery Canal in Jack Roberts'
memory, 29 April 2006, with (left) several family members present

157

Jack Roberts died on 31 December 1972, and was buried in Whitchurch with his wife.
Though the stone says that he was 79 years old, he was in fact 78.
The reverse of the stone has an image of a fly-boat by the family home at Grindley Brook

APPENDIX 1

INDEX OF BOATS MENTIONED IN THIS BOOK

All boats were Shropshire Union Company narrow boats unless otherwise described in this list. The abbreviation J.R. stands for the author of this book - Jack Roberts.

Photographs are denoted by a page number in *italics*.

Eric	ex-Pottery fly (later converted and re-named Shroppie Fly) skipper J.R. 133
Eva	(bricks, Shrewsbury 1906) 48
Express	Brumagem fly 15
Fairey	Newtown fly, skipper John Owen 105
Faith	Cheshire Farmers Assoc. narrow boat 70
Fancy	Newtown fly, skipper Jack Owen 1908 58, 80, 113
Firebrand	wide boat converted for passenger accommodation 156
Foxland	Salt Union Co fly, skipper G. Morris 77
Francis	skipper J.R. 1923 29
Fritz	Trench boat, skipper J.R. 128
Gertrude	Railway boat (Stourlifter) skipper Harry Goram 1908 66
Harold	Welsh boat, skipper George Hopwood 1910 93
Harriet	Market Drayton fly, skipper Edward Roberts pre 1890 12
Havana	LNWR railway fly boat 38
Hilda	Coal boat owned by Charlie the Mardu 23
Hogarth	Trench boat, skipper J.R. 147
Hope	Porth y Waen Lime and Stone Co boat 110
Inspector	Directors' packet boat 71
Khartoum	70
Kimberley	Wide boat 70
Kitchener	boat sometimes used as inspection boat 70
Ladysmith	Wide boat 70
Lord Clive	Mersey tug 20
Luna	Tug, Chester-Ellesmere Port 131
Mafeking	Cheshire Farmers' steam flat 70
Mail	Brumagem fly 15, *17*
Manchuria	skipper William Owen 90
Margaret	Hostel Craft passenger boat, skipper J.R. 6, *10*, *35*, *61*, *155*, 156, *161*
Mentor	Trench boat, skipper John Wood 1907-8 53, 65
Milner	tonnage boat, skipper Alfred Roberts 1908 82
Mons	Brumagem fly 15
Neptune	Director's packet boat 71
Opal	Trench fly, skipper Alfred Roberts 1906 48
Patriot	Trench boat, skipper J.R. 129, 145
Peel	Cheese fly 63, 122
Petrel	Cheshire Farmers' steam flat 70
Phoebe	Pottery fly, skipper Wood 117
Princess May	skipper Tom the Wern, later Moses Owen 81, 111, 156
Quail	General cargo boat, skipper Alfred Roberts, 1894 12
Ralph Brocklebank	Mersey tug 20
Rembrandt	Pottery fly 133
Rhoda	Shrewsbury fly, skipper Thomas Sutton 1908 63, 121
Rocket	Tug, Autherley-Tyrley 36
Ruth	Cheese fly, skipper Joe Jones, later Alfred Roberts 56, *71*, 100, 122
Saturn	Cheese boat, skipper J. Partridge *16*, *64*, *68-69*, 73, *87*, 101
Sedan	Pottery fly, skipper Sam Bell 110
Sheldrake	converted for passengers at Bryn Howell 96
Shroppie Fly	previously Eric, q.v.
Sirdar	Llangollen fly, skipper John Ellis 74, 104, 107

Sir William Robertson two cabin Welsh boat 145

Skye Gathering boat, skipper T. Scragg 42

Spot Trench boat, skipper Dick Wooley 1907, later J.R. 53, 128

Stephen ex-Llangollen fly, skipper Alfred Roberts, later J.R. 98, 129

Swallow Newtown boat, skipper John Wooley 79

Swindon Railway boat, skipper George Wood 1908 67

Tariff Brumagem fly 17, 142

The Dog Pottery boat, skipper Bill Grimes 101

The Equinox Cheese fly, skipper Joseph Jones 99, 100

The Gleaner Ceriog Granite Co boat, skipper Bill Baines 1908 63, 99

The Woodman Ellesmere & Chester fly boat (sunk 40 yrs.) 96

Times Brumagem fly, skipper Alfred Roberts 1908, later Tom Salmon 15, 58, 63, 65, 82

Tit Cheese fly, skipper Isaac Lowe, 1904 45, 122

Trentham Newtown fly, skipper Edward Owen 80, 111

Turk Fellows-Morton 'Greasy Ocker' 84

Usk Thos. Clayton tank boat, skipper Harry 53

Usk Trench boat (derelict) 22

Valentine Staffordshire weekly boat, skipper Tom Rush 123

Vesper Pottery fly, skipper James Morris 78, 102

Vulcan Chubbs' lime boat (donkey drawn) 23

Wappensal Ice boat 53

Wilden Fly boat on River Stour, skipper Joe Bradley 1908 68

Berriew *at Belan, August 1969*

APPENDIX 2

BOATS WORKED ON BY THE AUTHOR

In this book, Jack Roberts describes working on the boats listed on this page, but there may have been others. The boats are listed in the order in which they appear in the book.

Brett	timber carrying boat
Broxton	Newtown Fly, later a weekly boat
Crescent	ex-Brumagem Fly
Opal	Trench Fly
Times	ex-Brumagem Fly, later a North boat
Milner	Tonnage boat
Stephen	Llangollen Fly
Ruth	Cheese Fly, later a mileage boat
Sirdar	Cheese Fly
Princess May	Newtown Fly
Endeavour	Pottery Fly
Bee	Trench Fly (6' wide)
Rhoda	Shrewsbury Fly
(Name ?)	Whitchurch Fly

Valentine	South Staffordshire weekly boat
Spot	Trench boat (ex fly) – first boat as Skipper, aged 17
Fritz	Trench boat (ex fly)
Stephen	North boat, ex-Llangollen Fly
Patriot	Trench boat
Eric	North boat, formerly a Pottery Fly
Albania	North boat
Duma	North boat
Daisy	North boat
Blockade	Cheese Fly, until 06/1921

1915-1918 - War service

Patriot	Trench boat
Hogarth	Trench boat
African	North boat
Albania	North boat
Duma	North boat
Daisy	North boat
Blockade	Cheese Fly, until 06/1921

1921-1936 approx. - Railway work

Maintenance work, with various boats, based at Norbury, then Chester, and Ellesmere, then retirement for two years.

Margaret	hostelboat, 1960 - 09/1964
Aston	hostelboat, 1964

1964 - Final retirement

Jack Roberts on hostelboat Margaret

APPENDIX 3

TIMINGS OF FLY-BOATS

The author includes many details of departure and arrival details in this book, from which the following examples are taken. It must be borne in mind that Jack Roberts was writing from memory, so the timings can only be approximate. However, his long experience of boating must mean that these timings are realistic. They are presented in the main in the order in which they appear in the book.

The times in brackets are the time taken from the previous place in the list (not from the start of the journey).

•Ellesmere Port 08:30, Bunbury 18:00 (9½ hours), Barbridge 19:15 (1¼ hours), Swanley 21:00 (1¾ hours), Wrenbury 22:00 (1 hour), Bettisfield 06:00 (8 hours), bottom of Frankton locks 10:00 (4 hours).

•Belan 01:00, R. Rhiw aqueduct 03:00 (2 hours), Brynderwyn 05:00 (2 hours).

•Welshpool Wednesday 18:00, Aston at approaching midnight (just under 4 hours), Bunbury Thursday 18:30 (24½ hours), Ellesmere Port Friday 02:00 (7½ hours).

•Audlem wharf Wednesday 16:00, Goldstone wharf arrive 21:00 (5 hours), depart Thursday 04:00, Brewood wharf 15:00 (11 hours, so this must have included a stop), Wolverhampton Broad Street 19:30 (4½ hours).

•Autherley Junction 08:00, Wheaton Aston 12.00 (4 hours), Tyrley 20:00 (8 hours). Again, there must have been a break, as a non-stop trip would take under 8 hours.

•Broadheath, Bridgewater Canal 07:00, Manchester Castlefields 10:00.

•Manchester Castlefields 07:00, Preston Brook 15:00 (8 hours), Saltersford 17:00 (2 hours), Broken Cross arrive 20:00 (3 hours), depart 07:00, Barbridge 15:00 (8 hours).

•Kinver Thursday night, Shebdon Friday night, Barbridge Saturday 17:00.

•Ellesmere Port to Autherley Junction – the Company allowed 36 hours.

•Barbridge 06:00, Hampton Bank evening.

•Ellesmere 11:00, Wrenbury evening.

•Barbridge early Sunday, Norbury 20:00, Wolverhampton next day, Bridge Inn, northern Stratford Canal next day, Warwick flour mill next day 21:00.

•Autherley to Tyrley 5 hours, 27 miles.

•Barbridge 04:00, Knighton 14:00 (10 hours, 23 miles, 27 locks).

•Pontcysyllte lunchtime, Ellesmere evening, Barbridge next evening.

•Audlem flight of 15 locks (over 1¼ miles) – under one hour, with other traffic on flight.

•Barbridge to Manchester Castlefields, 13 hours (51 miles).

•Pontcysyllte 14:00, Ellesmere 20:00 (6 hours), Blackhoe next day 01:00 (5 hours), Calvely 09:00 (8 hours).

•Ellesmere Port 08:00, Llangollen next day midnight (40 hours).

•Birmingham 16:00, Autherley Junction 22:00 (6 hours), Wheaton Aston midnight (2 hours), Audlem at dawn (presumably 5-6 hours).

•Wolverhampton Wednesday 20:00, Beeston (Cheshire) Thursday evening.

•Ellesmere Port Saturday morning, Pontcysyllte Sunday night.

•Junction of Newcastle-under-Lyme Canal at Stoke-on-Trent (now covered by the Civic Centre) Tuesday 23:00, Ellesmere Port Wednesday 16:00.

- Ellesmere Port Monday late morning, Newport Tuesday afternoon, Trench Wednesday morning.

- Ellesmere Port 11:00, Cox Bank (Audlem, top of flight) 06:00.

- Chester 09:30, Trench next day 18:00.

- Wappenshall 04:00, Norbury Junction 09:00, Tyrley 12:00, Barbridge 21:00.

- Wolverhampton 14:00, Wheaton Aston evening, above Hurleston locks next evening, Abermule next day.

- Ellesmere Port 09:00, Shrewsbury next day evening.

Audlem stables at the winding hole at the bottom of the locks, with ex-steamer Viceroy *(1909)*

APPENDIX 4

LOCATION OF BOATHORSE STABLES

Canal horses needed to be kept well fed to work hard, and each needed to be kept warm and dry whilst resting, to avoid chills and sickness. Stabling for these animals was an essential part of the canal infrastructure, and the Shropshire Union Company maintained a range of stabling all over its network. Many were large, with stalls for ten or twenty horses, with a paid ostler or horsekeeper in attendance, particularly when looking after the change horses for the fly boats described in this book. Some were smaller, and many were provided by canalside pubs, lock-keepers or private owners, who would charge a fee for the night for the slow boats or bye-traders with their own horses. A few boatmen maintained their own. Wherever boats stopped, there had to be stabling, and in emergency the boatman might have to ask for space at a local farm. Jack Roberts mentions over forty separate stabling locations in this book but there were many more. Only the main ones are listed below.

Shropshire Union Canal - Main line
Ellesmere Port
Chester
Bunbury
Barbridge
Hack Green
Audlem
Tyrley
Norbury Junction
Autherley Junction

S.U.C. - Middlewich Branch
Minshull Vernon (especially for Pottery fly boats)

Birmingham Canal Navigations
Birmingham Crescent Wharf (standing for 30 S.U.C. horses)
Birmingham Gas Street/Worcester Bar
Wolverhampton Broad Street

Welsh Canal (Llangollen Canal)
Hurleston
Baddiley
Wrenbury
Blackhoe
Hampton Bank
Pontcysyllte Depot
Llangollen

Montgomery Canal
Frankton
Aston locks
Maesbury
Carreghofa
Burgeddin
Welshpool
Newtown

Shrewsbury and Newport Canal
Wappenshall
Trench
Shrewsbury

Bunbury staircase locks, and fly-boat horse stables, with fly-boat Saturn *(1906) on right in lock*

APPENDIX 5

PAYMENT SYSTEMS

This book contains several references to the payment system at the time the author was carrying and the following notes provide a brief introduction. The Shropshire Union canal boatmen's wages were paid either for the tonnage carried, or for the mileage covered each trip. Occasionally, and confusingly, it was a combination of the two. The fly boat services, boats working to a pre-arranged timetable to regular destinations, were paid mileage, as the weight of the loads carried could vary from trip to trip. Regularity and reliability were the prime considerations for this service. Before the First World War, most of the mileage rates that the author quotes are around $3^1/_2$d per mile if using the company's own horses, or 6d or $6^1/_2$d if the skipper supplied his own. This reflects the contemporary cost of horse haulage, not just the original capital outlay but the constant costs of feed and stabling, and regular shoeing. Most routes required two or three horses and the services of someone else to keep an eye on the resting animals.

Payment for 'tonnage' loads was paid per ton carried, but different rates could apply to different categories of cargo, all complicated by many other variable components – the capacity of the boat, the destination and even the state of the canal. Bulky cargoes might be quite light, in which case the skipper might be paid tonnage for what the boat could nominally carry. In most cases, a higher payment usually applied if the boatman provided his own horse, rather than use a Company horse. Jack Roberts notes that the Shropshire Union Company tried to avoid paying on a tonnage basis, as the trip tended to attract a higher payment than if it was done on a mileage basis. He also noted that a boat might be tonnage on the Shroppie, but mileage on other canals it travelled on to. The weight of a load was calculated by gauging the boat – see the definition in the Glossary of Terms.

Payment was only made to the skipper of the boat, who then had to find and pay the necessary crew to keep up to the agreed delivery schedule. When the author started boating in the early 1900s, a skilled boatman's wage was around 9 or 10 shillings a week, with all food found by the skipper.

The critical document was the Time and Way Bill. Sometimes, the author refers to it as if it were one document, sometime as if two. The Bill had to be signed for all goods delivered – by the wharf staff for goods delivered to wharves/warehouses, or the person to whom the goods were delivered, if it was not a Company address. The signature provided evidence for the final payment stage that the goods had been correctly delivered. Besides a signature, the date and time of delivery were also written down. The Bill was coloured either white or pink. White Bills were used for cargoes for which there was no specific timing laid down for delivery. However, there were some time-critical loads, and the author refers to some he carried, such as a cargo of stone, and for these the Time Bill was pink, although it was known as red. The latest permitted delivery time was specified, and there was a reduction in the pay rate if the load was delivered late.

The Time and Way Bill also had to be signed at all the Company toll offices and stables on the route, with the time of passing. It also had to be shown at the first toll office on other canals, to obtain a permit to go on to the canal. Until nationalisation just after the Second World War, the canal system was made up of a large number of completely independent companies, each operating their own toll systems.

There was no universal boat licence, as there has been now for well over 50 years. The author regularly traded on to the Staffordshire & Worcestershire Canal and the extensive Birmingham Canal Navigations (which join the Shroppie near Wolverhampton) and the Trent & Mersey Canal (joined in Middlewich).

A key point to note, was that all the boating carried out by the author (apart from his post-retirement work on hostel boats) was on Company owned boats. The Shropshire Union Company was unusual in that it owned a large number of the trade boats on its system; at one stage it had more than 400 narrow boats and barges. It was unusual for a canal company to be allowed to operate its own trade boats – this work was normally left to a variety of independent by-traders, to avoid a trade monopoly.

APPENDIX 6

CHEESE FLYS

An important part of the carrying trade of the Shropshire Union Company in Cheshire and Shropshire was cheese, made on individual farms but delivered to local canal depots for rapid transit to Manchester for home consumption, and to Ellesmere Port for export.

Cheese marketing fairs were held at Market Drayton, Nantwich and Whitchurch on alternate weeks, where designated cheese boats were promptly loaded and dispatched overnight. Other boats collected cheeses from other company warehouses, and the other regular fly boats would load cheeses as part of their mixed cargoes, transhipping into specific cheese boats at Barbridge.

Fresh cheese could not be stacked more than two high without damage, so the cheese boats were fitted with a special set of numbered floorboards and bearers to create two extra levels. This meant that a cheese fly could load 17 or 18 tons, where an ordinary boat could only carry 6 or 7 tons. When off-loaded, these fittings had to be dismantled and stacked in the hold, to allow the boat to load any general back cargo, for delivery anywhere on its way to its next regular collection point.

Ellesmere Arm - the canal basin, general goods warehouse, and crane

APPENDIX 7

GLOSSARY OF TERMS

Baccering

A boathorse working alone along the towpath without a driver. Many horses worked the same route regularly and knew the 'road' well and could be trusted to go by themselves, but this practice was only possible on a very quiet piece of canal or when the boat had right of way, working uphill. Then the drivers of any downhill boats had the responsibility of clearing their towlines over or under the horse and boat.

Big Lock

The double width bottom lock of the Middlewich flight, built to enable wide boats from the Bridgewater Canal and the River Weaver to reach the town centre wharves.

Butty

An accompanying boat (from colloquial meaning of friend or mate). 'To butty' another was to work with or alongside, particularly sensible when working up the broad locks from Ellesmere Port to Nantwich, saving time and labour. In later years, it became the common name for an unpowered boat towed by a steam or motor powered boat.

Cill (or Sill)

The stonework against which the bottom edge of the top gate closes and seals. It protrudes into the lock by up to two feet, and boats locking downhill have to ensure that the rudder or stern of the boat does not hang up on the cill as the water empties.

Driver

The person on the towpath responsible for driving the horse and clearing the towlines of the traffic coming in the opposite direction.

Duke's fly

Fly boat operated by the Bridgewater Canal Company (named after the canal's promoter, the Duke of Bridgewater).

Flat

A barge built for the rivers and canals of the North West, the Rivers Mersey and Weaver, and the Bridgewater Canal for example. Flats were generally about double the width of a narrow boat and could work up the Shropshire Union Canal from Ellesmere Port as far as Nantwich.

Fly-boat

A cargo boat working to a timetable, frequently non-stop round the clock with a change of horse at appropriate intervals. Fly-boats were normally operated by three or four men with two on duty, the driver and steerer, at any one time. The crew at rest were 'sleepers'.

Gathering boat

A boat that collected various goods from several local wharves, bringing them together to the fly boat for onward long distance transmission.

Gauging

Measuring the draught of a boat to determine the weight of the load being carried. By measuring at four points the average draught could be calculated, which was then checked against a reference book. Boats were gauged at 'stops' (canal narrows) to identify the weight carried, so that the toll payable could be calculated. (see Indexing a boat below).

Greasy Ockers

Nickname for Fellows, Morton and Clayton steam narrow boats and their crews, after the nature of one of their regular traffics to

Guillotine gates

Most canal locks have gates which are hinged to the lock walls, but a few had single bottom gates which were winched up vertically in a rectangular frame, as on the old Shrewsbury Canal. Shropshire Union boatmen called these guillotine gates 'pictures'.

Half legged horse

A strong draught horse with relatively short legs, like a cob - strong enough for a canal boat but low enough to work through all the low canal bridges.

'Hampton boat

Largest capacity S.U. narrow boat, for use on the main line between Wolverhampton and Ellesmere Port. On the Wolverhampton level of the Birmingham Canal Navigations, 'hampton boats' were 40 ton capacity coal boats that could only operate on the Hednesford-Wolverhampton-Birmingham route. They were too wide and long to go through any locks, but are not mentioned in this book.

Ice boat

A specially heavily built boat with a pronounced raking bow for breaking the ice to keep the canal open for the trade boats. Some were constructed of iron, whilst many were of wood sheathed with iron plating. Drawn by as many as a dozen horses if necessary, the boat was rocked from side to side by several men holding on to a central rail to smash a wide enough channel for the cargo boats.

Indexing a boat

The process of loading a new boat with measured gauging weights, whilst recording progressively the draught for future reference (see Gauging).

Inside

The towpath side of the canal.

Outside

The non-towpath side of the canal.

Peg, pegging to

Attaching the towline to the horse harness. The towline had a wooden toggle spliced in at the end, that was pushed through a loop of rope hanging from the spreader bar at the back of the horse harness. It was simple and efficient, but was quick to release in an emergency.

Pickford's fly

Fly boat traffic mainly between London and Manchester. These boats were originally operated by Pickfords in the early 1800s, but were probably part of Fellows, Morton and Clayton's business by the time of Jack's memory.

Ponty

The author's abbreviation (and also in common usage) for Pontcysyllte, the Ellesmere Canal aqueduct that crosses the River Dee in North Wales. Built in 1805, it is 125 feet high and just over 1000 feet long, but is only wide enough for one boat to cross at a time.

Provender

Bagged horse food, such as crushed oats and chopped hay.

Raddle

Iron ore imported into Ellesmere Port in coasters from Westmorland harbours. Red raddle is also a term for red ochre, the basis of red oxide paint.

River hauling rope

A very long towline, so that the boat can be steered well away from the bank in the deeper water, avoiding the shallows on the inside of river bends.

Sleeper

A fly boat crew member at rest when not required to steer, drive the horse or work the locks.

Standing horses

The editors are unsure of the precise meaning of this expression, but think it simply means reserve horses that are resting, ready to replace others at the end of their working period. The author sometimes uses it as an adjectival phrase to describe the capacity of the stable.

Thrum

The silk cord and tassle at the end of the boatman's 'smacking whip' that makes the crack of the whip. This was to give a sound warning to other approaching boats as well as to encourage the horse, and the thrums wore out and had to be replaced regularly.

Tub boats

Small square-ended flat bottomed boats carrying about five tons of coal, used on the Shropshire Canal and associated waterways. They were 20 feet long by 6 foot 4 inches beam and were pulled in trains, but worked individually up and down the inclined planes of the area.

Two cabin boat

A boat fitted with a small cabin at the fore end as well as the usual one at the stern. This increased the legal allowance of the number of people permitted to live on the boat. Also sometimes known as a 'two decked boat'.

Valley

A canal trade expression for a canal embankment that crosses a valley, a colloquial reversal of its usual meaning.

CURRENCY
Pre-decimal money (up to 1971)

There were 12 pence (d) to the shilling (s), and 20 shillings to the pound. One shilling is therefore equivalent to the current 5p (forgetting inflation).

Whilst there were no set rules on how to write monetary values, ten pence was usually written as 10d, one shilling and sixpence as 1/6, and four pounds eight shillings as £4 8s 0d or £4/8/0.

As a guide, £1 in 1920 had roughly the same purchasing power as £40 when this book was published (based on retail price indices).

LENGTH, WEIGHT, VOLUME
Imperial measures

Length - one foot (1') is approx. 30cm. Three feet make one yard (90cm), and 1760 yards make one mile (1.61km).

Weight - 112 pounds (112 lb.) make one hundredweight (1 cwt., or about 50kg), which is one twentieth of a ton. Many bulk products that were not carried loose in bulk, were bagged and transported in hundredweight sacks.

Volume - One gallon is 4.55 litres.

INDEX

(See Appendix 1 for index of boat names)